THE CALIFORNIA WINE INDUSTRY
1830-1895

1830   1895

THE CALIFORNIA WINE INDUSTRY
A Study of the Formative Years

VINCENT P. CAROSSO

UNIVERSITY OF CALIFORNIA PRESS
BERKELEY, LOS ANGELES, LONDON

University of California Press
Berkeley and Los Angeles, California

University of California Press, Ltd.
London, England

Copyright 1951 by
The Regents of the University of California
California Library Reprint Series Edition, 1976
ISBN: 0-520-03178-4

TO
JOHN D. HICKS

Preface

THE DEVELOPMENT of commercial viniculture in California forms an important chapter in the state's history. In the years between 1830 and 1895 California was transformed from a pastoral to an industrial and commercial agricultural community. Viniculture epitomizes this transformation, and this book is intended as an introduction to the study of the agricultural and economic history of what has become one of California's major sources of revenue.

Although the pre-1830 period has the typical romantic flavor of early California history, grape growing and wine production were commercially unimportant. For this reason the early period has been treated only in broad outline. The prologue is based very largely upon secondary works and monographic material. Only in matters where my own study of the sources has been thorough have I ventured to disagree with the chief secondary authorities. I have chosen 1895 as the terminal date of this study because by that time the wine industry was well established and recognized. The 'nineties found California viniculture well on its way to becoming "big business." Between 1890 and the passage of the Eighteenth Amendment there were few major structural or commercial changes in the industry. Between 1895 and 1915, when the prohibition movement began to gain momentum, the California wine industry made steady progress. National prohibition and a series of fluctuations in the business cycle after 1920 disorganized and demoralized the whole industry, and not until 1940 was any stability achieved. World War II, however, created new problems and accentuated old ones. The California wine industry has been operating under abnormal conditions since 1918.

In a study of this nature a few words on the sources used are, I believe, in order. Whenever possible I have used

Preface

source materials, and even when these were not obtainable I have tried to make as thorough an investigation as possible of the evidence obtainable. Obviously, however, in the study of so large a field, exhaustive research cannot be made into all the sources. Where my own investigations have been relatively complete, I have not hesitated to reach conclusions differing from those of other students; where they have not, I have subordinated my views to those of investigators who have probed deeper. The different types of source materials and secondary works cited in the bibliography are indicative of the materials used in making this study. The bibliography is in no wise exhaustive. I have cited only those works which were specifically used in the preparation of this book. Many of the manuscripts, books, and periodicals consulted are available in the Bancroft Library and the several other libraries of the University of California, the California State Library, and the Henry E. Huntington Library and Art Gallery.

It is with genuine appreciation that I take this opportunity to thank Professor John D. Hicks, under whose guidance the study was made. His constant advice, his wide knowledge, and his sympathetic encouragement have proved invaluable. My debt to him is indeed great. Gratitude is also expressed to Professors Walton E. Bean and Murray R. Benedict for critically reading the manuscript and for their excellent suggestions. I would also like to acknowledge my indebtedness to Mr. John Gildersleeve and Mr. John H. Jennings of the University of California Press for their advice and criticism. Professor Allen A. Gilmore, head of the History Department, Carnegie Institute of Technology, and the Research Fund Committee of the Division of Humanistic and Social Studies, facilitated in various ways the final preparations of this work. For their help and that of numerous other friends I am very grateful.

Vincent P. Carosso

Berkeley, California

Contents

Prologue	1
I. Jean Louis Vignes, William Wolfskill, and the Beginnings of Commercial Viticulture, 1830–1848	7
II. The Pre-Haraszthian 'Fifties	16
III. Charles Kohler, Pioneer Wine Merchant	29
IV. The Age of Haraszthy	38
V. The Committee on the Improvement of the Grape Vine in California	49
VI. The Anaheim Coöperative and the Sonoma Corporation	60
VII. Industrial Development and Organization, 1860–1870	74
VIII. Prosperity, Depression, and Recovery, 1868–1878	86
IX. Tariff Reciprocity, 1875–1879	102
X. The Phylloxera	109
XI. Founding of the State Board of Viticultural Commissioners, 1880	120
XII. A Business Cycle, 1880–1895	130
XIII. National Problems, 1880–1895	145
Epilogue	160
Notes	171
Bibliography	207
Index	227

Prologue

WINE-, RAISIN-, AND TABLE-GRAPE production are the three interdependent parts of the viticultural industry of California. In value, grapes and grape products today constitute the second most important fruit crop of California; the state produces more than 90 per cent of the commercial wine crop of the United States. In the crop year beginning July 1, 1948, and ending June 30, 1949, more than twenty-five thousand farmers were engaged in prosperous viticulture, and from more than 500,000 acres of vines of all ages California produced in that year more than 2,750,000 tons of grapes.[1] The wine yield of the state was estimated to be more than 100,025,000 gallons, of a total United States production of 139,845,000 gallons.[2] The farm value of the 1948 grape crop was $101,797,000. The average return to growers for all grapes was about $36 per ton. The average price of wine grapes was $30.29.[3] The industry has played an important part in the economic development of the state, and its history must be understood to appreciate fully the vicissitudes accompanying its progress.

The history of grape growing parallels the history of Western culture. Since early times the vine has accompanied civilization. The Phoenicians brought the vine from Asia and propagated it on the Mediterranean islands. From there it moved westward with the spread of civilization; first to Greece, then to Rome, Spain, and France. Dr. J. Arthaud, a historian of the vine, believed that before commercial relations existed between nations it was possible to determine the degree of a people's progress by a study of their knowledge of wines (oenology).[4] Arthaud traced the history of civilization from ancient China and Japan to nineteenth-century Europe, and his studies show the existence of a high

---

[1] For notes to prologue, see pp. 171–172.

The California Wine Industry, 1830–1895

correlation between these two factors. Mankind has made its greatest progress between the thirtieth and fiftieth parallels of latitude, and it is here also that viticulture has flourished. Upon the basis of his studies Arthaud concluded that wine is the *"agent excitateur de l'activité physique et morale de l'homme."*[5]

All European and American grape varieties originally came from the Asiatic vine. In America there are two types of vines: the indigenous American, numerous varieties of which are found in their wild state in many parts of the United States, and the *Vitis vinifera*, or the European variety. It is the *Vitis vinifera* with which we are primarily concerned, since upon it are based both the wine industry of Europe and that of California. In the United States, it is only in California that this vine has found soil and climate similar to those of its native habitat. This has been the most important single factor in making California the vineyard of America.

Wine making is not only one of the oldest commercial agricultural enterprises in California, but probably the oldest in all of western America. Its history may be traced to Cortez (1524) in Mexico. The Jesuits introduced the grape into Baja California from Mexico;[6] Father Juan Ugarte was probably the first person (c. 1697) to plant a vineyard there, but it is very doubtful that wine was produced for other than sacramental and personal use. From there came the first slips (*Vitis vinifera*) for the vineyards of Alta California, concurrent with the establishment of the Spanish missions. The Franciscan fathers cultivated it, with other fruits, during the middle of the eighteenth century, and to them is due credit for the beginnings of California's horticulture. As far as can be determined, the first vines were planted at San Diego about 1770,[7] and grape culture followed the northward march of the missions along El Camino Real. By 1823 the Spanish padres had brought it to the small town of Sonoma, which grew up around Mission San Francisco Solano, the most northerly of the missions.

The exact origins of the grape introduced by the Spanish

Prologue

priests are veiled in mystery. George A. Pettit, a member of the staff of the University of California College of Agriculture, believes it to be a seedling of the Monica variety, a species popular among the Mediterranean monasteries of the eighteenth century; this hypothesis, however, has not been unanimously accepted by oenologists.[8] Its exact origins and classification are not essential, however, for within a few years it became known as the Mission, and as such it is still known today.[9] It was not one of the best wine-grape varieties, and the quality of California's wines throughout the Spanish period suffered as a result. Although this grape dominated California viticulture for more than eighty years, its prolificness rather than its quality determined its popularity.

While there has probably been a vintage in California each year since 1784, there are no reliable statistics available for the early period. The history of viticulture between 1770 and 1830 is essentially the history of the missions, and wine production was determined by the needs of the friars. The degree of success of a mission determined the condition of grape culture and wine making in its locality.[10] Although wine making spread northward with the founding of new missions, concentration and expansion of vineyards during the 1820's and 1830's were largely limited to southern California. The pioneer vineyards of Sonoma County were planted after 1823—most of them after 1830.[11] New areas were cultivated annually, but there is little evidence that before 1840 wine was an important article of trade. The Mission grape was the prevailing, if not the only, variety grown, Indians performed field labor, and the product was designed to meet the demands of local consumption. There were no facilities for export, and had there been any, the shortage of casks and bottles would have prevented it.[12] Until the early 1830's few vines were planted by private individuals. California agriculture was mission agriculture.

Although viticulture extended as far as the missions did —from San Diego to Sonoma—Los Angeles was the vine-growing region of the 1830's. In 1831 more than 100,000

The California Wine Industry, 1830–1895

vines were growing within the present city limits of Los Angeles, fully one-half of those in the state.[13] The largest producers were missions San Gabriel and San Fernando, San Gabriel producing annually from 400 to 600 barrels of wine and about 200 barrels of brandy.[14] Although most of California's wine and brandy came from the missions, some wine was being made by individuals, and by 1840 several privately owned vineyards had been planted as far north as Napa and Sonoma counties.[15] As early as 1824 Joseph Chapman, one of the first American settlers in Los Angeles, planted 4,000 vines. Although he did not continue to grow grapes very long, he was probably the first American wine grower in California.[16]

In 1833 the Mexican government issued the decree that began the secularization of the mission lands. Its immediate effect was to bring to an end the domination of the missions over the whole of California's economy, and after 1834 the vineyards and orchards, which had been important sources of mission wealth, were gradually abandoned.[17] This act hastened the end of pastoral California, and the decline of the missions and consequent neglect of their vineyards mark the beginning of modern viticulture.

More than good land and climate were necessary, however, to make grape growing and wine making an industry. In 1839 Alexander Forbes wrote that California needed intelligent and trained persons to make superior wines.[18] Several of them came in the 'thirties, and it was to be the knowledge of Europe and the energy of America that were to create California's wine industry.[19] Climate, soil, and other conditions conducive to grape and wine production in California duplicate those of almost every celebrated viticultural region of the world. California's seven hundred square miles of vineyards extend over mountains, irrigated deserts, coastal plains, and inland valleys, in an area 595 miles long from north to south, with an average east-west breadth of approximately one hundred miles.[20] Forbes stated that California offered a "wide and promising field for the cultivation

Prologue

of the grape in all varieties."[21] The advertising literature of nineteenth-century California proclaimed the commonwealth to be one of the few promising viticultural regions of the world; European horticultural and viticultural journals echoed these sentiments.[22] California's virgin soil, temperate climate, long summers without rain, and the reasonable—if not cheap—price of land were its greatest attractions.

Chapter I
Jean Louis Vignes, William Wolfskill, and the Beginnings of Commercial Viniculture, 1830-1848

"NOTHING IS WANTING but intelligent persons, to make wine of a superior quality..."[1] Forbes wrote this in 1839, six years after the Mexican government had initiated a policy that was ultimately to destroy the missions, which had been the chief centers of California viticulture, and thus prepare the way for commercial production. Since southern California had dominated grape growing and wine making under the Spanish missions, it was natural that this region should continue to lead in commercial viticulture. Visitors, travelers, and settlers have left a large amount of memorabilia that indicates beyond doubt that southern California of the 1830's led the rest of the state in wine culture. Before the organized immigration of the 'forties, new settlers in California tended to congregate in the southern part of the state. What little economy California possessed under Spanish and Mexican sovereignty was concentrated around Los Angeles, and it was only natural that immigrants interested in commercial agriculture and business should make southern California their home.

The first of the "intelligent persons" whom Forbes felt California viticulture needed arrived at Monterey in 1829.[2] Appropriately his name was Vignes—Jean Louis Vignes, born at Cadillac, France, a small town near the famed wine

---

[1] For notes on chap. i, see pp. 172-174.

region of Bordeaux.³ He came to Monterey from the Sandwich Islands, and in 1831 moved to Los Angeles, where he remained until his death in 1863. To Vignes must go the credit for being the first man to make the manufacture of wine and spirits a business in California.

In 1833 Los Angeles had six wine growers owning nearly 100 acres of vineyards and approximately 100,000 vines.[4] Upon arriving at Los Angeles, Vignes purchased 104 acres of land and set up a commercial vineyard where the Los Angeles Union Station stands today. The presence of a large alder caused him to call the ranch El Aliso; this, in turn, led the neighbors to call him Don Luis del Aliso.[5] At Los Angeles Don Luis began importing foreign grape cuttings, which were packed with great care and shipped from France to Boston, thence around Cape Horn to California. Although the cuttings were used primarily for experimentation, several shipments of different varieties in quantities large enough to be used in wine making arrived in California in the early 'thirties.[6] William Heath Davis claimed that Vignes was the first person to bring foreign cuttings to California. Davis declared, "I regard him as the pioneer not only in wine making, but in the orange cultivation, he being the first man to raise oranges in Los Angeles and the first to establish a vineyard of any pretension."[7]

It is impossible to ascertain the exact date of Vignes' first vintage, but it is safe to say that it was not later than 1837. After that year Don Luis manufactured wine and *aguardiente* regularly and in considerable quantity. Probably as early as 1834 a nephew, Jean M. Vignes, who seems to have been the first of at least eight relatives to emigrate, joined his uncle, who was now one of the most popular men in Los Angeles, taking an active part in city affairs.[8] In April, 1836, Don Luis signed the roll of vigilantes, and he worked constantly to make Los Angeles a more orderly city—a city that would attract immigrants.

His success in growing grapes and in making wine caused him to advertise the potentialities of California to his coun-

Beginnings of Commercial Viniculture

trymen. He wrote to France asking his relatives, friends, and his "more intelligent countrymen" to come and settle near Los Angeles, for he believed California was destined to rival France, not only in the quantity of wine produced, but also in the quality of its wines.[9]

In 1839, by which time Vignes' enterprise consisted of more than forty thousand vines and a good cellar with oak casks he had constructed from nearby oak trees, a second nephew, Pierre Sansevain, later to become one of the famous pioneer wine merchants of California, joined him at Los Angeles.[10] In the year after his arrival Vignes began regular shipments of wine to other parts of California. In 1840 the ship *Mooson*, loaded with wines and brandies manufactured by Don Luis and Pierre Sansevain, was sent to Santa Barbara, Monterey, and San Francisco.[11] The white wines sold for two dollars a gallon, and the brandy for four dollars, a good profitable price. In 1842 Vignes could look with satisfaction upon a thriving coastwise wine trade. Always cognizant of the fact that the quality of his product would in the long run determine the quantity of his profit, Don Luis felt it was not too much expense to send his wines for an ocean trip—usually from California to Boston and back—to improve their quality before putting them on the market. The practice of improving choice wines by sending them on long sea voyages was customary and was also practiced by Eastern wine merchants. On January 19, 1843, Commodore Thomas ap Catesby Jones, U.S.N., arrived at Los Angeles to apologize to Governor Manuel Micheltorena for his attempted seizure of Monterey. Jones gave such a creditable performance before the governor that Micheltorena gave him a banquet at Sanchez Hall, at which the wines of Don Luis helped to efface any enmity that had resulted from Jones's diplomatic *faux pas*.[12] Before leaving California, Jones visited the El Aliso vineyard, and Vignes gave him several barrels of wine to take to President Tyler. There is no record that the president ever received this wine, which was reputed to have been of excellent quality.[13] Several years

The California Wine Industry, 1830–1895

later another American, Brevet Major W. H. Emory spoke for the quality of Don Luis' wine:[14] "We drank today the wine of the country, manufactured by Don Luis Vigne, a Frenchman. It was truly delicious, resembling more the best description of Hock than any other wine. Many bottles were drunk leaving no headache or acidity on the stomach."

Don Luis continued to manage his vineyard and winery until 1855, when he sold it to his nephews Jean Louis and Pierre Sansevain for $42,000.[15] This is reported to have been the highest price paid for any piece of Los Angeles real estate up to then. At the time of the sale Don Luis' vineyard was the largest in California, with more than 32,000 bearing vines and an annual wine production of more than 1,000 barrels.[16] The *Southern Californian*, commenting on this transaction, stated that the price was "a small sum in comparison with the intrinsic value of the property."[17] The sale of El Aliso to Jean Louis and Pierre Sansevain marks the beginning of the pioneer firm of Sansevain Brothers, which later became famous for the quality of its wines.

In 1831 William Wolfskill, whose activities in California parallel those of Vignes to an unusual degree, arrived in Los Angeles.[18] Wolfskill was born in Madison County, Kentucky, on March 20, 1798, of German and Irish parents.[19] When he was eleven years old his family moved to Missouri, to what is now Howard County but what was then the Indian country. The family returned to Kentucky in 1815, but the years on the frontier had aroused in William the same kind of curiosity that the sea arouses in a boy who lives near the ocean, and in 1822, after a few years of school and intermittent work at various trades, he set out on his own as a trapper.[20] Between 1822 and 1830 he trapped beaver in New Mexico, descended the Rio Grande to El Paso del Norte, and was a member or leader of other expeditions in the Southwest. In 1830 he was made leader of an expedition of twenty-two or twenty-three men that set out from New Mexico for the Tulare and Sacramento valleys of California to hunt beaver. George C. Yount, who was

Beginnings of Commercial Viniculture

later to become the first American viticulturist of Napa valley, was a member of the expedition. Wolfskill's route, "northwest to Green River thence across the Wasatch Mountains to Silver River and down Virgin River entering California by way of Tehachapi and Cajon passes," was an extension of the Santa Fe Trail, known as the "Old Spanish Trail."[21] The impossibility of crossing the northern mountain passes in winter forced the expedition to turn south, and in February, 1831, it reached Los Angeles.[22]

When lack of money forced the party to disband at Los Angeles, Wolfskill, with several partners, built a schooner and obtained a hunting and trading license from the Mexican government. Although a technical error on the part of the authorities enabled them to hunt the valuable sea otter as well as the beaver, the venture did not prove profitable. In 1831 Wolfskill gave up his career as trapper and scout for the less romantic but more remunerative occupation of horticulturist. In 1838 he and his brother John, who had come to California in 1837, purchased the first of the several vineyards he was to acquire in the heart of what is today downtown Los Angeles. Wolfskill acquired with his vineyard less than 4,000 vines, but by continued purchases of adjacent land the Kentucky trapper had by 1858 increased his holdings to 145 acres with 55,000 vines.[23] He had also a wine cellar with a capacity of 60,000 to 100,000 gallons. With Vignes as his only major competitor, Wolfskill was able to make from grape growing the profits he had failed to make from hunting beaver and sea otter. Between 1838 and 1846 he planted 32,000 vines. Although there is no evidence as to what varieties he planted and to what extent he made use of foreign vines, the sale and popularity of his product among Californians indicate that his wine was at least tolerable. Wolfskill's viticultural enterprise was, for his time, extensive, but he also took great interest in horticulture generally, in this field surpassing Vignes.[24] In 1841 he planted his first orange tree, and from that date he experimented with many kinds of fruits. He built a nursery and

The California Wine Industry, 1830-1895

carried on many experiments to determine what fruits were most adaptable to the soil and climate of California.[25]

The horticultural possibilities of other sections of California were not overlooked by Wolfskill. Although his greatest holdings were in Los Angeles, as early as 1841 he went to northern California to look over real estate in what was then the public domain. In 1842 Governor Juan Bautista Alvarado gave Wolfskill a grant of four square leagues of land on both sides of Putah Creek, which today is part of Yolo and Solano counties. In the same year John Wolfskill started a stock ranch on the newly acquired property, which he maintained until the time of his death. In 1831 a fruit orchard was planted, and although the vineyard contained more than 3,000 vines in 1854, the extensive planting of grapes here did not begin until the early 'fifties.[26] Another of Wolfskill's vineyards, in Napa County, produced probably the first northern California grapes sold on the San Francisco market. All through the 1840's and 1850's Wolfskill was able to command profitable prices for his Napa grapes, usually selling them on the San Francisco market for twenty-five dollars a hundredweight.[27]

During the period in which his ranches in the Napa valley and on Putah Creek were becoming established, Wolfskill was second only to Vignes as the largest grape and wine producer of California. In 1846 and 1847 Wolfskill produced 180 casks (2,880 gallons) of wine and an equal quantity of *aguardiente*.[28] Edwin Bryant, visiting the Wolfskill ranch at Los Angeles in 1847, stated that it was a "model of its kind" and that the quality of his wine compared "favorably with the best French and Madeira wines."[29] Grapes and wines from Wolfskill's Los Angeles ranch sold throughout California, and although, in the San Francisco market, Vignes concentrated on selling wine, Wolfskill sold grapes and fruit as well as wine.[30] Sailing vessels that called at Los Angeles on their way to San Francisco from other ports provided the only means of shipping fresh grapes and fruit to San Francisco. The cost of preparing the grapes for a sea voyage was

Beginnings of Commercial Viniculture

high, and there was always a possibility that they would spoil en route and arrive at their destination a total loss. Yet there was more profit in this period from the sales of grapes in San Francisco than from the sale of wine, for San Francisco in the 1840's was still largely dependent upon southern California for most of its grapes and deciduous fruits, and Wolfskill shipped as many grapes as the limited transportation facilities could carry.

Although before 1840 Los Angeles could claim very little more than a languid interest in commercial viticulture—beside Vignes and a few small producers there was no viticultural business; for that matter, no commercial agriculture of any kind—by the middle of the decade the production of wine and the growing and marketing of fruit of all kinds had become an important element in southern California economy. In 1841 the Los Angeles area is said to have produced 24,000 gallons of wine;[31] Bryant credits California with a total production 1,600,000 gallons in 1847, most of which came from southern California. The United States Census Office, however, reported the total wine production of California for 1850 as only 58,055 gallons. To attempt to reconcile the two figures with any degree of accuracy is almost impossible. Bryant's estimate for 1847 is undoubtedly an exaggeration; the official census figure is indubitably low, for it admittedly excludes all wine production outside Los Angeles and Santa Barbara counties. All that can be said with surety is that the amount of wine produced increased rapidly every year.[32] Bryant, who visited Los Angeles in 1847, stated that the San Gabriel River was "skirted with numerous vineyards," some with 20,000 or more vines, which produced large amounts of wine and brandy of good quality.[33] Both John S. Hittell and Guido Rossati substantiate his statement that in 1847-1848 California had approximately 200,000 vines.

Vignes and Wolfskill were the two greatest figures in California viticulture in this period—it was not until the advent of Colonel Agoston Haraszthy in the 'fifties that anyone was

The California Wine Industry, 1830–1895

more important—but they were not the only ones. Their success served to popularize the cultivation of grapes and to attract competitors. New settlers came to Los Angeles, new vineyards were planted, new wineries were built. Throughout the 'forties the Los Angeles area maintained its position as the foremost viticultural region of California.

There were, however, a lively interest and widespread discussion of the viticultural potentialities of other sections. The *California Star*, a San Francisco newspaper, published an article in 1847 on the adaptability of the vine to California, the wealth that was to be gained from wine culture, the relatively easy work that the culture of the grape demanded, and the increase in land value that accrued from planting vineyards on uncultivated lands.[34] The same paper followed this with another article, by the Ohio viticulturist Long, on the practical aspects of grape culture and wine making. Other papers in both northern and southern California devoted considerable space to the subject.[35]

Los Angeles wine growers controlled the prices of grapes and wine in the San Francisco market through the late 'forties and into the early 'fifties, and the profits they made provided the necessary stimulus for others to plant vineyards in northern California. With the discovery of gold the valleys surrounding San Francisco Bay became new centers of viticultural activity.[36] George Yount had planted a small vineyard in Napa valley in the middle 'thirties; Wolfskill's vineyard in the same valley was in bearing in the early 'forties; in 1846 a Dr. Marsh, a New Englander and Harvard graduate, had an extensive vineyard on the slopes of Mount Diablo.[37] When Edwin Bryant visited California in 1846 and 1847, he found the vine the one common characteristic of northern and southern California. From San Francisco the vine spread in all directions, and by 1849 Sacramento City had a prosperous grape and wine business.[38] All that viticulture needed to make it an important part of the economy of the state was a market. The gold seekers who came in such great numbers increased the demand for wine to such

Beginnings of Commercial Viniculture

a degree by the middle 'sixties as to cause northern California to outplant southern California.[39]

With the American colonization of California begins a new period in the state's viticultural history, a period marked by renewed interest on the part of Californians generally and by the large-scale development of vineyards and wineries. Guido Rossati, a member of the Italian Ministry of Agriculture, has called the post-1847 expansion of commercial agriculture and viticulture the distinctive contribution of Anglo-Saxon colonization to the rural progress of the state.[40]

Chapter II
The Pre-Haraszthian 'Fifties

THE GOLD RUSH of 1849 was the principal stimulus to commercial viticulture in the early period, for it was grape growing and wine making that, above all other agricultural pursuits, received the greatest encouragement from the miners.[1] The wine industry of California today is largely the product of developments that began in the decade 1850 to 1860.[2] The increased consumption of wine as a result of the discovery of gold led to an unprecedented expansion in grape culture[3] that continued until the 'seventies, when a worldwide economic depression and the phylloxera brought a temporary setback.

Probably at no other period in the history of California has there been such a demand for viticultural products in general as in the early 'fifties. Yet the gold rush made grape growing, rather than professional wine making, an industry in California. With a few notable exceptions, persons attracted to wine making in this period were not qualified either by experience or training to be called viniculturists; moreover, their search for immediate profits damaged the name and reputation of California wines for nearly fifty years.[4] Most of the wine made by the novices hardly deserved its name, although a few of them did succeed, usually by trial and error methods, in producing an article that was both palatable and sound. As early as 1849 some good wine was being produced along the coast within a hundred-mile radius of San Francisco.[5] After the immediate excitement of

---

[1] For notes to chap. ii, see pp. 174–177.

The Pre-Haraszthian 'Fifties

the discovery of gold had subsided, many of the gold seekers, who had come originally from the wine countries of Europe, returned to their previous occupation.[6] These pioneers, predominantly French and German, began to grow grapes and to make wine systematically on a commercial basis.[7] It was to be these early trained vintners who as agriculturalists rather than as miners were really to find their El Dorado in California. Finding organized viticulture in general totally neglected—for there had been individual rather than organized interest in grape culture since the secularization of the missions—the European immigrant "resuscitated and propagated it."[8]

The influx of population into northern California made it imperative that new areas closer to the market be cultivated. The viticulture of California before the gold rush had been characterized by the supremacy of the Los Angeles district, with only a few serious attempts at vine culture in northern California, but the increased demand for wine in San Francisco and the mining regions led to a period of energetic planting of grapes in the vicinity of San Francisco Bay.[9] In the early 'fifties two new viticultural areas emerged, the counties north and south of San Francisco Bay and the mining regions of the Sierra Nevada. Although vines had been planted along the Bear River before the gold rush, it was not until the early 'fifties that grape culture spread to Sutter, Yuba, Butte, Trinity, and El Dorado counties.[10] The major northern wine areas of present-day California started commercial grape culture in this period; Stockton began its cultivation on a large scale in 1850;[11] Lake County farming began in 1854, but because of the high cost of transportation, viticulture in this area was confined to domestic demand for several years;[12] Merced planted its first vineyard in 1855;[13] and Napa County is reported to have shipped its first wine (six casks and six bottles) to San Francisco in 1857.[14] The *California Farmer* estimated in 1856 that Sacramento County possessed 52,000 four-year-old vines.[15] When Horace Greeley visited California in 1859, he saw "patches of vines" throughout the mining region and claimed that California already possessed more mature vines than any other state in the union.[16]

Although there are no reliable statistics upon which to base an accurate estimate of the extent of California's viticultural investment in the early 'fifties, grape growing and wine making were far more important than horticulture between 1850 and 1860.[17] Wine making was carefully "nursed" by the California newspapers, and even before the establishment of the California State Agricultural Society in 1854, the California dailies and weeklies carried many articles advertising the possibilities of California as a wine and grape land, as well as technical articles on grape culture and wine making.[18] In the early 'fifties the press of the state already called California the greatest wine country of the world. It claimed that California's vineyards produced three times as much wine per acre as those of Europe; that one California variety—the Mission—produced several types of wine; and that the climate of the commonwealth was unequaled throughout the world for cultivating grapes. Bancroft, writing on the agriculture of the early 'fifties, says, "Chief among all first products . . . is the grape, the cultivation of which has . . . roused the interest of the entire community and absorbed the chief attention among the inflowing land tillers. . . ."[19]

If the articles in the San Francisco papers and the successes of such men as Vignes and Wolfskill had not been sufficient to attract farmers to grape culture, the shipment of wine from Ohio to San Francisco, and its immediate and profitable sale, might have produced the same result. At any rate, more and more persons were attracted to viticulture.[20] The State Agricultural Society had discovered with alarm that in the period between 1850 and 1856 the cellars of California were "filled exclusively from the vineyards of France, Germany, and other European countries."[21] This, however, was soon to be remedied, for at the third annual state fair in 1856, speakers on the progress of grape culture in Cali-

The Pre-Haraszthian 'Fifties

fornia stated with pride that an increasing interest in this branch of agriculture was evident throughout the whole state, and that "considerable progress" had been made in popularizing the grape in many districts that had heretofore either neglected or overlooked entirely the possibilities of viticulture.[22]

By 1855 the idea that the Los Angeles area alone was adapted to the vine was no longer tenable, for in that year many wine growers with extensive vineyards could be counted throughout the northern counties.[23] In October, 1855, the *California Farmer* listed the major vineyards of California. Quoting from the *Report of the Committee on Farms, Vineyards, and Orchards* of the California State Agricultural Society, this weekly left little doubt where the future great wine districts of the state were to be.[24]

The financial rewards to be gained from grape culture were forcefully publicized by the California press; the difficulties and hardships of starting and bringing to maturity a vineyard were discovered by many beginners with limited capital who had been attracted to viticulture with the hope of immediate profits. Among the greatest disadvantages facing the beginner was the high cost of experienced labor. Although a great deal of the vineyard work could be done by Indians and Mexicans, the numerous opportunities available made all labor costly, and experienced cellar men were scarce at any wage.[25] Caring for a vineyard did not ordinarily require as much work as caring for many other crops, but most American farmers had never followed viticulture closely, and to them grape growing presented formidable problems. There was much more to profitable grape culture than planting and pruning vines; most vineyards required (or at least the common belief at the time was that they required) irrigation, and this was expensive, inconvenient, or both. The farmer who had to borrow money to begin his vineyard or to bring it to maturity was faced with the added burden of extremely high interest rates. By no means uncommon was the vintner who was forced to sell his wine before it was properly aged, in order to meet his financial obligations. In the years immediately following the gold rush a market was usually available, since the supply never approached the demand, but when supply and demand approximated each other it became increasingly difficult for the debtor vineyardist to turn his immature wine into cash.

The initial cost of purchasing suitable vineyard land varied throughout the 'fifties according to location, adaptability of the soil to vine culture, and the general conditions of the grape and wine market. In 1858 one acre of bearing vineyard was reported to be worth a thousand dollars.[26] Even if the cost of suitable land could not be considered a major disadvantage at this time, and the cost of planting was not prohibitive, the time required for a vineyard to bear grapes (usually four years) represented a long period of unnremunerative investment. In 1858, according to Matthew Keller, a distinguished vineyardist of Los Angeles, it cost $1,604.64 to plant 100 acres of vines.[27] The upkeep for 100 acres of vineyard for the first three years was outlined by Colonel Haraszthy as: $2,349.64, $805.00, and $865.00 respectively.[28] Once this initial investment was met, the profits to be gained were considerable. Usually one acre with 1,000 vines yielded $200 annually, and in 1856 the *California Farmer* estimated 60 cents as the cost to the producer of one gallon of wine that he sold for 75 cents to $1 at the vineyard.[29] Despite the scarcity of labor, high rates of interest, and the initial cost of planting a vineyard, the 'fifties were characterized by a constant increase in the number of vines set out and the number of gallons of wine produced.[30]

The energy with which the northern counties entered upon the cultivation of the vine caused Los Angeles papers to advertise their area as an ideal grape and wine locality with greater forcefulness. Los Angeles publicists claimed that the grape grown within their county was by far the best in the state, and that since southern California was responsible for propagating grape culture, Los Angeles was obviously the most promising region for commerical grape growing.[31]

The Pre-Haraszthian 'Fifties

To attest to the viticultural productivity and adaptability of southern California, Los Angeles newspapers and Los Angeles vintners could point to the giant vine at Montecito in neighboring Santa Barbara County. Matthew Keller described the history and crop of this vine romantically and pointedly.[32]

A poor woman in the adjoining county . . . has but one vine. It bore last year five thousand bunches of beautiful grapes weighing over a pound each, yielding her the handsome sum of $4oo. When a girl, and leaving Monterey to remove to her present home, she picked up a vine cutting to drive her mule. The cutting she planted upon her arrival, and, after the lapse of seventy years, such is the result.

The tremendous development of grape culture in northern California attracted the attention of visitors to the state and of the majority of Californians as well. Extensive planting of vines continued in the Los Angeles area, however, and as far south as San Diego grape planting was pressed vigorously.[33] Despite this northern California was soon to surpass the south in the annual number of vines planted. Several articles that appeared in northern California papers —later copied by Los Angeles papers—describing the rapid extension of grape culture in the productive soil of northern California, left a serious impress upon the southern California viticulturists, for grapes and wines were a major source of their income in this period. In 1858 the *Southern Vineyard* stated that Los Angeles vintners would shortly meet formidable rivals in every northern mining and mountain region.[34]

The new counties, to be sure, attracted a great deal of public attention during the early 'fifties; but Los Angeles continued to lead the state in the quantity of its viticultural product. The investment of this county in grape growing and wine making in 1855 was estimated at a million dollars;[35] furthermore, Los Angeles had become the center of a viticultural area that included the southernmost counties of the San Joaquin valley. It was not until the vineyards and orchards of northern California came into bearing on a

The California Wine Industry, 1830–1895

large scale in the early and middle 'sixties that the viticultural supremacy of Los Angeles was seriously threatened. By 1856 Los Angeles claimed 592,000 bearing vines and 134,000 young vines;[36] in 1858 the total wine crop was estimated at 500,000 gallons, and in the same year this county shipped to San Francisco and other northern areas many tons of fresh grapes.[37]

Throughout this decade almost every wine district of California showed an annual increase in the total number of vines set out from year to year. Although some counties showed decreases in certain years, the statistics available for 1855 to 1859 indicate, beyond doubt, substantial increases in total grape acreage.[38] Although it is almost impossible to determine with accuracy the number of vines under cultivation in the years 1850 to 1855, more reliable statistics from which to draw sound generalizations are available for the latter part of this decade. In 1856 there were more than 1,500,000 vines under cultivation in California; in 1857 the total for the state increased to more than 2,200,000, an increase of nearly 50 per cent; in 1858 the number increased to 3,900,000, an increase from 1857 of approximately 74 per cent, and an increase of nearly 150 per cent over 1856.[39] Although more and more acres were planted to grapes, the production of wine was still largely in the hands of a few southern *vignerons*, with northern California not beginning to compete seriously in wine production until after 1857, when Colonel Agoston Haraszthy settled at Sonoma.

The major pre-Haraszthian vintners were in southern California, especially in the Los Angeles area. The Sansevain brothers, proprietors of the vineyard and winery originally owned by Jean Louis Vignes, and the firm of Kohler and Frohling had the largest establishments and continuously purchased large quantities of grapes from surrounding vineyards to make into wine.[40] There were other large producers: William Wolfskill, to whom wine making was second to fruit and grape growing; the Irish vineyardist Benjamin D. Wilson, who in 1855 and 1856 was reported to have had

The Pre-Haraszthian 'Fifties

a vineyard of more than 25,000 vines, and regularly manufactured wine on a large scale;[41] Matthew Keller, who took an active part in shipping grapes to San Francisco as well as in making wine, and after 1857 produced approximately 50,000 gallons of wine annually;[42] John T. Rowland; and Dr. T. J. White, who after 1855 was competing with Keller in the quality as well as the quantity of the wine made at his winery. The *California Farmer* described Dr. White as the ideal *vigneron*, for White was, to the editor of that journal, the most "industrious and scientific vintager" of California.[43]

Large vintages, however, were the exception rather than the rule. Much wine was made by small vineyardists in small quantities. Commercial viniculture during the 'fifties was, in spite of glowing journalistic accounts, still largely primitive. Foot power was still the most common method of crushing grapes.[44] Although progress was being made, a general lack of capital and the limited facilities for production and distribution favored the existence of substantial numbers of small domestic producers, each satisfying a limited local market. The most succinct statement on the commercial aspects and problems of this area during the 'fifties was made by one of its leading vintners, Matthew Keller, who wrote:[45]

More capital is needed to make proper cellars, produce necessary materials, and to enable us to hold our wines till they have age [*sic*], when they would compare favorably with the best. Another great want is a bottle manufactory, that we may store our wines, and prevent counterfeiting, which is now going on extensively.

Los Angeles accounted for most of the professional wine men of the state in this period, but the growing demand for wine resulted in an increase in the number of commercial vintners in other districts, and in the importation of approximately 15,000 cases of French wine in both 1856 and 1857.[46] In 1853 a group of five Frenchmen established a vineyard on the outskirts of Sonora, Tuolumne County. By industrious and intelligent work they were able to harvest, in 1858, more

The California Wine Industry, 1830–1895

than sixty tons of grapes from nearly 30,000 vines.[47] In 1857 Russell B. Blowers, better known for his work with raisins than with wine, planted ten acres of grapes in Yolo County.[48] Charles Krug, later to become one of the famous wine men of the 'eighties and 'nineties, began his Napa County vineyard in 1858.[49] The most popular vineyardist of Sonoma County was General Mariano G. Vallejo, who in 1854 claimed an income of $20,000 from the 5,000 vines planted on his property. By 1863 he had increased his holdings to 40,000 bearing and 15,000 nonbearing vines, not counting 3,000 foreign varieties in bearing and 12,000 nonbearing foreign varieties that were grown mainly for experimental purposes.[50] Vallejo can justly be called the first commercial vintner of Sonoma County.

The most popular wine-grape variety in this period was the Mission. Its prolificness as well as the low cost of Mission cuttings were its greatest attraction. Despite the statements and opinions of many California vintners as to its all-around usefulness and quality, the wine that California produced from this variety was not particularly good. Partly because of this and partly because many Californians did not know how to treat the grapes or how to make wine, California wine fell into disrepute.[51] The few vintners who did make good wine aided in damaging California's reputation by selling much of their product before it was properly aged. Professor Eugene W. Hilgard, of the University of California, commenting on the bad name given California wine, placed the responsibility for a large part of the prejudice against the California product on the early wine men of the 'fifties and 'sixties.[52] Another contemporary source stated that California's wine "found little honor in its own country," and accounted for what sale there was in the 'fifties to the "adulterated nature of the whiskey and brandy supplied by the San Francisco jobbers." The article continued, "Travelers fondly thought that in drinking California wine they at least could not hurt their insides, however insipid or sour the beverage might be."[53] A more honest and just appraisal

The Pre-Haraszthian 'Fifties

of the quality of California wines was made several years later by Professor George Husmann, a leader in the development of phylloxera-resistant vines and a resident of Napa County. He attributed the prejudice against California wine to inexperience.[54]

The important points lost sight of . . . were that rainless summers produced a fruit very high in sugar, and . . . the wines made from it were "heavy" and "heady." The French and German vintners fell into the error of letting the grapes hang on until they were very ripe, as was the custom in their native countries, where they could hardly obtain a thoroughly ripened product except in the best of seasons.

Another injurious practice was that of selling the entire product of cellars or wineries, good, bad, and indifferent, at an average price. The dealer having invested his money, had to devise means to get it back; and thus many poor wines, which injured the reputation of the young industry, were sold.

Falsification of labels was another reason for the general low regard in which wine produced in California was held. The better California wines were often bottled under foreign labels in order to command higher retail prices. The common nineteenth-century practice was to bottle cheap foreign wines under California labels. This was, from the beginning, done in both New York and San Francisco, and was doubly injurious to the name of the native product.[55] It deprived California of due credit and created between grower and merchant an unhealthy relationship that was to last until the twentieth century. Although these practices were often beyond the control of California wine makers, the vineyardists themselves were solely to blame for their continued attempts to imitate certain favored classes of European wines rather than produce a distinctively California product. This policy retarded the introduction and popularization of true California wines and led many to believe that California could at best produce only inferior imitations of foreign varieties. The attempt to imitate carried with it a certain amount of adulteration that spoiled good California wine and resulted in a rather vapid counterfeit. In 1859 the *Southern Vineyard* editorialized,[56] "The true policy of our wine makers is to make the best wine which the grapes of our soil, and the climate of our country will produce, without any regard to its peculiar aroma or flavor."

Despite the bad reports on the general quality of the product, certain experienced wine men produced a tolerably palatable wine, and the French viticultural journal, *Revue Viticole*, in 1862, credited California with being the only wine-producing area of North America capable of competing with the product of Europe.[57] Much excellent white wine was produced in Los Angeles throughout this period; the red wines on the other hand were usually strong, earthy, and heady, resembling more the heavy Italian wines.[58] The heaviness and deep coloration of these wines was attributable to the rich, virgin soil of California. Agoston Haraszthy later proved that this could easily be remedied by planting the red-wine varieties on the less-rich hillside soils of northern California. Possibly his greatest contribution to California viniculture was to introduce and to emphasize the idea that a study of soil adaptability together with the planting of better varieties of grapes provided the basis upon which to begin successful viniculture.

The various types of wine made in this period included champagne. Champagne was made at San Gabriel before 1856,[59] but it remained for the firm of Sansevain Brothers to popularize the manufacture of this product.[60] Calling the product made in their San Francisco cellars "Sparkling California," this firm was able to produce a reasonably good native sparkling wine,[61] but attempts to imitate the famous French brands were less than gratifying,[62] even though the *Alta California*, discussing the product of another Los Angeles *vigneron*, Benjamin D. Wilson, who has been credited with producing the first champagne in California, called it champagne of the "first quality."[63]

Although most reports were not complimentary to the quality of the viticultural products of California—and cer-

The Pre-Haraszthian 'Fifties

tainly these products were not always the best that could be produced—the wine and grape trade of this period was quite profitable. From 1850 to nearly 1860 Los Angeles monopolized the San Francisco grape market. The sale of grapes in San Francisco and the cattle trade were for that southern county the two most important sources of its revenue.[64] Grapes sent to the bay city, when properly packed, found a ready and profitable market.[65] Every *vindemia* (harvest) found ships leaving Los Angeles for San Francisco carrying large quantities of fresh grapes as well as wine, and the southern grape men "realized all the way from one to two bits (reales) a pound for their grapes."[66] One ship alone in January, 1853, brought 5,825 packages of grapes, estimated at 3,000 tons, which sold for 20 cents a pound.[67] By 1860 wine had become much more important commercially than grapes, and as the northern vineyards came into bearing, the cost of transportation forced the Los Angeles vineyardists out of their lucrative northern grape trade. It became quite evident to Los Angeles vineyardists that it was more profitable either to make wine or to sell their grapes to neighboring wineries,[68] and the growth of San Francisco made wine shipments more frequent. To facilitate further the wine trade between Los Angeles and San Francisco, many Los Angeles wineries established cellars in San Francisco.[69] By 1859 most of the twenty-three commercial *vignerons* of the southern metropolis possessed wine depots there.

Lack of adequate transportation was one of the major obstacles confronting wine men at this time. Keller summarized this when he said, "Let us have a railroad, and we shall supply the union with grapes and wine."[70] Shipping costs were too great to permit the acquisition and maintenance of a large Eastern market. Although the first Los Angeles grapes shipped east were sent by Dr. William Osborn to an agricultural convention in Albany, New York, in October, 1854, it was to be some time before California was to derive any substantial profit from this trade.[71] The cost of transportation and packing, and the danger that the

The California Wine Industry, 1830–1895

grapes would spoil en route, prevented a commercially profitable transcontinental trade. In 1855 several boxes of grapes were sent east from Los Angeles by express. They arrived in good condition, but the cost of shipping alone— more than 25 cents a pound—brought the price to $1 a pound retail on the east coast.[72] It remained for Charles Kohler, a German musician, to begin, in the late 'fifties and early 'sixties, the marketing and distribution of California wines on a substantial commercial basis. There was little danger, of course, that wine, in casks or carefully bottled, would spoil during shipment, but although some fairly large shipments were sent east—in 1858 one shipment of 1,230 packages was valued at $13,700, and a shipment of 1,849 packages valued at $33,582 was made in 1859[73]—the high cost of transportation, the inadequate shipping facilities, and the lack of competent means of distribution made such a venture unattractive to the average wine producer.

Chapter III
Charles Kohler, Pioneer Wine Merchant

THE CALIFORNIA WINE INDUSTRY was founded by vineyardists who were usually merchants as well as growers and manufacturers, but by the middle 'fifties it became impossible for one person or one firm to carry on successfully all these activities. As wine production began to take on the characteristics of a profitable industry, as production began to surpass local and state demands, and as the industry faced new marketing problems, it was evident that individual wineries could no longer handle all the aspects of wine marketing from the growing of the grapes to the final retail sale. The wine traffic indicated a profitable future for viticulture, and many people were attracted to grape growing and wine making. Some were experienced vineyardists, wine makers, or cellar men, but a substantial number were vinicultural novices. Having to face the problems inherent in any new business undertaking was in itself formidable. The added burden of competition with foreign wines as well as with a growing number of professional California wine men presented to the new vintner serious production and marketing problems that taxed his resources and his time. The decade of the 'fifties was an auspicious period for an astute merchant, and California as a whole profited from the business acumen of Charles Kohler.

The son of a German agricultural-tool maker, Charles Kohler (1830-1887), was born in Grabow, Mecklenburg, Germany on July 18, 1830.[1] Educated in German schools,

---
[1] For notes to chap. iii, see pp. 177–178.

The California Wine Industry, 1830–1895

Kohler showed signs of more than average musical ability. Upon completion of his secondary education, he studied music and the violin for five years. The unsuccessful attempts of German liberals to establish a representative and responsible government for the Germanies, and the final triumph of reaction under Prince Felix von Schwarzenberg, coupled with the success of the English export trade and the crop failures in the Rhine valley in 1850, which meant economic depression for agriculture, led Kohler to join the host of other migrants to America.

In September, 1850, the twenty-year-old youth arrived in New York with a sound musical education, a violin, and no more.[2] If he did not sweep the musical world of New York off its feet, Kohler became a member of the Italian Opera Company, accompanist for Jenny Lind, Ann Bishop, and other mid-nineteenth-century divas. The rumor of greater opportunities on the Pacific coast "drew his thoughts to California," and in 1852 the German violinist sailed for San Francisco.[3] Crossing the isthmus, he arrived in the boom town on February 5, 1853.[4]

Kohler's first undertaking in San Francisco was to organize the German Glee Club and the even more important German Concert Society. With what he claimed to be the twenty-eight best musicians of the state, he introduced the "music of Mozart, Haydn, and Beethoven on the coast."[5] Thirty-five years later a critic of Kohler's musical accomplishments concluded that the German had a wholesome effect on the men of California, stating:[6] "Rough as the Californians of those days were, the softening influence of virtuous women being almost entirely absent, they found a partial substitute in listening to Kohler's reproduction of those thrilling tones, which can subdue the most savage heart."

The incident that turned the German *émigré* from musician to wine merchant has more the qualities of fiction than of reality.[7] Kohler, his flutist, John Frohling, and a third friend, Beutler, also a musician, took daily morning walks to the Cliff House. On one of these promenades Beutler

Charles Kohler

bought some California grapes, and while eating and admiring the luscious fruit was struck with an idea—they should build "an altar to the God Bacchus and go into the wine business." He was certain that their future in California would be more secure with Bacchus than with Orpheus.[8] Several weeks of discussion ensued, and in September, 1853, the three musicians decided to forsake their music to become wine men. In May, 1854, Frohling was sent to Los Angeles by his two partners to investigate the possibilities of purchasing a vineyard and to report on his findings. He soon reported, "I have purchased a vineyard, send me down four thousand dollars."[9] Their acquisition consisted of twelve acres of old Mission vines that had been cared for by Mexicans.

While Frohling managed the vineyard in Los Angeles, Kohler opened and operated a five-hundred-gallon wine cellar in San Francisco to distribute their product.[10] From the start these two Germans (Beutler was called east to care for his sick wife and sold his interest to his partners) displayed the business acumen and perseverance that were ultimately to make their firm one of the largest wine houses in California.[11] Although the manufacture and distribution of wine were their major concern, music was not entirely abandoned. The sixteen-dollar fee Kohler received for each of his evening performances was used to finance the cellar at 102 Merchant Street, San Francisco, to import foreign vines, or to meet other financial obligations.[12]

In spite of their avowed aim to "produce an article that should compete in quality, quantity, and price with the wines of the old world," their business for the first two years was poor, largely because of their own inexperience and the lack of knowledge as to the type of wine most in demand. But as they became more experienced, business grew better and in 1856 the *California Farmer* credited Kohler and Frohling with a good, sound wine that age would further improve, and complimented the two partners for beginning the serious production of good wine for general consumption

The California Wine Industry, 1830-1895

rather than attempting only to produce "wine for the connoisseur."[13] The *Farmer* went on to add that the firm possessed a vineyard of 20,000 vines and several thousand gallons of wine, and had already shipped wine to New York, England, Germany, the Sandwich Islands, Australia, and China.[14] In 1857 Kohler, when it had become evident that their business was established on a sound basis, had the two largest casks ever to be used for wine built for the firm,[15] and in 1858 he ended his public musical career—for four years he had played every evening to make up for the losses incurred on Merchant Street during the day. Their business had increased enough to warrant the full-time hiring of a wagon and a team of horses; previously Kohler had been able to accommodate their trade by making personal deliveries on foot, carrying the wine in a basket on his arm.[16] From a modest total production of 15,000 gallons in 1856,[17] their wine crop for 1857 jumped to 60,000 gallons,[18] and in 1858 their total vintage was more than 100,000 gallons, of which 72,073 were white wine, 8,093 angelica, and 20,000 brandy.[19] In 1860, 120,000 gallons of wine were stored in San Francisco alone,[20] and in the next year more than 130,000 gallons were sent to San Francisco for distribution.[21] By 1860 the firm had shipped over $70,000 worth of wine outside California and had established a branch office in New York under the management of Perkins, Stearn and Company, the only exclusive California wine house in that state.[22] The New York management was given the "right to establish sub-agencies in all cities of the Union."[23] Foreign agencies and distributors were created in Shanghai and Hong Kong, China; Hakodate, Japan; Amur, Russia; Lima, Peru; and various other South American cities.[24] By 1862, ten cellars on Montgomery Street were required for their San Francisco stock. In Los Angeles they rented the entire basement of the city hall as well as storage vaults at the Wolfskill vineyard and other nearby wineries. Kohler and Frohling had 500,000 gallons of wine and 20,000 gallons of brandy in storage in 1862.[25] Beside the produce from their 22,000 bearing vines in Los Angeles, they annually purchased the grape crop of more than 350 acres of Los Angeles vineyards and during the vintage employed more than 150 men to pick, crush, and prepare the wine for fermentation. The cellar in Los Angeles was prepared to handle wines of all types. Fermentation and storage tanks were constantly being built.

The success of Kohler and Frohling, the popularization of vine culture by Colonel Agoston Haraszthy at Sonoma, and the initial success of a coöperative experiment at Anaheim aroused an interest in viniculture along the entire California coast. Nearly every farmer and small landowner of this period "caught the vine fever." The profits in this new business attracted many, few of whom looked closely enough to discover that the success and the profits made by men like Kohler were built on more than chance and increased production. The success (and the later fame) of this firm rested primarily on Kohler's skill in marketing and distribution, and it was his pioneer work in this field that raised it far above the general run of prosperous first class mid-nineteenth-century California wine houses. Frohling, at Los Angeles, kept pace with the progress and farsightedness of his San Francisco partner. He ran the vineyard on a profitable basis, the vines were well cared for, and the cellar, always the most important feature of the southern branch of the firm, received, as such, marked attention. In the field, experiments with various foreign varieties increased the soundness of the wine, and the importation of Spanish sherry and port varieties not only provided successfully adaptable grapes for California but permitted a wider range of wine production. White wines and brandy were major items, and the brandy made possible the manufacture of fortified sweet wines—angelica, port, sherry, and muscatel.

The out-of-state trade in California wines—with its accompanying problems—is in many respects the story of the export trade of the firm of Kohler and Frohling, for this company was the first major out-of-state shipper of California wines and brandy. Both the quantity of wine and brandy this firm shipped to New York and the profit from such trade were, at first, small. The demand for California wine grew slowly, and the cost of transportation, the scarcity of suitable containers, and the lack of experience in packing tended to make out-of-state marketing difficult. But by 1863 California's eastern exports had increased by more than 100 per cent over 1860, Kohler and Frohling showing the greatest individual increase.[26] To facilitate this traffic and extend the scope of their operations, Kohler and Frohling, in 1867, merged with Perkins, Stearn and Company, and in the following year established an agency in Chicago; the Midwestern trade, however, was not great until the transcontinental railroads provided easier access to that market.

California wines had strong competition to face in the East. The New York wine trade was controlled by the Ohio and other Eastern producers. All efforts to introduce California wines on that market met with strong opposition from both the Eastern producers and Eastern dealers.[27] The Ohio and New York vintners joined forces in their concerted attacks on the quality, soundness, and color of Kohler's wine; Kohler and Frohling, the managers of their New York office, and all other California wine exporters were accused of fraud, adulteration, and falsification of labels. The president of the American Wine Growers Association joined the attack and accused Kohler and Frohling of putting Eastern wines on the New York market under California labels. The fight continued for several years until Perkins, Stearn and Company forced the issue into the newspapers, where finally the "accusers were wholly discomfited."[28]

As California became better known as a wine-producing area, however, and the demand for its wines grew, Eastern traders stopped calling California wine men counterfeiters. Instead, Eastern merchants in this period bottled anything that looked and smelled like wine under a California label, a practice that considerably damaged California's out-of-state trade as well as the general reputation of California wines. The many prizes, medals, and honorable citations

Charles Kohler

California wine received at Eastern exhibits and fairs did not dispel the idea that the state produced mainly worthless imitations. The fight to gain a national pure-wine law, which began at this time and lasted until the middle 'nineties, indicates the length of the battle to prevent adulterations and to impress upon the Eastern market the real character of the California product.

From 1862, when Frohling died, until 1865, when a new partner was taken into the firm, Kohler carried on alone with his prosperous and expanding business, and extended its operations until it had connections in every principal country of the world. In 1868 Kohler and Frohling wines were sent to Germany, Denmark, and to other European countries. These wines proved to be equal to the best German varieties, with the long sea voyage adding to their quality.[29] The principal varieties produced by this firm were:[30] white wines—hock, reisling, muscatel; red wines—tokay, gutadel, burgundy, malvoisie; sweet wines—sherry, port, angelica.

Brandy had been produced commercially since 1858 and enjoyed the same popularity as the firm's various wines, however, the 90-cent federal excise tax retarded any large-scale development of commercial distilleries in California.

Among the early difficulties that restricted the California wine trade was the lack of suitable containers, for both domestic sale and out-of-state shipment. There was no large California glass manufacturer, and transportation costs made it unprofitable to import empty bottles. Consequently, bottles that originally contained foreign wine were used over and over. The increased production of California wine and the attendant decrease in the importation of bottled wine drove the price of bottles to as much as eleven or twelve cents apiece.[31] Kohler joined forces with Taylor and Company of San Francisco, and the Pacific Glass Works was incorporated in October, 1862, with a capital of $50,000, later increased to $100,000, of which $70,000 were "levied and paid in assessments."[32] Kohler and Frohling had a sixth

The California Wine Industry, 1830–1895

interest.³³ Although at first financially unprofitable, the company was able so to reduce the price of glassware that Kohler compensated for his loss through his increased profit on wine. The corporation produced all types of glassware, but it was the wine men who made the most consistently large demands for its products. The first wine bottle was blown on June 16, 1863, and from that date twenty glassblowers and forty-five other workers were employed full time to meet the demand for wine bottles and glass containers of all types.³⁴

Charles Kohler, the guiding spirit of the largest commercial wine house of California, vice president of the Pacific Glass Works, and proprietor of extensive vineyards in Los Angeles, Sonoma, and Fresno counties, still found it possible to take an active part in the political and social life of his city and state. Slavery made him an avowed unionist and a Republican, and when the Civil War broke out he battled successfully to bring the Germans of California to the side of the Union.³⁵ He remained a unionist for the rest of his life, but left the Republican party in 1880 because of that party's stand on the questions of temperance and monopoly. Admitted as the ninety-third member of the Committee of Vigilance, one of the original incorporators and directors of the San Francisco cable car system, founder and director of the San Francisco (later California) Insurance Company, an original incorporator of the German Savings Bank Society of San Francisco, member of two San Francisco charter conventions, member of the San Francisco Board of Education, director of the San Francisco Public Library for seventeen years, and member of many other civic organizations, Kohler left behind him a tradition of public service.³⁶

There have been at various times arguments over who established the first commercial wine house in California, with Kohler and Frohling and the firm of Sansevain Brothers as the chief contestants. The *Alta California* stated in 1862 that Kohler and Frohling "were alone in the wine business for two years before Mr. Sansevain also entered into busi-

Charles Kohler

ness."[37] In 1861 C. Ladrey, in an article in the French journal *Revue Viticole*, credited the German house with one year's seniority over the Sansevain firm.[38] Pierre Sansevain, in a letter to Arpad Haraszthy, dated June 22, 1886, states, on the other hand, that his uncle, Jean Louis Vignes, whose business the Sansevains took over, was the first California wine merchant.[39] Although conclusive evidence on this point is lacking, the claim of Kohler and Frohling seems most tenable.

However that may be, the estate left by Kohler on his death in 1887 is ample proof of the wealth that could be derived from California viticulture. Kohler left his heirs (two sons and a son-in-law) the largest wine-distributing firm of California, with an annual business of considerably more than $500,000;[40] the original Los Angeles vineyard; the Glen Ellen vineyard of 800 acres, of which 350 were in vines, with extensive cellars, buildings, and a winery; a one-third ownership of a 2,080-acre Fresno County ranch with 600 acres of young vines; interests in the Natoma Mining and Water Company of Sacramento County, which had 9,000 acres of land with 2,000 acres in vines; and shares in the Italian Swiss Colony at Asti.[41] To his heirs he left great material wealth, to California wine makers a heritage of practical and intelligent viniculture, and to California wine merchants a heritage of ethical as well as sound business practices. His contemporaries later stated:[42]

> To the intelligence, enterprise, and perseverance of Mr. Kohler, and his friend, is largely due the credit of having first directed public attention to the marvelous capacities of our favored state; of turning men's minds from the fevered search for the precious metals to the more healthful, more beneficient, and extremely more profitable pursuits of husbandry.

Chapter IV
The Age of Haraszthy

ONE OF THE MOST INFLUENTIAL and colorful figures of California viticulture's formative years was the Hungarian exile Colonel Agoston Haraszthy de Mokesa, regarded by many as the father of the modern California wine industry. Working with pen, capital, and skill, Haraszthy was able to arouse the "Legislature and the people of the State to an active interest in improving the original stock of Mission grapes," and his experiments with foreign varieties at Sonoma "changed the whole trend of California viticulture."[1] No other person worked so long and so diligently to establish a sound basis upon which to build California's grape and wine culture. The vigorous industry of today is a tribute to the perspicacity of this *émigré*.

Agoston Haraszthy was born at Futtak, in the Comitat of Bacska, Hungary (now part of Yugoslavia), on August 30, 1812, the scion of an old, influential, and noble Hungarian family.[2] After receiving the traditional education of the Hungarian nobility, he studied law, and at sixteen entered the personal service of the Austro-Hungarian Emperor, Francis I. As a member of the Royal Hungarian bodyguard he acquired the title of colonel. Leaving that service, he became an important civil servant, chief executive officer of his county with the title of count, and then served as secretary to the viceroy of Hungary. Haraszthy was in his own right a Hungarian country squire and wine grower.[3] Like Kohler, he was an advocate of representative government, and

[1] For notes to chap. iv, see pp. 179–181.

The Age of Haraszthy

his devotion to the "cause of liberty . . . and patriotism" involved him, spiritually if not actively, in the Hungarian nationalist movement.[4] His vociferous liberalism as well as his close friendship with the Hungarian nationalist Louis Kossuth made Haraszthy *persona non grata* to the Austrian government.[5] Escaping in disguise from Hungary, he went to Vienna, Hamburg, London, and finally in 1840 to New York.

While negotiating the release of his family from Hungary, Haraszthy traveled throughout the United States with General Lewis Cass, and one result of his travels was a book on "the resources of the United States, which was designed to invite emigration from Hungary, and was the first work upon that subject ever printed in the Hungarian language by a Hungarian author."[6] Unable by long-distance negotiation to free his family, Haraszthy, through the intervention of General Cass, was given permission to return to Hungary and guaranteed safe return to America; Cass held important state papers and documents to insure that the Austrian pledge was kept. His Hungarian properties and wealth were confiscated, but Haraszthy and his family—mother, father, wife, and three sons—returned to America in 1842 and settled in Wisconsin.

In Wisconsin, Haraszthy constructed roads, built bridges, founded settlements, established ferries, and experimented with various branches of agriculture. Although his first American attempt to cultivate grapes, in Sauk City in 1845, proved a failure, the colonel was the first man to grow hops successfully in Wisconsin.[7] The agricultural opportunities in America, particularly in Wisconsin, caused him to advertise the resources of this new land to the depressed, toil-weary farmers of Europe. He became chairman of the Emigration Association of Wisconsin and was responsible for the migration of a large number of Germans, Swiss, and English colonists to America.[8] When the Hungarian revolutions of 1848 broke out, he took the lead in collecting money, ammunition, and arms for the Hungarian liberals. Through his efforts Haraszthy was able to satisfy many of Kossuth's material requests.[9]

The California Wine Industry, 1830–1895

A severe asthmatic condition, and the opportunities that California of 1848 promised, caused Haraszthy to leave Wisconsin, and in 1849 he and his family set out for California via the southern route.[10] Upon arriving in San Diego (December, 1849), Haraszthy was greeted with the news that his Wisconsin agent had sold all his estate and property on the basis of an unfounded rumor that the whole family had been massacred en route by Indians. Haraszthy could have found no better place than California at the turn of the decade to reëstablish himself.

San Diego in 1849 and 1850 was a typical provincial town whose inhabitants were nearly all self-sufficient diversified farmers. Grapes, though not the predominant crop, were cultivated with other fruits. The spring following his arrival, Haraszthy, on the 160-acre lot which he had acquired, planted a garden, fruit trees, and vines.[11] In 1850 he was elected sheriff, but he was still able to devote his leisure to viticulture, and in 1851 he received his first shipment of imported cuttings, which consisted of several Hungarian varieties.[12] He was elected to the state legislature of 1852, where he "distinguished himself by his opposition to all schemes of fraud and monopoly."[13] After serving in the assembly, he purchased a large tract of land thirty miles from San Francisco, near Crystal Springs, in what is now San Mateo County.

The Hungarian grape varieties of the 1852 shipment were first planted at San Francisco, then transferred to Crystal Springs, and after 1857 the same species were extensively cultivated in Sonoma valley.[14] The first two casks of wine manufactured from the now famous Zinfandel, a variety that was later to flood California with its wine, were not made until 1862.[15] The imported vine cuttings and fruit trees were set out in an orderly fashion at Crystal Springs after 1853, and in the same year Haraszthy started a prosperous nursery business.[16] An earlier purchase of fifty acres near Mission Dolores in San Francisco in 1852 further expanded the nursery, and here as in San Mateo County the imported

The Age of Haraszthy

vine cuttings formed the nucleus of his growing business. While in the bay area Haraszthy was appointed assayer in the United States Mint by President Franklin Pierce; later he took over the responsible positions of melter and refiner. When Haraszthy resigned from the mint, he was charged with an excessive shortage of gold, and during the investigation that followed (ultimately all charges against him were proved to be totally unfounded) the colonel pledged all of his San Francisco and San Mateo landholdings as security. During the period of escrow, squatters settled on the property and appropriated everything they found including the land. Only after six years of court litigation and expenditure of $25,000 was Haraszthy able once again to receive clear title to his property.[17]

While occupied with his duties at the United States Mint, the colonel continued experiments with foreign vine varieties at San Francisco and San Mateo. He soon noticed, however, that the San Francisco fog, which was most frequent during the months when the grapes needed sun and warm weather to ripen, prevented the fruit from maturing and acquiring the necessary sugar for wine purposes. Already convinced that the best wine was made from the foreign varieties, Haraszthy now attempted to find a more suitable locality for an extensive vineyard. Early in 1857, before he resigned from the mint, he purchased the nucleus of his Buena Vista property at Sonoma. Several important vintners already had discovered that the soil and climate of this locality were ideal for grape growing and wine making. The Ohio journal *Horticultural Review and Botanical Magazine*, in an article published in 1854, credited this valley with some of the finest vineyards of northern California, and substantiated its claims with statistical examples from the large and prosperous vineyard of General Vallejo.[18] Already acquainted with Vallejo's success, Haraszthy was also influenced by the proximity of Sonoma to the San Francisco grape market in his purchase of the Sonoma property.[19]

The final transfer of the Buena Vista property was ac-

The California Wine Industry, 1830-1895

complished in May, 1857, and Haraszthy and his son Attila, superintendent of the Sonoma ranch, began to transport their rooted vine cuttings from San Mateo and San Francisco. The 560-acre Sonoma ranch was located on the floor of the valley and in the Mayacamas Mountains. Sixteen acres of Mission grapes (about 8,000 vines), some of them planted as early as 1832 and 1834, were still in bearing. The condition of these vines, the profit from the sale of fresh grapes in San Francisco, and the excellent quality of some of the wine made in this valley determined Haraszthy to make viticulture his sole business and interest from this time forward.[20] Within one year he planted 85,556 vines in the vineyard and 462,000 rooted cuttings in his newly constructed nursery. Fourteen thousand were foreign varieties,[21] "the most extensive single plantation of its kind ever made in the State up to that time." Already the possessor of the largest foreign vine collection in California, Haraszthy continued importations on a large scale, and in 1858 his vine imports included 165 varieties.[22] Through extensive use of Chinese labor, Haraszthy within one year built a stone cellar in a hillside and produced 6,500 gallons of wine in addition to large grape shipments to San Francisco.[23]

The rebirth of Sonoman prosperity coincided with the arrival of the Hungarian exile in 1857. Once Sonoma had lost all hopes of becoming the state capital in 1850 and 1851, a general period of decay and depression set in, lasting until 1857. After unsuccessful attempts to supply San Francisco with fresh vegetables—onions, cabbage, and potatoes—and upon the failure of profitable wheat and barley culture, the population of that county within five years (1852-1857), dropped 50 per cent.[24] Little economic progress was made until Haraszthy and the enthusiastic French and German émigrés he attracted caused Sonoma County land values to jump from $6 to $150 an acre.[25]

During the first few years at Sonoma Haraszthy was busily engaged in acquiring more land, planting newly imported vines, and correcting the erroneous conception that all wine

The Age of Haraszthy

vineyards needed irrigation.[26] He was the first Californian to demonstrate in a practical way the superior wine from nonirrigated grapes. The effect of his discovery on California has been likened to that of the cotton gin on the South.[27] In 1852 he entered his nonirrigated vineyard in the annual state fair competition and won first prize. Not satisfied with personal triumphs, Haraszthy started a campaign to induce such later prominent viticulturists as Colonel A. J. Butler, Charles Krug, Major Jacob R. Snyder, General Charles H. S. Williams, Emil Dresel, Jacob Gundlach, and George L. Wratten to settle near him. All these men, directly influenced by the colonel, added to the number of foreign vines planted in this period.[28]

The many inquiries coming from all parts of the state to Colonel Haraszthy made Sonoma "the fount of knowledge in viticultural matters" as well as the foreign vine nursery of the state. It was from here that the Zinfandel, the Flame Tokay, the Black Prince, the Emperor, the Seedless Sultana, the Reisling, the Traminier, the Black Morocco, and numerous other varieties were distributed throughout California.[29] The practical success Haraszthy met with growing all kinds of grapes without irrigation, the superiority of hillside culture for wine grapes, and the use of redwood casks to alleviate the oak shortage made the Sonoman the most eminent *vigneron* of the state.

From 1769, when the Spanish priests introduced the Mission to California, with the exception of the few scattered attempts of such men as Vignes and Kohler, the Spanish vine was, for all practical purposes, the only extensively cultivated variety in California. The practical introduction of foreign vines on a large scale dates to the original 160 cuttings and 6 rooted varieties Haraszthy set out in 1852 in San Francisco. He, more than any other person, popularized the idea that Europe's choicest *viniferas*, although a total failure in the eastern United States, could be grown successfully in California. The outstanding as well as the most outspoken advocate of imported grape varieties, Haraszthy

The California Wine Industry, 1830-1895

felt that only through imported vines planted with due consideration to their adaptability to soil and climate could a better wine be produced. He distributed many of these choice vines to friends, viticultural *dilettanti*, and to inquirers to Sonoma in general after 1857. Many of the non-Mission varieties found in California after 1857 came from the colonel's importations. Yet, in spite of the generally recognized superiority of wine made from the choice imported varieties, and in spite of the publicity attracted to Haraszthy's continuous importations, a very large number of the new vines set out in the late 'fifties were still of the far inferior Mission variety.[30] Its productiveness and the unceasing doubts of some vineyardists, as well as its continued support by the State Agricultural Society,[31] caused the Mission to continue to be the most popular wine grape of California until the 'sixties and 'seventies, in spite of Haraszthy's statements to the contrary.[32]

The fevered plantings of the late 'fifties from Los Angeles to the foothills of the Sierra Nevada brought out one of the first major attempts on the part of the *Alta California* to warn the new vineyardists as to the requirements of successful grape culture. The necessity for a competent study of soil, climate, and variety was for the first time seriously discussed with reference to better wine production.[33] The following year (1859) the *California Farmer*, in an article on the future of California viticulture, urged all new vineyardists to set out only foreign varieties, for the future marketability of California wine depended on an article of better grade than the Mission could produce.[34] To satisfy inquirers and to establish the culture of the grape on a sound basis, Haraszthy also published a series of articles in various California weeklies and dailies. To aid further the scientific establishment of viticulture in Sonoma County, and for the benefit of California as a whole, the Horticultural Society of Sonoma County was founded in 1860 under the supervision of Haraszthy. Within three years more than 60,000 cuttings of various imported varieties represented in the ex-

The Age of Haraszthy

perimental garden of the society were distributed throughout California, but lack of support and patronage soon forced the dissolution of the Horticultural Society and its valuable experimental garden.[35] In 1860, at the Petaluma County Fair, Haraszthy pleaded for a state college of agriculture with a school of viticulture to give practical instruction to all who requested it. The Sonoman believed only ignorance and prejudice were responsible for California's viticultural backwardness.[36] Haraszthy, in 1858, wrote a lengthy article covering every detail of setting out a vineyard as well as a comprehensive treatise on wine making. This work was published as a part of the proceedings of the State Agricultural Society of that year, but a large edition was issued under separate cover and circulated throughout the wine areas of California. Haraszthy's monograph soon became, and for years remained, the best guide to practical viticulture and viniculture in print, and was responsible for many new "converts" to grape growing and wine making.[37]

In 1860 the Buena Vista estate of Colonel Haraszthy embraced nearly 5,000 acres of hillside land with 8,000 fruit trees and 260 acres of vineyard, of which 80 were in bearing and yielded in 1859 4,000 gallons of wine.[38] A strong and clamorous advocate of Chinese labor, Haraszthy was opposed to all forms of restriction of Chinese immigration and taxing of coolie labor. With this same Chinese labor, Haraszthy planted 70,000 vines in 1860 and 135,000 in 1861. Chinese vineyard labor cost Haraszthy only $8 a month and board, but white labor commanded $30 a month and board and was no better than the former for planting and caring for vines and for general work in the winery.[39] Most of the Buena Vista produce was sold as fresh grapes in San Francisco at prices ranging from 9 to 10 cents a pound, and Haraszthy's wine, as early as 1860, brought from $1.50 to $2.00 a gallon in San Francisco. The prosperity of the Sonoma vineyardist led the *Southern Vineyard* to list the "rich warm, light, red soil" of that valley, the large stock of foreign vines, and the little or no irrigation required as the chief

The California Wine Industry, 1830–1895

advantages of Sonoma over other California wine districts; the slow growth and maturing of vines and grapes, the expense of fencing, and the more abundant crops produced in Los Angeles were Sonoma's chief disadvantages.[40]

The success of Colonel Haraszthy; the publication in the California press of articles, pamphlets, and treatises on wine culture and grape growing; and the active support and promotion of viticulture generally by the State Agricultural Society—all resulted in a widespread interest toward increasing the cultivation of the vine.[41] The expansion of Ohio's wine industry in the late 'fifties had a definite and appreciable effect on the California vintners. The popularity of Catawba wine resulted in serious attempts to introduce this wine in California, and quantities of Ohio wine and grape cuttings were imported during the 'fifties to California.[42]

To add further to the impetus initiated by the success of the Ohio wine men and the press of California, every ship coming to California brought news of the destruction of the European vineyards by disease. The California newspapers echoed the prevalent sentiment that their state was to replace Europe as the wine producer of the world. The existence of the mildew and a vine pest in Los Angeles neither affected the setting out of new vineyards nor aroused the fear that a vine disease could ever attack in California. A. Delmas, a prominent San Jose wine man, assured the vineyardists, through the *Alta California*, that the use of sulphur three times a year would check the mildew and continued use would eliminate the danger.[43] The *California Farmer* became the militant crusader of California viticulture and the most outspoken advocate of the necessity of increasing the wine production of California. In a series of articles on the profits to be derived from commercial viticulture, the low cost of grape lands, the small operating costs of vineyards, the excellent market for grapes and wine, and the necessity of making California viniculturally self-sufficient, this journal pointed to the wealth of France as a symbol of what this industry could do for California.[44]

The Age of Haraszthy

The increased production of wine in the period after 1855 and the consequent decrease in the amount of wine imported into San Francisco,[45] the vociferous and persistent demands of the California press, and the increased wealth and investment in viticulture resulted in the active support of the state to aid this new industry. Before 1859 the legislature had taken no active or positive interest in promoting grape culture, but in that year Henry Hancock, assemblyman from Los Angeles, introduced in the assembly a bill "to exclude vineyards . . . from taxation."[46] This "wise policy" provided[47]

> No tax of any nature whatever, shall be hereafter assessed or collected from the owners, managers, or agents, of newly-planted vines or olives, on account of the same, until the vine shall have obtained the age of four years and the olive seven years; *Provided*, that this act shall not be so construed as to exempt such vines and olives from such assessment and taxes as it may hereafter be deemed necessary for the purpose of irrigation.

The close of the 'fifties chronicled the first great advances in California viticulture. Approximately 2,000,000 vines were set out annually for the next twelve years;[48] the distillation of brandy, which had been until 1858 largely an obscure art and a more or less neglected branch of viticulture, became at the turn of the decade an important and remunerative part of the industry; and the legislative act of 1859; as well as the noble work of Haraszthy—all made possible the development of a really important commercial viticulture. Haraszthy not only stimulated planting and increased production of grapes and wine, but he was determined from the start that the new industry should be built on viniculturally sound foundations. Inexperience, the search for immediate profits, and indifference toward choice vine varieties, soil, and location postponed the realization of the Haraszthian ideal for nearly two decades. The career of this "exile, town-builder, . . . farmer, politician, . . . and viticulturist" from 1859 to 1868[49] is the history of the major developments of the viticultural industry of California, and any attempt to separate the two would sacrifice both.[50]

The California Wine Industry, 1830–1895

The passage of the act of 1859, and the success and fortune of men like Haraszthy, Kohler, Sansevain, and others, led to wildly optimistic speculations about the future. The New York journal *Cozzens' Wine Press* predicted that within a few years California would become the first wine-producing country of the world and that viticulture would yield more to this state and its people than all the gold that was taken "from the bowels of her mountains."[51] Authorities and self-styled authorities assured the world that the virgin soil of California prevented any vine disease, such as the phylloxera, from destroying the vineyards.[52] In less than twenty years the disease was to raise havoc with the vineyards of this state. The most promising report on the future of California viticulture came from Haraszthy himself. The colonel stated in 1864 that California had five million acres suited to grape culture, and continued to say that ". . . in a generation or so, . . . the wine product . . . will be worth, on the spot, at only twenty-five cents per gallon more than five hundred million dollars.[53] Such a statement from such an authority was not ignored, and the new decade witnessed more positive state interest as well as more vines planted and more wine produced.

Chapter V
The Committee on the Improvement of the Grape Vine in California

It was indeed paradoxical that California, whose natural features were so strikingly agricultural, should be forced to depend upon South America for most of its breadstuffs, beans, peas, and barley. Apart from viticulture, which yielded abundant crops and substantial profits, the farm produce of mid-nineteenth-century California was decidedly limited and primitive. The negligible production of legumes and the commoner varieties of deciduous fruits accompanied by the scanty supply of seeds, cuttings, and fruit trees were factors concomitant with the lack of competent farmers. Faced by these problems the legislatures of the 'fifties and 'sixties adopted policies explicitly aimed to encourage agriculture. In harmony with such a course the committee to investigate the culture of the grape vine in California was appointed in 1861. The establishment of this committee was a major factor in the development and history of California wines in the formative years.

Before the appointment of the committee Haraszthy, through the support of various California newspapers, urged that a commission be sent to Europe to acquire technical and scientific knowledge, to examine horticultural and viticultural practices and processes, and to collect choice varieties of vines and fruit trees. Since the value of a large-scale project of this nature would more than compensate for the expense involved, the *Alta California* advocated immediate legislation toward this end.[1]

---
[1] For notes to chap. v, see pp. 181–183.

The California Wine Industry, 1830–1895

In February, 1861, Assemblyman Murray Morrison introduced and caused to be passed a concurrent resolution requesting and authorizing Governor John G. Downey to appoint three commissioners to report at the next session upon "the ways and means best adapted to promote the improvement and growth of the grape vine in California."[2] The appointees, to serve without pay "or other considerations," were to be qualified agriculturists. The three commissioners were Colonel Agoston Haraszthy, Colonel J. J. Warner, and a Mr. Shaw, who left for South America shortly after his appointment and never reported for duty.[3] Haraszthy convinced Governor Downey that a trip to Europe to collect the choicest vines and cuttings was the most profitable way in which to increase the number of select varieties in California. Although an assembly committee favored and approved such a project, Haraszthy never received explicit authorization.[4]

The failure of the legislature to appropriate any funds or guarantee any reimbursement for incurred expense inspired Haraszthy to outline a scheme to defray part of his costs. Several weeks before he left for Europe, this plan appeared in different California newspapers. It proposed payments in advance to Colonel Haraszthy from twenty-five to five hundred dollars on the basis of the number of vines and trees contracted for. This money would enable him to purchase extensively, and it would guarantee each contributor, on the basis of the amount paid, the culled varieties of Europe. Unfortunately there is no evidence to determine either the interest this proposal evoked or the amount of money the colonel was able to raise. That such a scheme was outlined was an indication of the difficulties Haraszthy was to face when he attempted to collect from the legislature the freight and purchase price of the importations.[5]

Convinced that only through accomplished agriculturists could California ever hope to equal Europe, Haraszthy sailed from San Francisco on June 11, 1861, with the blessings of the legislature, his own money, and the dubious un-

Committee on Improvement of the Grape Vine

derstanding that he was to purchsse vines and fruit trees for distribution in California. In New York he arranged with Harper & Brothers to publish, upon his return, a diary of his travels including detailed accounts of the viticulture and viniculture of the famed vineyards and wine houses of Europe and a catalogue of the vines of Europe and Asia. In five months—from July to December—he visited every major European wine area in France, Germany, Italy, Spain, Prussia, and England. Haraszthy published a series of articles in the *Alta California* aimed to instruct and inform the grape growers and wine makers of California on the extent and progress of continental viticulture. The following year (1862) he published his results and recommendations in the now famous treatise *Grape Culture, Wines and Wine-Making: with notes upon agriculture and horticulture.*

The American Secretary of State, William H. Seward, provided Colonel Haraszthy with a letter to United States consuls in Europe instructing them "to extend to him any facilities . . . necessary" for the successful completion of his mission.[6] The consular offices made possible meetings and conferences with the distinguished vintners of Europe and also served as temporary depositories for the vines and trees Haraszthy gathered. Immediately upon his arrival in France, Haraszthy opened profitable correspondence with many of the national and provincial horticultural societies of that country. He requested and received valuable specialized and systematized data on the various aspects of grape and wine culture. This material was published periodically in the *Alta California.*[7] At Dijon, France, home of the influential *Revue Viticole: annales de la viticulture et de l'oenologie françaises et étrangères*, Haraszthy was able to obtain valuable cuttings as well as instruction in the wine-making processes of that celebrated region.[8] The publication of such data in the California press not only attracted wide attention but contributed materially to increasing the number of vines set out after the slump in prices of 1859 and 1860.[9]

Haraszthy returned to San Francisco, 1861, more convinced than ever that the "quality of the grapes governs, in great measure, the quality of the wine." He also believed that California required only the excellent grape varieties of Europe and the "same care and science" in the manufacture of its wine to produce an equally "generous and noble" article.[10] Fortified with the experience and knowledge of the best wine makers of the Old World, the colonel presented his report and recommendations to the state legislature. He outlined the procedure of his recent European mission as follows.[11]

... I determined to make arrangements to purchase a quantity of vines, and also to examine every celebrated wine-making establishment within the limits of my tour, so as to learn and describe the newest and best methods of making wine. I did not limit my observation and study to the manufactories alone, but procured the reports of scientific committees, appointed by different governments to investigate the subject by means of practical experiments, continued through a series of years. I also obtained the proceedings of the Congress assembled, by order of the government of France, for the purpose of comparison and consultation, and which was composed of the most scientific chemists and practical wine-makers. I availed myself of reports of similar assemblies held annually in Germany, and of the newest and best works in various languages, written by able men, who had spent their lives in the business of vine-culture and wine-making.

The 200,000 cuttings and rooted vines represented the finest selections of France, Germany, Italy, Spain, Portugal, and Hungary.[12] They were catalogued under 499 names and embraced 1,400 varieties.[13] A gardener cared for the collection en route; at New York they were examined, packed, and shipped by Wells Fargo steamer to California. They arrived in San Francisco "in the very best condition" in February, 1862.[14] From San Francisco the valuable collection was taken to Haraszthy's Buena Vista ranch at Sonoma, where the more "exquisite varieties" were planted in hotbeds and the others set out in the vineyard.[15] The result of this work guaranteed 300,000 rooted vines ready for distribution the following fall. Since there was neither machinery nor estab-

Committee on Improvement of the Grape Vine

lished precedent to follow in distributing such a large number of vines and trees, Haraszthy suggested that Governor Downey ask the legislature to direct how the vines and trees should be made available to the vineyardists of California. The United States Patent Office distributed many of its plants on the basis of the number of representatives each state had in Congress. This seemed a likely formula, since there were few counties in the state that were not adapted to the vine. Although Haraszthy was interested in securing immediately permanent and well-distributed areas for the imported varieties, Downey and the legislature procrastinated for several months before deciding upon the policy to be followed.

During the period of indecision Haraszthy outlined a six-point program aimed to encourage grape culture in California.[16] Basing his recommendations upon his recent European experiences, he strongly urged the legislature to take a paternalistic attitude toward agriculture. Only through the aid of the state government could viticulture prosper and be financially profitable to the vineyardist and the state as a whole.

The all-inclusive Haraszthian program visualized a state appropriation for the purchase of land to establish an experimental garden under a qualified, state-appointed horticulturist. After this initial grant, the legislature was to appropriate annual funds sufficient to allow the garden to purchase seeds, vines, and trees for experimentation. Haraszthy was convinced that the success of European agriculture was largely the result of having liberal governmental funds at the disposal of the agricultural societies engaged in research and experimentation. In the United States, on the other hand, this duty rested with the individual states. To supplement the work of the experimental garden, "a joint-stock company, with a capital of a million dollars for the planting of vines, almonds, mulberries, etc. in the southern part of the State," was to be created.

The marked difference between European and American

The California Wine Industry, 1830-1895

agriculture was the greater interest the governments of the Old World took in this important branch of their economy. Through agents authorized to collect the choice fruit specimens of the world, Europe secured for itself a wide collection of valuable vines and trees. Haraszthy suggested that California follow such a course. Complementing the work of the horticultural societies and the governmental agents was the recognized position of husbandry in the universities, technical schools, and colleges of Europe. Alert publicists and agriculturists maintained that there was a great need in California for a state-supported agricultural college giving practical instruction in horticulture and viticulture.

To insure confidence in and to prevent the adulteration of California wines, Haraszthy asked the legislature to pass an act providing for the appointment of a general agent for California,[17]

... who would reside in San Francisco, and to whom the wine producers could send their wines to be sold; the agent to sell the wines at prices fixed by the manufacturer, with the proprietor's label on the bottles, or, if in barrels, with his name attached thereto. This agent, so appointed, to receive from the owners of all wines or brandies sold a commission, to be fixed by law, and not to exceed the commission usually received by merchants; the agent to defray the expense of office and cellar out of the commission he may receive. The law creating said office might also impose heavy fines and confiscation of the liquor belonging to any individual who would send for sale adulterated articles. Such an office would be no burden to the State nor to the wine-growers, as it would be optional with them to send their wines to this office or dispose of them in any other way. Every producer, ... would find it to his advantage to avail himself of this medium, as he would meet a ready sale, and pay no more than the usual commissions, while he would aid in preventing frauds, and thus create confidence in the genuineness of our wines. The agent would have to be strictly impartial. The agent should be required to give ample bonds for the faithful and impartial performance of his duty, and for the prompt payment of all receipts on account of sales.

The successful execution of this program would have required a large amount of money; moreover, it would have

Committee on Improvement of the Grape Vine

required practical and qualified men to fill the various responsible positions. With the money-making opportunities California offered during the 'fifties and 'sixties, only exceptionally high salaries would have attracted the right men. Haraszthy understood this; furthermore, he believed that the state was willing to underwrite such a long-term program. In this he was mistaken.

The *California Farmer* approved Haraszthy's report and recommendations and urged the legislature to take the initiative in distributing the unparalled collection of vines. Colonel James Warren, editor of this weekly, strongly endorsed the whole program and hoped to see it realized.[18] He was particularly anxious to see an agricultural college established in California, for as early as 1853 he was instrumental in urging the legislature to provide for such an institution. Then the *California Farmer* reopened a vigorous campaign along the same line. Warren was a one-man pressure group until 1868, when the University of California was founded.[19] In April, 1862—after nearly two months of wrangling—the Senate Committee on Agriculture submitted its final report.[20]

Early in February, 1862, Haraszthy informed Governor Downey of the expense he had undergone in making the collection. He asked that an appropriation be passed to refund him the expenses already incurred—$12,000 to cover the original cost of the collection, freight, and the planting and care of the vines at Sonoma.[21]

The divided attitude of the legislature manifested itself as soon as the subject of an appropriation was introduced. The debate began with a resolution authorizing the Assembly Committee on the Culture of the Grape Vine and a committee of three from the Senate to go to the Buena Vista ranch and report to the legislature on the number of vines, their condition, and what ought to be done with them. This resolution indicated very early the form and substance of the debates that were to follow. The opposition attacked the resolution on three grounds: that it was neither politic nor

The California Wine Industry, 1830–1895

just to encourage one industry at the neglect of others; that the "grape vine interest should be left, like everything else, to seek its own level by the laws of political economy, without any extraneous aid from traveling committees"; and that a resolution to send eight or ten men to Sonoma, where one would do as well, for no other purpose than to get their mileage, was to inaugurate a policy of "expensive extravagance."[22] More significant than the pecuniary objections was the attitude voiced by Assemblyman Dudley of Solano County. Dudley's opposition to the resolution was characteristic of the denunciatory spirit of many of the representatives of the mining counties. He was opposed to state purchase of the vines because he felt that the culture of the grapes should be left to viticulturists with no subsidy from the state, and because he was convinced that it was no more appropriate for the state "to go to speculating in grapes than for it to speculate in thoroughbred stock." Therefore, it was not surprising that any resolution guaranteeing some form of state aid should be set aside by the substantial vote of thirty-five to eighteen. The resolution authorizing a committee of the assembly and senate to visit Haraszthy was passed only after the initial motion was amended so as to allow the committee not more than "their traveling expenses and their per diem."[23]

In April, 1862, by a majority of three to two, the Senate Committee on Agriculture refused to report by bill, and the inaction of the legislature ended all hopes of state purchase and distribution of the vines.[24] The *California Farmer* and the Sacramento *Union* were distressed with the results. Both papers felt that a great injustice had been done, not only to Haraszthy, but to all of the vineyardists of California. The committee's final action was prompted by the fear of losing votes by showing its "willingness to worship Bacchus" as well as by the reluctance of the state to go into business.[25] Two members of the minority succeeded in introducing a bill recommending: distribution of the vines and trees by county according to population; a payment of $8,457 to

Committee on Improvement of the Grape Vine

Colonel Haraszthy for the original purchase; and an appropriation of $1,549 to Wells Fargo for the cost of transportation. The opposition, however, shelved the bill by the overwhelming vote of twenty to nine. Haraszthy never received a cent.[26] Two decades later, Arpad Haraszthy, the colonel's son, attributed the action of the predominantly Republican legislature to an attack upon his father, who at the time was chairman of the state Democratic committee. During the Civil War, Haraszthy was accused of being a secessionist, and it is very likely that this accusation also mitigated against him.[27]

Assured of no aid from the state legislature, Haraszthy held the vines for a year and then offered them for sale. The primitive manner in which they were distributed and the lack of knowledge on the part of many buyers resulted in a general confusion that held the industry back twenty-five years.[28] To the shortcomings of the legislature of 1862 is largely due the muddled nomenclature of California wine varieties today. The failure of the state to take an active part in preserving and propagating the vines resulted in a tremendous loss, since very few vineyardists were qualified to train the new, delicate varieties successfully. Many of these choice vines were forced to yield to the "test of quantity by short pruning."[29] Although the Haraszthian collection was sacrificed to political expediency, the interest attracted to sounder wine production and choicer varieties had a healthy, if somewhat retarded, effect on California viticulture. In spite of the fact that many vineyardists continued to plant inferior but productive grape varieties and to produce nothing but *vin ordinaire*, a few did profit from the vast new store of information from Europe.

The interest aroused by Haraszthy's trip, his articles and book, and the bickering in the legislature following his return unfortunately overshadowed the conspicuous significance of Commissioner Warner's report. Warner outlined to the legislature the development of viticulture in California and recommended that the state actively aid the wine

The California Wine Industry, 1830–1895

industry by protective legislation as well as by distributing viticultural information among the farmers of the state.[30] The creation of a state institution to extend technical and commercial knowledge formed the theme of the commissioner's report. Only through such an organization, Warner maintained, could the agriculture and viticulture of California attain the important position it deserved.[31] He urged the state to undertake Colonel Haraszthy's "liberal offer ... to teach, without compensation, the several branches of grape culture and the manufacture of wine to delegates from the various counties of the State," and to use Haraszthy's services to inaugurate an extended program of viticultural education. The properties of wine grapes, the planting, pruning, and training of vines, the racking of wines, and the organization of cellars were to be the major subjects of the new state-supported educational program.[32] The new system of education was to utilize the information Haraszthy had recently brought from Europe, and was to be based upon European horticultural experiences. The immediate problems of scientific grape culture and wine making were to be attacked by creating a bureau to disseminate information on a state-wide basis.

Although progress had been made in producing wine, the California product still lacked distinction, and the wine trade of the state suffered as a result. Warner attributed this to the myopic policy of an uninformed legislature. Although the Act of 1859 excluded vineyards from taxation for four years, Warner recommended that this policy be augmented to include wine as one of the tax-free commodities. The expansion of grape culture, with the consequent increase in the production of wine accruing from such legislation, would in the not too far distant future more than compensate the state for its momentary loss of revenue.[33] Such legislation would not only attract many new colonists but would enable California to compete advantageously with foreign wines as well as to improve the quality of its own product. It would no longer be necessary to sell unripe wines to avoid

Committee on Improvement of the Grape Vine

an annual tax, and this fact alone would materially improve the wines of California. This was undoubtedly the most cogent reason, for California wine throughout the nineteenth century—and a good portion of the twentieth—was seldom properly aged.

Commissioner Warner's report, although in many respects quite excellent, would have been much more effectual if he had had the necessary funds to investigate the exact status of grape culture and wine making in all the major viticultural counties of California. Although the resolution authorizing Warner's report encompassed a state-wide investigation, it also provided that the commissioner "should receive no pay, nor ask for any compensation." This latter provision not only compelled Warner to abandon any hopes of procuring reliable and scientific data but seriously curtailed the effectiveness of his whole project.

That the Committee on the Improvement of the Grape Vine in California accomplished what it did is a tribute to Haraszthy and Warner. Financially repudiated, and in the face of legislative indifference, both men succeeded in accomplishing a great deal more than might have been expected under the circumstances. The choice Haraszthian collection of vines and the scientific and systematic data he brought back to California served as the basis upon which the modern industry of the state was built. Warner's researches and investigations in California viticulture clearly indicated the path toward profitable commercial viniculture.

Chapter VI
The Anaheim Coöperative and the Sonoma Corporation

BETWEEN 1857 AND 1863, the policy of the state government to encourage agriculture coincided with a new development in commercial viticulture. The attempt at coöperative wine growing in 1857 at Anaheim and the corporate experiment of 1863 at Sonoma indicated a new trend in commercial grape growing and wine making. The coöperative viticultural ventures of the 'eighties and 'nineties and the later corporate big business growth and organization of the wine industry were sequels to these two early experiments. They are important because they indicated—very early—new tendencies in the business and commercial organization of the industry; they are equally significant as studies in the early history of large-scale wine production.

The German experiment at Anaheim was one of the more successful mid-nineteenth-century attempts to set up coöperative communities in America. The abundance of cheap land, the lack of industrialization, and the high degree of political and religious freedom in the United States attracted many European immigrants. Although strictly coöperative in its origins, this German community, twenty-six miles southeast of Los Angeles, contained elements of the pre-1850 utopian and humanitarian socialism. The belief in the "perfectibility of society through rational effort," and similar politico-economic theories were, however, always incidental

---

[1] For notes to chap. vi, see pp. 183–186.

Anaheim Coöperative and Sonoma Corporation

to the more immediate and material needs of the community. This was first and foremost a business venture.

The idea of a German wine colony was conceived in 1855 by four prominent California Germans: Charles Kohler, John Frohling, Otto Weyse, and George Hansen.[1] In the mid-'fifties the demand for wine so far exceeded the supply that the success of such a venture appeared assured from its inception. Hansen (a Los Angeles lawyer, civil engineer, and for six years a deputy supervisor of Los Angeles County), Otto Weyse (editor of the San Francisco *Democrat*), and Frohling met with Hansen in Los Angeles in 1855 and discussed plans for establishing a German colony in southern California.[2] The scheme aroused immediate interest, and within a few weeks the Los Angeles *Star* warned the vineyardists of Los Angeles County to postpone all sales of wine lands until more definite results of the Hansen, Frohling, Weyse meeting were known. The *Star* maintained that the large number of San Francisco Germans who planned to raise vineyards in the Los Angeles area would insure better prices in a few weeks.[3] Upon his return to San Francisco, Hansen became the general agent through which the German colony of northern California made its interests in coöperative viticulture known. Largely through his efforts the 1855 meeting materialized into the definite plans of 1857.[4]

In the summer of 1857 the Anaheim association was organized and incorporated at San Francisco under the name of the Los Angeles Vineyard Society with a capital stock of $100,000.[5] According to the society's constitution and bylaws the experiment was to maintain its communal organization for six years, but by 1859 the coöperative features of the enterprise had come to an end. The 50 two-thousand-dollar shares were purchased by fifty Germans—forty-one residents of San Francisco and nine of Los Angeles—many of whom, according to Kohler, were practical viniculturists from the Rhine Valley.[6] More recent investigation has proved Kohler entirely wrong.[7] Only one of the original settlers had any grape-growing or wine-making experience. Harris New-

The California Wine Industry, 1830–1895

mark, a contemporary, called the colonists a "curious mixture," and the occupations they represented—carpenter, watchmaker, blacksmith, engraver, brewer, bookbinder, poet, miller, and musician—were a far cry from practical viniculture.[8] Since Hansen had been the prime mover and organizer, this "man of keen judgment and remarkable foresight" was chosen to select the site of the colony, purchase the land, and complete the transfer of title and deed. The bylaws gave Hansen, as supervisor and general factotum, wide powers and unlimited authority over the initial work to be inaugurated. From the construction of the first fence to the building of the society's offices, Hansen was in complete charge.

On September 12, 1857, Juan Pacific Onteverras sold a portion of his rancho—1,165 acres—to Hansen and Frohling for approximately two dollars an acre. Included in the deed was a thirty-two-foot right of way to the Santa Ana River for an irrigation ditch.[9] At the time of purchase, the only vegetation on this "barren, dry, sandy plain" was cactus.[10] Although the inherent qualities of the soil might be excellent, its barrenness at first seemed portentous. The large turnover of the society's stock during the first few years attests to the lack of confidence in the outcome of the venture among some of the shareholders,[11] granting that some purchases of Anaheim stock were speculative.

Division of the tract was begun immediately upon acquiring title. After a preliminary survey fifty rectangular twenty-acre lots were laid out—one for each shareholder.[12] In addition each member was given a town site for building a home. Ten lots were set aside in the center of the tract for schools and other public purposes.[13] While this work was being done, the shareholders continued at their various occupations in San Francisco and Los Angeles.[14] Hansen's abilities as an engineer were successfully tested when he directed Indian, Mexican, Sonoran, and Chilean labor to construct an irrigation ditch. Providing irrigation was the most immediate problem, since without water it would have been impossible

Anaheim Coöperative and Sonoma Corporation

to introduce successful grape culture on such arid land. Water was so important to this area that when the original venture came to an end in 1859, it was only natural that a water company should succeed the corporation.

In September, 1857 Hansen began work on the irrigation canal to the Santa Ana River.[15] Within six months the canal was completed. It was six miles long, eight feet wide, and from two to three feet deep. To prevent excessive evaporation during the hot summers, willows and sycamores were planted on both sides of the ditch.[16] Before setting out the vines it was necessary to fence off the whole tract, since cattle and sheep roved the countryside. This was the second most pressing problem, and Hansen solved it with equal ability. The entire tract was fenced with live six-foot willow cuttings one foot apart.[17] Since willows grew quickly, they served a twofold purpose: as fencing and as an economical source of fuel.

The general interest aroused by this experiment caused many Californians, both vineyardists and speculators, to offer as much as 33 per cent above par for a share of Anaheim stock. Hoping to keep out speculators and to restrict the profits to its original investors, the Los Angeles Vineyard Society did not offer any stock for sale. In spite of the fact that the members "bound themselves by a promise not to sell a share to non-members," a certain amount of stock did fall into the hands of speculators.[18]

From 1857 until the final subdivision among the shareholders in 1859 the land was cultivated in common. Very few members took any part in setting out the first vines. Like all the other work at Anaheim, this was done by laborers under Hansen's direction. In 1858 the first vine was set out.[19] Within a year eight acres of grapes, averaging between 900 and 1,000 vines to the acre, were planted on each of the fifty lots. More than 400,000 vines were set out the first year.[20] The cuttings, almost entirely of the Mission variety, came from the various Los Angeles and Santa Ana vineyards. A few cuttings of Spanish Barcelona grapes were also

The California Wine Industry, 1830-1895

planted, but their number was insignificant.[21] The *Revue Viticole* commented that the sandy soil of Anaheim was not only the most ideal for cultivating grapes but the most easily irrigated. An acre of vines, under the conditions set up by Hansen, could produce annually 10,000 pounds of grapes or 800 gallons of wine.[22] At the end of the first eighteen months the Sacramento *Union* called the irrigation canal, the fence, and the half million vines planted one of the greatest agricultural achievements ever performed in California.[23] Undoubtedly it was the most extensive attempt at viticulture undertaken in the state, and as a strictly coöperative settlement of agriculturists it was certainly the most unique.

The scarcity of labor, cuttings, and building materials made such a large-scale operation expensive. Within two years approximately $60,000 were spent on labor and improvements. Labor cost more than $300 a week. From 1857 to 1859 the society paid $20,000 for 22,789 days of field labor alone.[24] Non-European labor was paid between fifty and seventy-five cents a day. It soon became apparent that Indians and Mexicans were more profitable than the four German and one American workers hired by the society. The latter averaged between thirty and thirty-five dollars a month, but the former never earned more than twenty dollars a month.[25] Such an initial outlay of money resulted in a large indebtedness.

Increasing difficulties, lack of harmony among the shareholders, and the lack of confidence in Hansen's work and policies caused a distribution of the common property in 1859. Although Hansen had done substantial work, the cost of the experiment and the inability of the society to pay any dividends disheartened some of the members.[26] The distribution of the vineyard and town lots took place at a drawing held in San Francisco on September 12, 1859. After estimating current vineyard prices, the Anaheim lots were appraised at about $1,200 apiece.[27] To prevent any injustice and to assure an equitable distribution, a common fund was established. Its purpose was to pay holders of lots valued

Anaheim Coöperative and Sonoma Corporation

at less than the estimated average the difference in cash, and those who drew lots valued at more than $1,200 were to pay the difference to the treasury. The lottery was an attempt to insure each shareholder the opportunity of drawing a choice piece of property or to receive the equivalent of $1,200. Once the distribution of lots was completed, the Los Angeles Vineyard Society sold its other property and effects to the Anaheim Water Company. Thus the coöperative features of the enterprise came to an end. Before passing out of existence the society was able to pay a dividend of more than a hundred dollars to each stockholder. This brought the cost of an individual subdivision down to a little more than $1,000—a nominal sum for a vineyard of 8,000 vines and a townsite 150 by 200 feet.[28] The investors assumed individual control of their vineyards on December 15, 1859, but only twelve families moved to Anaheim in that year.[29]

The Germans who founded and settled Anaheim came from all parts of Germany except its eastern border, the majority being from Hanover, Schleswig-Holstein, and various Rhenish provinces. They had one thing in common—they were all poor. Not until they settled in California did the idea of a coöperative wine colony originate.[30] When the first settlers arrived in 1859, they found a "crude frontier settlement." Their first problem was to establish some form of community life. Once this was accomplished, the colonists planted the remainder of their lots in vines, and in 1861 they harvested their first crop—500 pipes of wine (approximately 70,000 gallons) valued at nearly $23,000.[31]

Many non-Germans looked upon the experiment with keen interest, but the founders made it exceedingly difficult for outsiders to acquire property within the tract.[32] The settlers were happy among themselves, as shown by the fact that only one of the fifty original investors left the colony.[33] They made their own laws and dispensed their own justice "with no other restraint upon their actions than that of a sense of stern justice and a desire to do what was right." The medieval qualities of the experiment continued for more

The California Wine Industry, 1830–1895

than a decade, when despite the disapproval of the "elders" the colony grew to nearly 1,200 inhabitants and the original tract was no longer sufficient. To satisfy the needs of a rising population, 1,500 additional acres were acquired in the early 'seventies, most of which was planted in wine grapes.[34]

The first decade found the vineyardists of Anaheim faced with serious problems, the most pressing of which was the difficulty of making and selling their wine at a profit. Although production increased from nearly 70,000 gallons in 1861 to over 600,000 gallons in 1868, the marketing of the wine presented obstacles not easily surmounted.[35] The inferior wine produced from the Mission variety, as well as the trial-and-error methods of Anaheim production, resulted in an article too strong to be agreeable. The bad reputation of California wines generally added to the difficulty of selling the Anaheim product. Then too, the San Francisco market was too distant and transportation too expensive for profitable exploitation. Then a serious flood in 1862 greatly damaged many vineyards. The severity of the damage reduced the crop of that year substantially, and many of the town homes were inundated under four feet of water.[36]

By 1860 the extent of the grape acreage and the productivity of vine and soil made Anaheim one of the leading viticultural areas of California.[37] The product was at the time almost entirely purchased by Kohler and Frohling, but it was impossible for the vineyardists to continue to depend upon any one firm for their market. The evident necessity of some form of reliable transportation between San Francisco and the new township of Anaheim—created in December, 1860—resulted in the establishment of the Anaheim Lighter Company for the specific purpose of building a wharf and port for the community. The Anaheim Landing—as the wharf became known—was completed in October, 1864.[38] A twelve-mile road was built from the center of the town to the wharf. The slough, seven feet deep at low tide, was able to accommodate small ships. With coast steamers stopping here weekly, the transportation problem was partially solved

Anaheim Coöperative and Sonoma Corporation

but remained critical until the railroad was established in 1874 and 1875.

The story of Anaheim from 1870 to 1888, when a mysterious vine disease killed virtually all the vines, is one of growth, expansion, and increased production.[39] These years of interest and progress were the results of hard work, perseverance, and thrift. The importance of Anaheim goes beyond the immediate history of California viticulture. At the same time that it stimulated interest and attracted attention to the grape industry in its experimental stage, the Los Angeles Vineyard Society was also one of the first attempts in California—although by no means the last—to found a coöperative agricultural community. The frontier qualities possessed by these German pioneers gave them within twenty years comfortable incomes, beautiful homes, and sound agricultural investments. Although the vine disease of 1888 marked the complete destruction of the community's grape industry and financially crippled Anaheim, the subsequent cultivation of walnuts and oranges made possible a new period of prosperity.

The founding of Anaheim and the establishment of the Buena Vista Vinicultural Society in March, 1863, were comparable only in that both organizations originated as fundamentally coöperative ventures immediately concerned with grape growing and wine making. At this point the similarity ceases. In direct contrast to the viticultural inexperience of the founders of the Los Angeles Vineyard Society, the B.V.V.S. was established by the undisputed and foremost master wine maker of California, Agoston Haraszthy. The viticultural tradition, practicable experience, and vinicultural knowledge of Haraszthy; the recognized adaptability of Sonoma soil and climate; the superior collection of *viniferas;* the proximity to the San Francisco market; and the substantial winery, cellar, and equipment inherited by the B.V.V.S. made its beginnings antithetical to those of Anaheim.

In 1863 Haraszthy sold his winery, 400-acre vineyard,

The California Wine Industry, 1830–1895

and 6,000 acres of land in Sonoma County to the society.[40] As early as 1860 he had conceived the idea of subdividing his lands into ten-, twenty-, and thirty-acre lots set out with choice vines. His plan was to care for the vineyards for three years and at the end of that time to sell the various tracts for approximately $200 an acre to the workers on his estate, friends, and other interested persons.[41] The final disposition did not follow the original idea, and, in lieu of small independent wine farms, a corporation, hiring Chinese and other day laborers to work the vineyards and cellar, was created.

At this time the corporation laws of California forbade any society or land company from holding more than 1,440 acres of land. However, in 1863 special legislation was enacted exempting the B.V.V.S. from this provision. On March 27, 1863, the society was incorporated, with William C. Ralston, wealthy and prominent Californian, as its disguised patron.[42] The society, composed chiefly of San Franciscans, was capitalized at $600,000 divided into six thousand shares. Five out of eight of the trustees were German, and three—Haraszthy, Dresel, and Landsberger—were prominently concerned with viticulture.[43] The object of the corporation was stated to be:

> ... the purchase of lands in Sonoma and Napa Counties; improving, developing, working, and cultivating the same; raising all kinds of fruit, grain, and plants thereon; making wine, brandy and other liquors; burning lime, quarrying, and selling building stone; and generally, to make such use of said lands, with whatever may be found thereon, either in the shape of minerals, water, stone, or other things as may be deemed proper or advantageous.[44]

At the time of incorporation the Buena Vista estate, the most noted and prominent wine ranch of northern California, contained extensive and valuable improvements, and its wine-making facilities were unequaled in the state. With more than 150,000 permanently planted foreign vines, nearly 30,000 choice one-year-old European varieties, and 186 kinds of abundantly bearing grapes, the society was able

Anaheim Coöperative and Sonoma Corporation

to enter upon large-scale production from the beginning. In 1862 Haraszthy produced 30,000 gallons of red and white wine and 1,000 gallons of brandy. He estimated the estate's wine crop for 1863 to be 100,000 gallons. The cellars included every "convenience and requirement" necessary for manufacturing wine and brandy. Its most celebrated possessions included a steam-operated crusher with a capacity of 50,000 pounds of grapes a day, a complete set of machinery for making and processing champagne, a modern distillery, excavated rock cellars, and eleven 4,000-gallon storage and fermentation tanks.[45] Beside the vinicultural assets, the property possessed "inexhaustible quarries of white and red stone," 40,000 cords of standing wood, and five sulphur springs whose waters were "known, and ... successfully used by invalids." (If necessary, a substantial income could also be secured by constructing bathhouses and resorts.) In short, the financial potential of the estate was unlimited.[46] The organization of the B.V.V.S. as an incorporated grape-and-wine company aroused great interest among the vineyardists of the state, and the *Alta California* stated that its success would determine the advisability of adopting similar plans elsewhere in California. Although Colonel Haraszthy had at first visualized a coöperative organization, the B.V.V.S. was from the start a corporation with all the appurtenances and fixtures thereof.

In early 1863 the B.V.V.S. prepared to become the major wine producer of the state. The colonel had put his son Arpad in charge of the society's cellars. This twenty-two-year-old youth had in 1862 returned from France, where he had studied grape culture, wine making, and champagne processes. Under his supervision, experimentation with sparkling wines was begun at once. In 1863, B.V.V.S. champagne was exhibited at the state fair.[47] Like earlier attempts to imitate that famous French wine, the society's champagne was not particularly good. The first experiments seemed to warrant optimism, but once the wine was bottled, it lost all its good qualities and had to be uncorked. This failure cost Colonel Haraszthy nearly six thousand dollars.[48]

The California Wine Industry, 1830-1895

The use of Mission grape—totally useless as a champagne variety—as well as inexperience in fermentation and bottling were the most likely causes of the early failures.[49] The company was unable to produce a palatable champagne for several years. Despite the praise of the California press and statistics of Eastern demand and sale, it was not until 1867, under the supervision of the French champagne maker, P. Debanne, and after continued large-scale experimentation, that the B.V.V.S. made a successful sparkling wine.[50] "Sparkling Sonoma" received an honorable mention at the Paris Universal Exposition in 1867. The manufacture of champagne was always unprofitable to the company, but its production increased general interest in the Sonoma corporation and gave it a more sophisticated position among the wineries of California. In 1868 and 1869 the B.V.V.S. produced nearly 120,000 bottles of champagne, which sold at twelve to fifteen dollars a case—a few dollars less than the imported article. The champagne of the society—and of California generally—was now reputed to be equal to the second-rate champagnes of France.[51] Despite his early failures Arpad Haraszthy was in many respects the founder of the present-day California champagne industry, and the Buena Vista Vinicultural Society was the first successful large-scale manufacturer of that article. In 1864, partly as a result of his expensive failures with sparkling wine and partly because he could not "effect satisfactory terms" with the directors of the society, Arpad Haraszthy resigned and formed an independent wine firm with a Swiss-Italian of San Francisco.[52]

Under the guidance of Colonel Haraszthy, supervisor of the whole estate, the corporation rapidly increased its production and sales. During one year the Sonoma corporation produced 100,000 gallons of wine, 5,000 gallons of brandy, 10,000 pounds of tobacco, and grain, wool, fruit, and hay valued at more than $10,000, the total value of all the B. V. V. S. produce during this year being more than $135,000. In the same year, the corporation spent more than

Anaheim Coöperative and Sonoma Corporation

$50,000 on permanent improvements alone.[53] The profits of the first year exceeded all estimates, and the colonel stated:

We consider our Society no longer an experiment, but as an established and successful fact: and we expect that a handsome dividend on the money invested will be paid in 1865.[54]

The work to accomplish all this was done largely by Chinese laborers. Haraszthy, long convinced that they were the most useful as well as the cheapest source of labor, employed them whenever they were available. Nearly a hundred Chinese, working in the field, on permanent improvements, and in the lime and stone quarries, cost the society no more than approximately a dollar a day each.[55] The heavy labor responsible for the three new cellars constructed after 1863 was done entirely by Chinese. When they were not working for the corporation, the Chinese were hired out to work in the different vineyards and fields of Sonoma County, thus furnishing a source of cheap labor for the whole county. Living in bunkhouses by themselves with their own cook, the Chinese at Buena Vista, although not slaves, were in many respects the American counterpart to the pre-1848 serf and agricultural field labor of eastern Europe.

Although the annual reports of the treasurer of the B.V.V.S. indicated increased assets and cash balances, the corporation was not so solvent as the profit-and-loss statements made it appear.[56] In 1864, as a result of increased indebtedness, the slow development of the business, and the shortage of fluid capital, the company issued more shares. An excise tax on wine and brandy added to the society's financial difficulties and forced the trustees to postpone further dividends accruing to the shareholders.[57] The following year Samuel Bowles, editor of the Springfield (Massachusetts) *Republican*, and Schuyler Colfax, Speaker of the House of Representatives and later Vice-President of the United States, visited the Buena Vista farm and commented upon the management of the estate and the quality of the wine.

We tasted the liquors, we shared the generous hospitality of the estate, and its superintendent; but we failed to obtain, here, or

The California Wine Industry, 1830–1895

elsewhere any satisfactory information as to the boasted success of wine-making, yet, in California. The business is still very much in its infancy, indeed; and this one enterprise does not seem well-managed. Nor do we find the wines very inviting; they partake of the general character of the Rhine wines and the Ohio Catawba; but are rougher, harsh and heady,—needing apparently both some improvement in culture and manufacture and time for softening. I have drank, indeed much better California wine in Springfield than out here.[58]

Bowles was quite mild in his criticism of the management of the estate, for in 1865 and 1866 Agoston Haraszthy was charged with extravagance, unfaithfulness, and visionary experimentation. The attacks became so frequent and so malicious that the trustees issued a statement defending the colonel's management and challenging anyone to prove any of the charges made.[59] Although Haraszthy was exonerated of all charges, the corporation was not paying dividends and the stockholders were becoming increasingly dissatisfied. In the fall of 1866 Haraszthy resigned his position and left the corporation.

The history of the Buena Vista Vinicultural Society for the next several years is the story of increased production, extensive planting of more foreign vines, new experiments in wine making, and limited profits. Although there is no evidence to substantiate the society's claim of 1863 that within a decade it would produce about three million gallons of wine annually, its own reports as well as official statistics do reveal material advances in subsequent years. In 1865 the *Alta California* approved corporate viniculture and recommended such extensive operations on the grounds that better wines and greater profits were the logical results of large-scale production.[60] Within four years the same newspaper was to attack the society for being neither profitable nor expedient. In many respects this criticism was deserved.[61] The world's largest grape ranch was certainly the most unprofitable and the most costly. The society never paid any dividends, but the fault lay neither in its size nor entirely in

Anaheim Coöperative and Sonoma Corporation

its management. The absence of experience, the cost of cultivation and production, the restricted California wine market of the 'sixties and 'seventies, and the pressure for profits were the causes of its chief difficulties.

Both the Anaheim experiment and the Buena Vista Vinicultural Society played an important role in the development of grape growing and wine making in California. The publicity given these ventures stimulated many farmers to enter upon viticultural careers, attracted immigration, and promoted a new interest in agriculture generally. Hillside lands in Sonoma, which had hitherto been regarded as worthless, were now attracting attention, and many of the distinguished Sonoma and Napa Valley vineyards of today were first set out at this time. The B.V.V.S. familiarized northern California with the importation of foreign vines, the excavated hillside cellar, the steamed redwood tank, and the nonirrigated vineyard. Both Anaheim and the B.V.V.S. served to focus attention and interest upon California viticulture from a business point of view. At the same time they called attention to the problems facing the vineyardist and the wine maker. Thus they advanced the organization of the industry.

Chapter VII
Industrial Development and Organization, 1860-1870

CALIFORNIA VITICULTURE, as a well-established commercial industry, dates from about 1860; only then did it begin to receive general business attention.[1] Before that time the relatively negligible commercial significance and the pioneer nature of the industry make the history of California wines largely a chronicle of romantic personalities and interesting events. By 1860, however, grapes, along with wheat and barley, were one of the three major agricultural products of the state. In the field of manufactures wine ranked seventh.[2] The rate of increase (both in acreage and in production) between 1850 and 1860 was exceptionally large.[3] The statistical evidence available for this period makes it difficult to determine the exact nature of the transition of wine making from the pastoral to the industrial state. However, the wine crop figures of 1850, 1860, and 1869 offer a reasonably reliable index of the nature and scope of this development. The federal census of 1850 showed that California had a total wine production of 58,055 gallons. By 1860 this production had increased to 246,518 gallons, and by 1869 it reached the quasi-big-business figure of 2,000,000 gallons.[4]

The flourishing wine industry of the 'sixties helped make grapes one of the most popular crops in California for over a decade.[5] Newspapers, journals, and numerous visitors had proclaimed California as an ideal vine land as early as 1839.[6]

---

[1] For notes to chap. vii, see pp. 186–189.

Industrial Development and Organization

The viticultural prosperity of the middle and late 'sixties was accompanied by a new wave of optimism that permeated and, in many respects, dominated the agricultural thinking of California.[7]

Significant during this decade was the emergence of the two separate viticultural interests characteristic of present-day California—grape growing as distinct from wine making.[8] Before this time the two had been inseparable. The vineyardist was grower, manufacturer, and merchant. The famous retailers of California wine—Kohler, Sansevain, Wolfskill, Haraszthy, Delmas—were also proprietors of extensive vineyards. The San Francisco grape market of the 'fifties, controlled mainly by these large manufacturers, was an outlet for both table grapes and wine grapes. (The latter was to meet the demand of the foreign populations of San Francisco.) Kohler, Sansevain, and a few others purchased some grapes and wine from vineyards and cellars other than their own, but it was the exception rather than the common practice. The dual aspect of the industry—the vineyardist essentially a farmer, and the wine maker primarily a manufacturer—became increasingly prevalent after 1860. Although this division marked the beginning of a new period in California viticulture, the typical California grower-manufacturer was never totally replaced. The various small independent wineries in California today are not only in contrast to the corporate big-business aspects of the present industry but are strong reminders of an earlier—certainly more colorful—period.

By 1860 the meager viticultural beginnings of the early 'thirties had become a substantial part of the state's economy. The greatest development, however, was made after 1857. Of a total of 12,000,000 vines in 1863, about 1,500,000 were set out before 1857.[9] The reasons for this expansion are easily understandable. In addition to the more obvious advantages of soil, climate, abundant yields, cheapness of vineyard land, and the comparative facility of cultivation, many farmers were attracted to grape growing by the confirmed

The California Wine Industry, 1830-1895

adaptability of foreign varieties, the successful experiments with nonirrigated vineyards, and—last but by no means least—the large demand for and the small supply of wine.[10] The failure of the Eastern states to cultivate any grapes other than their indigenous varieties and the virtual certainty that in the near future a transcontinental railroad would be established gave California viticulture hopes and confidence in a remunerative, noncompetitive Eastern market. Such conclusive evidence left very little doubt to the undecided farmer. Few other crops could offer so much as grape growing. Practical, conservative wine men stated that the demand for wine would not exceed the supply for at least a century.[11]

The increased duties on foreign wines, as a result of the tariff act of 1864, and the hopes of California viniculturists to replace the foreign article with a native one led to an enthusiastic planting of more grapes. During the early 'sixties, approximately 3,000,000 vines were planted annually.[12] The California wine makers hoped to cultivate the American taste for wine to the point of making it a national beverage. The genuine fervor of this early period was accompanied by an interest in selecting better wine, table, and raisin varieties of grapes.[13] Although it was almost universally recognized that the foreign vines produced a better wine, opportunity for immediate profits and doubt as to the relative success in cultivating the new varieties continued to sustain the popularity of the Mission variety.[14] During this period the most popular foreign vine—the Zinfandel—was more important experimentally than commercially.

Los Angeles, Anaheim, and Sonoma were the three major grape and wine areas of the 'sixties. They not only possessed the greatest number of vines, but grapes and grape products were the chief source of their revenue.[15] During this decade commercial viticulture had a significant northward advance.[16] The proved quality of wines from nonirrigated vineyards and the rise of San Francisco as the chief wine market of California were largely responsible for the rapid

Industrial Development and Organization

commercial development of northern viniculture. Grape growing and wine making were already established in northern California as early as 1855, but it was not until after 1860 that they became one of the more important and remunerative branches of agriculture. Before 1860, except for Haraszthy and Vallejo, only a beginning had been made in the commercial exploitation of the viticultural wealth of Sonoma, Napa, and Solano counties. The Buena Vista Vinicultural Society contributed materially toward the new trend of planting grapes along hillsides and mountains. These new northern vineyards set out the majority of the foreign vines in California, and in the future were to produce something better than *vin ordinaire.*

The search for immediate profits, and the inferior quality of the more common red wine types, made the California wine trade of the 'sixties largely a traffic in the finer grades of white, sweet, and sparkling wines.[17] By the end of the decade certain well-defined wine types peculiar to their native districts were recognized. Southern California sweet and sparkling wines—port, angelica, and champagne—and northern California dry white wines—hock, sauterne, and reisling types—were commercially important articles. Common claret was not important as an export article.[18] Since it could be—and usually was—produced by the most inexperienced wine makers, it was sold without proper aging or processing; and because it could be easily adulterated, it was the most inferior wine made in California. Under such conditions it was only natural that claret and the more common red wine varieties were the least important wines commercially.[19] More than $200,000 worth of European wines—largely red—were imported into San Francisco in 1861. This fact alone attests to the unpopularity of the California red wines.[20]

During the 'sixties the improved quality of certain wine types was reflected in a substantial increase in the export trade of California. From approximately $100,000 in 1864 the value of wine exports, by sea alone, increased to a little

The California Wine Industry, 1830–1895

more than $400,000 in 1869.[21] San Francisco was now not only the chief grape and wine market but the chief export center of California wines.[22] With a dozen or more major distributors and merchants located here, San Francisco became—and remained—the business center for California wines. Although the United States consumed four-fifths of the California product, foreign demand increased substantially after 1860.[23] In one year—1860-1861—foreign shipments increased more than 100 per cent.[24] Since it was not until 1866 that data of export values were kept, and not until 1869 that separate totals for bottled wine and bulk wine were recorded, the figures given are consequently estimates rather than exact statistics. The California Bureau of Labor has compiled a series of tables showing the approximate quantity and value of wine exports between 1864 and 1869. These figures show that during this period the amount of wine exported increased from 190,000 gallons to more than 450,000 gallons. This represents an increase in value from $100,000 to more than $400,000.[25] Shipments to South America, China, and Europe became more frequent, but the Eastern demand was the chief source of California's out-of-state revenue. Boston and New York received the greatest amount of California wine. The most serious obstacle to the development of this trade was the extensive adulteration and counterfeiting that went on in California as well as on the east coast.[26] After the transcontinental railroad was established in 1869 the central United States became a profitable market for California wines, but it never surpassed the demand of the Atlantic coast states.

The industrial and commercial developments of the 'sixties made wine growers conscious of the new problems facing the industry. The transition from pioneer to commercial agriculture was accompanied by a demand for state aid. The 1862 Committee on the Improvement of the Grape Vine in California, although not in itself too successful, did promote a new interest in grape growing and wine making and stimulated planting of new vineyards. Certainly an in-

Industrial Development and Organization

dustry that added to the commercial wealth and prosperity of the state, promoted immigration, and converted thousands of acres of rocky, bare, and otherwise useless land into fertile vineyards, merited encouragement from the state.[27] The efforts of Haraszthy in 1862 had resulted only in honoring viticulture with a standing committee. Obviously a permanent organization had to be formed. The necessity for such an organization to serve as the voice of the California wine men had already been discussed among the more prominent viniculturists. The discussion turned into action when in 1862 the federal government imposed a tax of five cents a gallon on wine and twenty cents a gallon on brandy. This was followed by a general discussion of the problems facing the industry and the formation of the first organization of wine men in the state.[28]

The California Wine Growers' Association was formed in December, 1862.[29] It was the first of several similar organizations that periodically made their appearance in California between 1862 and the formation of the Board of State Viticultural Commissioners in 1880. This association focused attention upon grape growing and wine making and marked the first real attempt at organization on the industry level. A meeting of vineyardists held in San Francisco in November, 1862, resulted in the temporary organization of an association whose immediate aim was to relieve the California wine men from burdensome taxes. The association supported the policies and aims of the State Agricultural Society to foster scientific agriculture in California.[30] The November meeting appointed a committee of three to report the following month at a general convention of the state's wine growers to be held in San Francisco. Since the new liquor and wine legislation of the federal government was immediately responsible for the convention, the December meeting discussed and formulated policies aimed to protect their common interests.[31]

With representatives from every major viticultural area of California, the convention tackled its first problem—the

The California Wine Industry, 1830–1895

tariff and California wines. The out-of-state wine traffic was suffering from European competition. The existing 50-percent ad valorem tariff on foreign wines was not enough protection for the California vineyardists. As early as 1860 the *California Farmer*, a journal that consistently and vociferously lent its support to furthering commercial viticulture in the state, advocated common action by California, Ohio, and Georgia. The representatives of these states in Congress were not only to fight all attempts at lowering the wine duties but were to unite with other interests to form a protectionist bloc in Congress. The *Farmer* further suggested that a national wine lobby (New York, Georgia, Ohio, and California) be created to fight for tariff protection and lower excise taxes. The first function of this lobby was to replace the ad valorem rates with specific ones.[32]

The cost of casks, the scarcity of competent and cheap labor, the exorbitant interest rates on borrowed money, the excessive costs of transportation, and the four to five years of expensive unproductive cultivation, all made the protective tariff the only means whereby California wine men could compete with foreign wines for the Eastern market.[33] In addition to the fact that the ad valorem duty of 50 per cent did not in itself afford enough protection, the common practice of foreign merchants of evaluating their wine with specific reference to the American tariff not only defrauded the United States government but nullified the primary object of a tariff—to protect home manufactures. Under the leadership of the major San Francisco merchants, a committee was appointed to recommend to Congress that the wine duty be a specific one and ". . . of such an amount upon each and every gallon of foreign wine imported into the United States, as shall afford the requisite protection, and at the same time afford reasonable revenue to the government."[34]

The importance of this issue to the producers and to the merchants caused the Buena Vista Vinicultural Society to send Colonel Agoston Haraszthy to Washington in 1863 and

Industrial Development and Organization

1865. The purpose of Haraszthy's mission was twofold: to replace the ad valorem duty with a specific one, and to obtain the repeal of the tax on wine and brandy. After considerable discussion and an eloquent presentation of the case of the California wine men, the Committee on Ways and Means of the House of Representatives recommended a specific tariff. In 1864 the duties on foreign wines were increased, and the issue subsided until the next tariff measure came up for discussion in Congress.[35] The wine men of California soon learned the efficacy of lobbying. Thus Haraszthy, in 1863 and 1864, was the precursor of the California wine lobby.

The 1862 excise tax on wine and brandy was as important to California wine men as the tariff.[36] The five-cent tax on wine was regarded as oppressive and impolitic because it was so high in proportion to the value of the article. Assuming an acre of vines to yield approximately six hundred gallons of wine, the tax per acre would be about $30.[37] Although the tax was high, many vineyardists failed to recognize that the dull market conditions of the years between 1862 and 1863 were largely the results of the feverish planting of vines after 1857 and the regression of the local and out-of-state market. The Civil War impeded traffic in luxuries, and wine was definitely a luxury. The tax on wine and brandy was in some respects a convenient way to rationalize an unpleasant situation.

By 1860, brandy had become an important branch of California viticulture, but not until 1865, with the increased production of wine and the decline in price, did it become commercially important.[38] The immediate effect of the tax on distilled spirits was to reduce its production drastically and virtually destroy its export. Such legislation not only seriously threatened to curtail the manufacture of brandy but threatened to reduce the production and trade of fortified sweet wines.[39]

The convention of wine men and grape growers meeting in San Francisco in December, 1862, asked the state legislature for relief from the federal tax. In February, 1863, the Assembly Committee on Grape Culture drew up a petition to Congress, and in June of the same year a second meeting of the California Wine Growers' Association was called to devise means to hasten federal tax relief. A second petition to Congress had the desired effect. The tax on wine was abolished, and in 1865 the tax on distilled spirits was reduced to 25 cents a gallon.[40] The following year the tax on brandy was raised to $2 a gallon. This threatened real disaster, since it was impossible to sell California brandy with an additional $2 tax.[41]

The leading vintners joined in calling an emergency convention in 1866.[42] The original California Wine Growers' Association was no longer functioning. It had originated as a protest organization against the ad valorem tariff, and general indifference among the state's viniculturists caused it to pass into oblivion once its purpose was accomplished. Before the formation of the second Wine Growers' Association, Sonoma, Napa, and Los Angeles counties had organized local conventions and associations to work for the repeal of the prohibitory $2 tax.[43] When the second association was organized in November, 1866, the county conventions merged with the state body.[44] The immediate aim of the new state association was to reduce the tax on brandy from $2 to 50 cents a gallon, but it also advocated the formation of a permanent organization to represent the California wine industry in Washington. By 1866, viticulture had become important enough to warrant a permanent body to guard its interests. The second Wine Growers' Association operated for several years as the guardian of the interests of the California wine men.

Through a series of petitions, special agents in Washington, and the material support of Thaddeus Stevens in the House of Representatives, the onerous tax on grape brandy was reduced to $1 in the spring of 1867.[45] The tax on all other distilled spirits remained at $2. This compromised tax reduction on brandy partially solved two other major prob-

Industrial Development and Organization

lems obstructing trade and commerce in California grape brandy. The heavy fines imposed on all who adulterated grape brandy in order to avoid the general $2 tax curtailed adulteration to a degree. The same law abolished the requirement that brandy be stored in government warehouses and that all government taxes be paid before its sale. The repeal of these two provisions was much more valuable to the distiller than an outright reduction of $1.50. The storage and advance-tax-payment requirements were in many respects more distressing than the tax itself.[46]

The general attitude among California distillers was favorable to the amended law of 1867. Matthew Keller, prominent Los Angeles distiller and wine maker, believed that the moderate tax would increase revenue and stimulate production. The effect of the $2 tax is shown by the following figures. The 1865 brandy produce of California was 89,490 gallons. In 1866 it dropped to 8,540 gallons; under the amended revenue law of 1867, brandy production jumped to approximately 169,811 gallons in 1868.[47] By 1867 the tariff and tax issues were solved. Through organization and unified action the wine growers of California had accomplished what they had set out to do. The specific tariff rates on foreign wines and the exemption of domestic wine from any excise assured the wine producers of the United States substantial profits. The California wine men enjoyed a double advantage since Europe was their only competitor in wine made from non-American varieties.

The 1866 meeting resulted in the formation of a permanent Wine Growers' Association, which was to hold annual meetings to discuss and suggest unified action. The object of the association was:

... to encourage the production of the Grape, the manufacture and introduction to market of Pure California Wines, Brandies, *etc.*, the promotion of the Wine-growing Interest, and the increase of Emigration to our State.[48]

Apart from representing the interests of the grape grower and wine maker in Sacramento and Washington, the association was to collect and disseminate technical viticultural and vinicultural information, collect statistics, and formulate and propose legislation favorable to the industry and the development of California wines.

As a part of its first session the question of adulteration and counterfeiting of wines and brandies was discussed and remedies proposed. In 1861 the state legislature passed a general adulteration act, which did no more than stigmatize and censure counterfeiters and manufacturers of spurious liquors and wines.[49] The greatest fault of the act was that it failed to define what constituted adulteration. The result was not only to nullify any benefits that could be derived from such legislation but to impose severe hardships upon legitimate manufacturers. The addition of sugar and brandy to fortify sweet wines and the watering of wine during fermentation — both legitimate practices — were not distinguished from the use of coloring matter or drugs, "the use of which is so nearly akin to fraud that no line of separation can be safely drawn."[50] The total accomplishment of the first session of the association was a series of talks on methods to test adulterated wines and brandies and a strict provision in the constitution of the association expelling any member found guilty of such practices.[51] The question of assuring pure wines was to be one of the major problems facing the California wine men for the next thirty years. Pure-wine bills were periodically sponsored, and some were enacted by the state legislature. In the 'nineties an antiadulteration act was passed by the federal government, but real protection was not achieved until the passage of the Pure Food and Drug Act during the administration of Theodore Roosevelt.

The formation of the Wine Growers' Association, the unified action of the grape growers and wine makers of California, and the beginnings of a wine lobby marked a new era in California viticulture after 1860. Within two decades wine making had grown into a real business. The pioneer character of the earlier period was succeeded by industrialization. Then legislation—both state and national—indus-

Industrial Development and Organization

trial organization, and trade and commerce became the main themes of California's viticultural development.

Relief from high taxes and protection from the tariff caused a general expansion in all branches of viticulture, from planting of more grapes to exporting more wine. More vines were planted in every California county, with Los Angeles losing its viticultural leadership to Sonoma. In 1869 Sonoma outranked Los Angeles by approximately 360,000 vines.[52] The better white and red dry wines of Sonoma and the distance between Los Angeles and the San Francisco market were the chief reasons for southern California's gradual decline. However, the boom of the early 'seventies overshadowed everything else, and it was not until after the depression of 1875 that southern California table grapes and raisins compensated for the loss of revenue from wine grapes.

Chapter VIII
Prosperity, Depression, and Recovery, 1868-1878

THE PROSPERITY THAT FOLLOWED the introduction of foreign varieties and the beneficial legislation of the state and national governments led to an era of unprecedented expansion. In 1870 the future of the California wine industry seemed assured. Grape culture employed more labor than any other branch of farming.[1] The state encouraged grape growing because it attracted "honest, industrious, and moral immigration"; the press advocated more wine farms because grapes and grape products commanded higher prices, required less labor, and yielded substantially more profits than any other agricultural pursuit.[2] In 1870 California's viticultural investment was estimated at over $30,000,000 in gold.[3] The wine and brandy crop of 1871 was valued at more than $2,000,000, and the capital invested in the 139 major wineries of the state was well over $500,000.[4]

The development and expansion of commercial viniculture in this period also contributed to the industrialization of San Francisco. The necessity for containers—barrels and bottles—contributed to the development of the cooperage and glass business of the city. As early as 1870, forty-three men were employed by two firms to make and to repair barrels alone.[5] The importance of casks, certain specific types of bottles, and wine machinery increased commerce and trade and advanced the fame of San Francisco as the major port of the Pacific coast.

---

[1] For notes to chap. viii, see pp. 189-192.

Prosperity, Depression, and Recovery

The prosperity of the late 'sixties and early 'seventies had all the earmarks of a boom. The annual number of vines set out increased continually and reached its peak between 1870 and 1875.[6] Foreign varieties were planted more extensively, and new varieties were introduced.[7] Wine cuttings cost from $7 to $25 a thousand, depending upon the variety. Vineyard lands sold from $5 to $2,000 per acre, depending on their proximity to the San Francisco market.[8]

The out-of-state exports of wine and brandy for the period 1870 to 1875 increased annually from 10,000 to 40,000 gallons. In 1870 approximately 800,000 gallons of wine were exported, and in 1873, according to the most optimistic sources, more than 1,000,000 gallons.[9] The establishment of the transcontinental railroad made possible the overland shipment of wine and brandy from Sacramento and other inland areas.[10] Several San Joaquin valley towns grew up during the 'seventies as shipping centers for wine and grapes as well as other fresh fruits. Later in the decade the raisin industry largely supplanted wine grapes as one of the chief items of the valley's Eastern trade. However, the great bulk of the freight movements of the 'seventies were still by ship. The railroad rates on heavy freight were so exorbitant as to render large-scale overland shipments unprofitable. It was not until after the depression of 1874 that the railroad became the chief wine carrier in the transcontinental trade.

The foreign wine traffic of the boom period increased slowly. Mexico and Central America were by far the largest foreign consumers of California wine, with the Far East, Hawaii, Europe, and Canada still only making nominal demands.[11] The greater portion of the foreign trade was carried on by a half dozen or more merchants situated in San Francisco. White wines, champagne, and sweet wines were the most important types commercially. Common red wine was becoming more important but still lagged behind the other varieties.[12]

Champagne enjoyed an unequaled popularity in California as well as throughout the United States. The largest

The California Wine Industry, 1830-1895

demand for California champagne came from the Eastern cities—Boston, New York, and Philadelphia.[13] Foreign exports increased at the same time. The California wineries, especially the Buena Vista Vinicultural Society, were producing a superior type. The Franco-Prussian War, in 1870-1871, by cutting off most European sources of champagne, contributed more to the increased demand for the California product than the inherent qualities of the wine itself.

The northern counties produced and exported more sparkling wine than southern California. In California, champagne was made by both the fermentation process—natural fermentation in the bottle—and by the "soda-fountain" process.[14] The latter method required the addition of carbon dioxide to give the wine its sparkling quality. Although the French and German vintners of California produced the greatest amount of this wine, the native-born wine makers were becoming equally skillful and successful.[15] The *Alta California Almanac* of 1874 maintained that the sparkling wines of California were "generally better than the French champagnes, save a few of the best and most costly brands."[16] Whether or not this was true, as soon as the Franco-Prussian War was over, French champagnes found little difficulty in regaining their American market.

The increased demand for California wine on the east coast was accompanied by a demand for California grapes. The early 'seventies marked the real beginnings of a new branch of commercial viticulture that continued into the early 1940's. The refrigerator car created an Eastern grape market in every city where large colonies of French, German, Italian, and Spanish resided. One of the first eastern shipments of grapes by rail was made in 1876, representing California viticulture at the Philadelphia Centennial Fair.[17] The following year L. W. Buck, of Vacaville, California, shipped several packages of grapes to Clinton, Iowa. Loaded in an ordinary dry car "with a few cakes of ice . . . in the center," the grapes arrived in good condition. These two first experiments were the forerunners of a new outlet for

Prosperity, Depression, and Recovery

the California grape grower which became increasingly more important.

The prosperity the grape growers and wine makers enjoyed in the period between 1870 and 1874 attracted more farmers to viticulture. The demand for wine was large enough to allow even the most inexperienced vineyardist to make a comfortable profit. Many vintners were convinced the industry could not be overdeveloped, and as long as there was a demand for wine new areas were planted with grapes. Thirty-five of the forty-four counties of the state planted vines on a large scale. Although Sonoma, Napa, and Los Angeles counties were still the most advanced viticulturally, the early 'seventies found El Dorado, Yuba, Solano, Santa Cruz, Santa Clara, Sacramento, and Tulare counties not far behind.[18] Public and railroad lands in Sacramento and El Dorado counties were bought, at prices ranging from $1.25 to $2.50 an acre, and set out with vines.[19]

Fresno County became one of the most promising viticultural areas of the 'seventies. The first vine in this county was supposedly planted in 1873, and grapes soon became one of the more important crops of this valley county.[20] In 1873 Francis T. Eisen discovered that Fresno lands, if properly irrigated, were adapted to the production of sweet wine grapes. When Eisen acquired his land, he had no idea that within five years raisins would overshadow wine grapes as the chief source of Fresno County's viticultural revenue.[21] The success of the prodigious wine business of the Los Angeles Vineyard Society and the Buena Vista Vinicultural Society convinced Eisen of the efficacy of large-scale production. He purchased 650 acres of land five miles east of the town of Fresno. Through irrigation he shortly turned this parched earth into a veritable vine garden. In the same year he planted 300 acres in choice foreign vines, and between the date of purchase and 1885 Eisen continued setting out more and better vines. He specialized in brandy and sweet wines—port, malaga, tokay, angelica, and muscatel.[22] The Eisen experiment was duplicated in many other parts

The California Wine Industry, 1830–1895

of California. Further south, the Cucamonga ranch, with a capacity of 130,000 gallons of wine, was competing with Eisen for the sweet-wine market of California and the United States. Under the competent management of Jean Louis Sansevain, a nephew of Jean Louis Vignes, the ranch yielded both good crops and substantial profits.[23]

Viticulture had indeed become a mania. While Eisen and others were competent viniculturists, many who made the attempt were not. During the boom, grape growing and wine making, as in the earlier period, continued to attract fortune seekers and speculators whose only object was to make money.

With so many inexperienced people continuing to make wine, it was not surprising that the general quality of the wine produced in California was poor. Much of the wine was strong, heady, and lacking in the finer qualities of its European counterpart.[24] Matthew Keller, experienced wine man of Los Angeles and producer of fine wines himself, blamed the Mission as the chief cause of the poor wines produced. Keller maintained that this variety produced a "strong wine ... fit only for sailors to drink."[25] This was only a partial explanation. Lack of experience on the part of the makers was a much more important reason for the poor wine. Much good wine has been made from this variety by experienced vintners in recent years. On the other hand, Arpad Haraszthy maintained that the Californians' lack of experience made possible wine production on a more scientific basis without the European attachments to age-old prejudices.[26] Unfortunately the quality of the wine did not confirm Haraszthy's opinion.

Much of the bad wine did not come from the wineries but from the grape grower who made his own wine. The costs of constructing and maintaining a modern, scientific winery were too great for the majority of California vineyardists.[27] Good wine making required a complex knowledge. Few farmers could afford to hire experienced wine makers. The wines of California would have enjoyed a far

Prosperity, Depression, and Recovery

better reputation if the grape grower had confined himself to farming and had sold his grapes or juice to large wineries possessing the skill and facilities for making good wine.[28] Major Sir Rose Lambart Price, visiting California at this time, had this to say:

> ... as most Californians are exceedingly proud of their supposed ability to produce a marketable vintage, and as they talk a great deal about wines, and know almost nothing, I may as well warn my reader against forming pleasing anticipations of good or cheap drinking when he visits their country.
>
> During my journey through California (which afterwards extended from the Mexican frontier to within a few miles of Oregon), I never once tasted a commonly decent glass of wine. Hardly anything was ever sold under a dollar a bottle, and though I martyred myself in tasting it on every possible occasion in hopes of something wonderful at last turning up, I never once came across even a moderately good specimen throughout the entire State.[29]

It is true that much of the wine produced was largely of an inferior quality, but California did make some good wine during this period. The boom of the early 'seventies found good and bad wine sold, but the depression of 1876 found the manufacturers of fine wines the least affected. A German vineyardist of Sacramento took some of his wine to Germany in 1870. It was found to be of excellent quality and in many respects equal to the best products of his native country.[30]

The commercial development of the industry and the attempts to increase the export trade in wines resulted in the rise of a number of local and state wine growers' associations. The prosperity and the Franco-Prussian War increased the demand for California wines, but the poor quality of much of the California article, as well as the necessity for continued vigilance against the enactment of harmful legislation, necessitated some form of organization. Moreover, it was imperative that practical viticultural information be disseminated among the many inexperienced grape growers

The California Wine Industry, 1830-1895

and wine makers that the "boom" had attracted to the industry.

In February, 1872, a general meeting of the Wine Growers' Association was held at Sacramento.[31] The aim of the convention that followed the meeting was to devise means to improve and to encourage the various branches of viticulture in California. Its immediate objective was to create an association of more practical value to the growers and manufacturers than the Wine Growers' Association. The older organization was primarily interested in preventing the passage of legislation hostile to the interests of the wine men.[32] As an agency aimed to distribute practical viticultural knowledge, it had proved itself totally unsuccessful. With the expansion of the industry and the infrequent meetings and conventions of the California Wine Growers' Association, the state organization did not meet the needs of the whole industry. Out of the talks and speeches of the 1872 meeting of the California Wine Growers' Association and the California Agricultural Society came the California Vine Growers' and Wine and Brandy Manufacturers' Association.[33] The committees appointed by the new association indicate its scope and function. The eight standing committees were concerned with the most vital issues facing the industry at the time. The mere names of these committees illustrate the extent of commercialization the California wine industry had undergone since the founding of the first Grape Growers' Association in 1866. The eight committees were concerned with the following important issues:[34] cultivation of the grape and pruning of the vine; wine making and the clarification of wine; manufacture of brandy from grapes; casks, vessels, presses, and machinery; statistics; memorials to Congress; best varieties of grapes for general use; and classification of grapes.

On the basis of its activities, the California Vine Growers' and Wine and Brandy Manufacturers' Association was the precursor of the technical and scientific work of the University of California College of Agriculture and of the State

Prosperity, Depression, and Recovery

Board of Viticultural Commissioners. The first and second wine growers' associations were primarily organizations of viniculturists for political purposes, lobbying being one of their main functions.

The work of the new association was aimed at a statewide audience of wine men. Local problems were always secondary. The result was the rise of a number of county societies whose object was to bring together, in smaller and more cohesive groups, vintners faced with common farming and manufacturing problems. In 1872 the Napa Valley Wine Company, a joint-stock association, was formed to introduce and popularize Napa wines in every major Eastern city.[35] Although high prices and general prosperity continued and the demand for wine seemed insatiable, the more conservative members of the industry were already preparing for less fortunate times. It was these local clubs, societies, and associations that assumed the leadership in an attempt to place the business of wine making on a sounder basis.

Essentially educational in purpose, the county organizations that began to appear during the last years of the boom added to the strength of the state associations. The latter were usually the capital motivators in the fights for protective legislation, but the local county associations never overlooked the opportunity to make their opinions known and felt. The threatened repeal of the Fence Law in 1872 brought forth the disapproval of every local wine society in the state.[36] Through organized pressure the wine men were not only able to prevent the repeal of the Fence Law but were able to extend the fencing requirement to several more counties.[37]

An equally important function of these societies was to promote agricultural immigration to California. The cultivation of grapes and the making of wines required trained if not skilled labor.[38] The boom period was marked by a shortage of competent field and winery workers. The more specialized aspects of wine making suffered from the inexperience of the majority of California vintners.[39] In 1871 a special appeal was made for European grape growers and

The California Wine Industry, 1830–1895

wine makers.[40] The State Agricultural Society, the Vine Growers' and Wine and Brandy Manufacturers' Association, and many county societies availed themselves of the viticultural prosperity to advertise and promote immigration. In 1870 a circular prepared by the wine men of the state demanded that the national government invite "by thousands the intelligent vine growers of Europe to come in multiplied numbers, bringing with them their experience, their industry, their families and their capital...."[41] This publicity of the 'seventies attracted not only many vintners from the wine-growing regions of France and Germany but also many Irish as well. The Irish immigrants and their descendants found remunerative livelihood in this new industry.[42]

The prosperity of the United States after the Civil War was reflected by the California wine industry. The Franco-Prussian War reduced the export of French wines, and a dependably high tariff assured the California wine men of a steadily growing market. The economic revolution that characterized the change in American industry and agriculture after the Civil War was duplicated in the development of the business, commercial, and industrial aspects of wine making. Moreover, the accelerated immigration to America after 1863 increased the consumption of wine. It was the European—or the American with strong European ties—who drank the most wine. Since wine was a luxury rather than a necessity in the United States, the general prosperity following the Civil War found many more people able to afford this beverage. In California the demand was interpreted as an assurance of a perpetual prosperity and the certainty that enough wine could never be produced.[43]

The failure of Jay Cooke and Company, on Thursday, September 18, 1873, precipitated one of the worst depressions in American history. The results of the economic and commercial dislocations after the panic of 1873 did not seriously affect the California wine industry until 1876. Although the industry began to lag seriously after the autumn

Prosperity, Depression, and Recovery

of 1873, the wine men of California hesitated to call the prosperous period they had just enjoyed a typical American "boom." The depression, which lasted until 1878, was worldwide, as were some of its causes—a series of European wars, overexpansion, and speculation. Other causes were peculiar to the United States—currency and credit inflation, governmental waste, and overinvestment in railroads, factories, and other enterprises. The world depression accentuated the weaknesses of the California wine industry and contributed to the deflation of the California wine bubble.

The most obvious explanation of the recession in California wines was overproduction.[44] The panic of 1873 had little immediate effect on the number of vines set out and the amount of wine made. Despite the diminishing demand after 1873, more vines were planted annually. In 1873 there were approximately 30,000,000 vines in California.[45] By 1876 the number had increased to 43,000,000.[46] The production of wine and brandy increased accordingly. The worst depression year for California wines was 1876. In that year the new vineyards planted at the turn of the decade came into bearing, and the out-of-state and foreign trade dropped to next to nothing.

Moreover, the internal revenue tax on brandy reduced the traffic in that article and increased an already large stock of unsold wines. The 50-cent tax on brandy became burdensome when the drop in prices after 1875 curtailed its sale.[47] Furthermore, the government had returned to its earlier policy of requiring distillers to pay their taxes while the brandy was still in bond. This, with the bankruptcies and financial losses of 1875 and 1876, made it impossible for distillers to afford to make brandy. The decline in production contributed substantially to increasing the wine surplus and maintaining low wine prices for several years.[48] In 1875 a committee of the San Francisco Wine Dealers' Association and the Vine Growers' and Wine and Brandy Manufacturers' Association held a meeting to recommend emergency legislation. The wine and brandy men drew up a petition

The California Wine Industry, 1830-1895

to Congress, and Governor Henry H. Haight of California urged the state legislature to present the wine men's written views to the House of Representatives. The governor further urged that the California delegation in Congress push the measure through.[49] Congress did not act upon the demand for a tax reduction or upon the appeal to relax the bonding requirement. In 1878 recovery had set in, and increased demand led to more brandy manufacture. What seemed imperative in 1875 and 1876 became by 1878 no more than desirable. The advanced prices and sales of wine and brandy caused the California viniculturists to abandon temporarily their fight for modification of the tax and brandy laws of the national government.

The increase in the production of wine during the boom period was accompanied by the sale of immature and indifferently made wines.[50] The most important single factor in promoting the crash of 1876—apart from overproduction —was the generally poor quality of the wine produced. On the other hand, the "doctoring" of wines on the east coast brought added discredit to California.[51] Further damage was done by the practice, becoming more and more prevalent after 1870, of dealers purchasing whole cellars regardless of quality. The good wine was disposed at high prices under foreign labels, and the poor was sold at cheap prices under the name "California wine."[52] It was only natural then that the people who could afford wine during the depression drank French and other imported varieties. During the middle 'seventies the American demand for wine was largely for imported wine.[53] Moreover, the Californians themselves drank very little of their own product.[54] Major Sir Rose Lambart Price, visiting several California bars and restaurants, remarked that while "Californians praise their wine to strangers, . . . they studiously refrained from drinking it themselves. . . ."[55]

The diminishing market and the large grape crops of 1874, 1875, and 1876 emphasized another major issue that had long annoyed California wine men—railroad rates.

Prosperity, Depression, and Recovery

Since 1869, when a committee of wine men and exporters attempted to gain rate reductions from the Central Pacific Railroad on overland freight, the poor facilities and the exorbitant rates for grapes and wine had reduced the amount of California's Eastern trade.[56] A case of wine valued at no more than $2.50 cost $4.80 to ship overland to Chicago.[57] These usurious rates deprived California of a large market in the middle United States. During the depression it was impossible to sell any wine at a profit unless it could be shipped by sea. Not only the out-of-state trade, but also the grape and wine produce of the northern California counties, had to be sacrificed because of the prohibitive railroad rates. Indeed, it was not uncommon for the railroad tariff to be more expensive than the actual value of the crop.[58] One of the purposes for the organization of the St. Helena Viticultural Club, in December, 1875, was to open new markets in the central United States by trying to reduce the railroad costs.[59]

Between 1875 and 1877 the wine industry reached its all-time low. Wine at 10 and 15 cents a gallon and brandy at 37 to 40 cents a gallon could not find a market.[60] The stock of wine on hand was so great and the prices so low that it was more profitable to let pigs, turkeys, and other barnyard animals harvest the crop of grapes than to attempt to sell it at a profit. Foreclosures on mortgages were not uncommon. Banks refused to make loans, considering vines of no value to the land whatever.[61] Many vineyardists dug up their vines and planted fruit and walnut trees. In 1876, wine was sold to vinegar manufacturers at 10 cents a gallon, and grape prices averaged between $2 and $10 a ton,[62] only the choicest varieties commanding the latter price. The productive and once successful Buena Vista Vinicultural Society was bankrupt, and the "goods and chattels" of the corporation were sold to satisfy a chattel mortgage.[63]

In the midst of this depression the Centennial Exposition was held at Philadelphia. At no other period in their history were the California wine men so dejected or so apprehensive

The California Wine Industry, 1830–1895

of the future. The Vine Growers' and Wine and Brandy Manufacturers' Association, which had shortened its name to the State Vinicultural Society in 1875, worked toward representing the California wine industry at Philadelphia.[64] However, most wine men were so financially embarrassed and so downcast that only a halfhearted effort was made to represent California wines at the exposition. Their exhibit had neither the sanction of the state nor the support of the State Vinicultural Society.[65] The wine at Philadelphia belonged to private individuals, who hoped it would further their own personal advantage. Coarse, earthy, and full of sediment, the wine damaged the reputation of California still further, and "it took nearly ten years to remove the bad impression created by that villainous travesty."[66]

The only advantage to California resulting from the Philadelphia Centennial was to advertise further the ideal wine and grape nature of the soil and climate of the state. The famous Montecito vine—the largest in the world—was cut, packed in seven boxes, and shipped to Philadelphia.[67] Set up in its natural position, this huge specimen attracted wide attention and comment.[68] Although the exhibit interested visitors from all over the world, it did very little to stimulate trade and commerce.

In early 1878 the clouds began to lift. Prices rose and the demand for wine began to increase. The Mission sold at prices between $7 and $10 a ton in 1876; by 1878 these prices had increased to $12 and $14 a ton. Foreign varieties showed proportionate advances. After 1879 the prices of fresh grapes increased rapidly. On the other hand, wine prices and profits improved slowly,[69] and it was not until 1880 that prices reached a quasi-prosperity level.

Recovery and revival of the industry after 1878 were largely owing to the steady improvement in the quality of the wine produced. The depression routed many of the novices and the speculators. Many of those who remained in the industry cultivated better wine grape varieties, matured their wines, and produced a generally superior article.[70] The

Prosperity, Depression, and Recovery

late spring frosts of 1879 and the occurrence of the mildew[71] in several California districts resulted in only a two-thirds grape yield for that year.[72] Most of the wine stock on hand in 1876 and 1877 had been either distilled or made into vinegar. Thus, in 1880 the price of wine increased, and the industry was once again on its way toward a new prosperity.

Probably the greatest single stimulus to California grape culture after 1879 was the failure of the French vineyardists[73] when the phylloxera, a genus of plant lice, devastated thousands of acres of French vines, assuring California wine men of new markets and diminishing competition. Empty cellars, advanced prices, and new customers led to a new era of planting.[74]

The havoc raised by the phylloxera in France and by the depression of 1876-1877 taught the California wine men a serious lesson. The producers of fine California wines suffered least from the drop in grape and wine prices; the advocates of Mission grapes and Mission wine suffered most. After 1878 the finer German, French, Spanish, Austrian, and Italian varieties became increasingly popular.[75] Better European grapes and improvements in cellar arrangements and manufacturing processes resulted in finer wines and advanced sales. In 1879, 3,364,407 gallons of wine and 93,500 gallons of brandy were received in San Francisco from the interior;[76] imports from France decreased from 7,000,000 gallons in 1872 to less than 2,500,000 gallons in 1879.[77] Professor George Husmann, noted authority on wine grapes, attributed this revision of trade to the "protective tariff, the ravages of the phylloxera in Europe, and to the genuineness and acknowledged merits of our wines."[78]

The State Vinicultural Society now began a threefold campaign to hasten and to secure the recovery of the California wine industry. The bases of its program were education, legislative protection, and advertising.[79] In the field of education, the society attempted to acquire books, periodicals, newspapers, and monographs from the major wine areas of the world. Its chief interest was to secure the ex-

The California Wine Industry, 1830–1895

perience and proposed remedies of French *vignerons* to combat the phylloxera. Moreover, since the poor quality of the California wine in the pre-depression era had contributed materially to the collapse of the industry in 1876, the society sponsored articles, speakers, and booklets on the best methods of grape culture and wine making in California.

In harmony with this program, Arpad Haraszthy procured from the first president of the State Vinicultural Society, Jacob R. Snyder, a commission authorizing Charles A. Wetmore, University of California graduate, viticultural enthusiast, and later founder of the Cresta Blanca Wine Company of Livermore, California, to represent California and the society at the Paris Exposition of 1878.[80] Wetmore was to "investigate and report to the Society everything of interest concerning viticulture and wine making. . . ." The articles Wetmore published in the *Alta California* contained some of the most valuable viticultural information ever received in California. They dealt with the major viticultural problems facing the industry—adulteration, vineyard methods, the phylloxera, fermentation, wine sales, clarification of wines.[81] One of the most important results of these articles was the formation in 1880 of the State Board of Viticultural Commissioners.[82]

A great educational service was rendered to America when Wetmore, upon his return to California, declared that 95 per cent of the French wine imported into the United States was adulterated *vin ordinaire*, and that very little high-priced wine came to the United States at all.[83] The popularity of imported wine suffered a severe setback from this statement. Although many Americans claimed the superiority of foreign wines over those of California, very few were capable of differentiating between French *vin ordinaire* and the better California varieties. Americans were—and in many cases still are—"drinking labels." There was a great deal of truth in Wetmore's statement that the popularity of foreign wines over the domestic ones owed more to sophistication than to the wine knowledge of the American public.

Prosperity, Depression, and Recovery

Apart from the educational value of Wetmore's trip, the free advertisement it attracted to California wines led the State Vinicultural Society to accept, in 1879, the offer of Dr. J. I. Bleasdale of Australia to exhibit samples of the various types of California wines at the Sydney Industrial Exhibition.[84] The opportunity of securing the Australian market was in itself enough justification for the expense involved in participation. Forty-three samples of different types of California wine from different parts of the state were sent to be tested, analyzed, tasted, and judged by a committee of experts.[85] The findings of the commission of experts confirmed the opinions of the more competent California and American manufacturers and merchants—although the California article was basically sound, it was heavier in body and color than its European counterpart. Moreover, it had a naturally higher alcoholic content. The fault was not in the wine but with the manufacturers and dealers. The harmful but persistent practice of Californians to sell their wine before it was properly aged and mature was the greatest drawback to increased overseas demand and sales.[86]

The publication of the findings of the experts at the Sydney Industrial Exhibition and the revealing articles of Charles A. Wetmore from Paris gave the California wine men a new impetus to better production. Moreover, the three years of depression had caused serious changes in the development and organization of the industry. The new era in California viniculture was characterized by a more general—as well as a more genuine—interest in improving the quality of the wine through planting better grape varieties and by utilizing the newly acquired knowledge from France in producing finer wines. The transition from adolescence to maturity after the depression was also carried over into the commercial and business development of the industry.

Chapter IX
Tariff Reciprocity, 1875-1879

SINCE THE EARLY ORGANIZATION of the industry on a business and commercial basis in the mid-'sixties, the tariff on foreign wines has been one of the major issues facing this California enterprise.[1] From the passage of the first tariff act of July 4, 1789, to the present time, imported wines have continuously been dutiable. It was not until 1875 that duties on imported wine became specific. Before that time, wine usually carried ad valorem rates. Indeed, by 1875, few issues could evoke as much consternation among the wine men of California, New York, and Ohio as the threat—or even the remote possibility—of a return to ad valorem rates. Since 1875 the wine men of the United States have been able to have enacted lower rates on bulk wine than on bottled wine.[2] Such rate distinctions not only protected American wines but increased the sale of packaged wines, which was the most profitable part of the trade and which the California merchants wanted most to cultivate.

The main argument of the viticulturists for protection in this period was the conventional one—protection for an infant industry.[3] This was true, but the vintners of America seldom differentiated between protection and prohibition. The act of 1870 carried specific rates "in conjunction with value brackets." The wine men of the state still found the act, which was enacted during a boom period, totally unsatisfactory. When business began to lag after the panic of 1873, the vineyardists blamed the tariff. Any attempt at a

---

[1] For notes to chap. ix, see pp. 192–193.

Tariff Reciprocity

downward revision consistently met determined opposition from the viniculturists.

Between 1878 and 1879 tariff revision dominated the thinking and actions of the state, county, and local wine societies of California. The first round in the fight was a victory for the California State Vinicultural Society. In 1878, by the organized pressure of the society, accompanied by organized bargaining in Washington, the grape growers and wine makers of California were able to defeat a bill introduced by Fernando Wood, a representative from New York, to return to ad valorem wine rates.[4] In 1875 the tariff on foreign wines was 40 cents a gallon. The revision sponsored by Wood would have reduced the duty on "all wines valued at less than 40 cents at the place of sale . . . to 25 cents per gallon. . . ."[5] Such an act would have deprived the California industry of sufficient protection. At the same time this initial victory was being gained, the French government was working to accomplish a reciprocal trade treaty with the United States.

The heavy indemnities France was forced to pay to Germany after the Treaty of Frankfurt in 1871, and the loss of revenue from the transfer of Alsace and Lorraine to the recently proclaimed German Empire, caused the French ministries of the 'seventies to look toward overseas trade and colonial expansion as a means to reëstablish the hegemony of France in Europe. The proposed reciprocal trade agreement of 1878 with the United States was one factor of this policy. The treaty anticipated a 50 per cent reduction of the American tariff on French wines and French cognacs.[6] As soon as news of this project appeared in the California press, the fight was on. The *California Farmer* commented at length on the economic disaster that would ensue if such a policy were enacted.

The movement for the reciprocal trade agreement between France and the United States was inaugurated by a group of Parisian manufacturers who hoped to secure new markets and recapture those they formerly monopolized and controlled.[7] This group of French manufacturers acted without the expressed approval of their government; moreover, they were not representative of the general business and trade classes of France. The proposed treaty demanded a general reduction of American tariff rates on all articles of commerce, but it specifically singled out and cited the rates requested by the producers of French wines, spirits, and silks.[8] Representing the interests of this group was Leon Chotteau, whose aim was to organize "a powerful party" of followers in the United States. The contemplated trade treaty further requested that America bind herself to a ten-year policy of low tariffs. Such a policy, the wine men argued, would not secure American trade any more privileges than they enjoyed at present. Furthermore, it would allow England, Germany, Austria, and every other major European power to dump their products on the United States. The basis of the wine men's thesis was that it would greatly increase American imports from all over the world and that it would relieve the congested European markets at the expense of the progress and development of American industries.

The spring of 1878 found Chotteau visiting every major American city on both coasts. His project was to explain in nontechnical language the supposed advantages the American people would derive from a treaty that granted the United States the "most-favored nation" status in its trade with France.[9] In May, 1878, Chotteau first visited San Francisco. At that time he was able to get the San Francisco Chamber of Commerce to approve the proposed treaty. Immediately the State Vinicultural Society, under the leadership of Arpad Haraszthy, called a meeting and issued a circular censuring the action of the San Francisco Chamber of Commerce.[10] By arousing the whole state against the resolutions, the State Vinicultural Society succeeded in having the San Francisco Chamber of Commerce rescind the obnoxious resolutions as well as adopt a new set. The latter stated:

Tariff Reciprocity

Resolved, that no part of the resolutions of May 20th, in reference to the French treaty, shall be construed into an endorsement of any change or reduction in the duty of wines and brandies. And be it further

Resolved, that this Chamber earnestly recommends to Congress that the present duties on foreign wines and spirituous liquors be left at the present rate.[11]

This action soothed inflamed feelings only temporarily. For several months Chotteau did not return to San Francisco, and the prosperity, the increased demand, and the advancing prices of 1878 served to push the French treaty from the front pages of the San Francisco papers. The officers and more active members of the State Vinicultural Society, however, did not accept this period of respite without action. Indeed, it was at this time that they prepared for the battle that started once again on April 2, 1879. Chotteau in the meantime was working in Washington and on the east coast. His policy was to try to gain the support of American free-trade and low-tariff advocates.

On April 2, 1879, a special meeting of the State Vinicultural Society was called in San Francisco. The society's expressed object was to defeat the proposed treaty and to prevent any downward revision of wine rates.[12] Aaron A. Sergent, United States senator from California, had already begun to investigate the importation of foreign wines and liquors into the United States. On February 11, 1879, he submitted a resolution in the Senate requesting the secretary of the treasury to investigate the importation of foreign wines and liquors into the United States and the revenue derived therefrom.[13] The evidence gathered was to be used in fighting the Chotteau treaty. It was also to be a guide for the internal revenue policy of the federal government.

When Chotteau returned to San Francisco in June, 1879, the California wine men were prepared to decide the fate of the state's wine industry on "the battlefield of free trade versus protection."[14] Wetmore likened the proposed agreement to the Portugese-British Wine Treaty of 1840, which made Portugal a virtual colony of Britain. If the present tariff pact was enacted, California would become economically subservient to France.[15] The reduction of the rates on brandy from $3 to $2 and on table wines from 40 to 20 cents would not only destroy California viniculture but would seriously dislocate the whole economy of the state. By 1879 grape growing and wine making were no small part of the state's economy.

On June 13, 1879, Chotteau presented his case before a special session of the San Francisco Chamber of Commerce.[16] The very fact that he appeared before this group indicates how important it was for him to dispel the fear he had aroused among the California wine men. If his scheme was to succeed, he would have to placate them. Unfortunately for Chotteau and the proposed treaty, his speech only added to the already growing indignation among Californians toward this Frenchman. Moreover, the San Francisco Chamber of Commerce passed three resolutions that not only emphatically placed the chamber, the city, and the wine men against any and all aspects of the proposed attempt at reciprocity, but caused them to become militant crusaders for protection.[17]

Chotteau's speeches before the Chamber of Commerce and at other places in San Francisco gave the California wine men ample opportunity for attacking the whole project. In contrast to Chotteau's generalizations on the increased trade that would accrue from such a project, and his general statements of the long friendship between the two powers, the representatives of California wines—Kohler, Wetmore, and Haraszthy—presented conclusive statistical evidence of the harmful effects such a treaty would have on the California industry.[18] Chotteau also failed to present a satisfactory case for the proposed treaty at an interview held for him at a special session of the State Vinicultural Society.[19]

Although the passage of the three resolutions by the San Francisco Chamber of Commerce destroyed all hopes of mutual understanding between Chotteau and the wine men

Tariff Reciprocity

of California, the struggle was still not over. The real fight was to take place in Washington, and, realizing this fact, the State Vinicultural Society appointed a committee of three to raise $4,000 to support a representative in Washington throughout the 1879-1880 session of Congress.[20] The delegate of the California wine men was to fight the proposed treaty and to prevent a downward revision of the existing wine and liquor rates. Coöperating with the society's delegate, the several California congressmen read and presented petitions and recommendations to both houses of Congress.[21] Many of the requests and petitions of the wine men reached the influential Ways and Means Committee and the Committee on Finance of the House of Representatives. The State Vinicultural Society was prepared to defeat the reciprocal trade agreement long before it came to a vote. With this in mind, the society furnished the various committees with ample evidence and sufficient grounds to defeat the proposed bill.

The most cogent case for the wine men was presented by the three leaders of California viticulture, Charles Kohler, Arpad Haraszthy, and Charles A. Wetmore. The addresses, writings, and appeals of these three men were aimed to arouse every Californian—landowner, merchant, and worker—in fighting the Chotteau treaty. In this they were successful. Wetmore appealed to all classes and all economic groups.[22] He defended protection on grounds that appealed to every wine drinker in America. Admitting the advantages a high tariff assured California wine, he credited protection with promoting and maintaining higher wages. Furthermore, the tariff protected the American drinking public from the "drugged, colored, flavored, and imitated wines of Europe."[23] Whereas Wetmore presented the California wine industry as an integral part of the state's economy, Haraszthy and Kohler were more interested in discussing the development of the industry itself. The papers and speeches of these two men form an important part of the source literature of the industry.

The California Wine Industry, 1830–1895

When the Forty-fifth Congress adjourned in 1879, the State Vinicultural Society could—and did—claim its victory. The proposed reciprocal trade treaty with France had not passed beyond the committee stage, and it was indeed doubtful whether it would be discussed further. The defeat of this proposal was the most obvious and the most material accomplishment of the organized wine men of California to that time. Although it was highly improbable that any Congress would commit itself to a general low-tariff policy, the mere threat of unlimited, tax-free competition of European wines was a serious challenge to the wine men of California. The frenzied activity of the California viniculturists during 1878 and 1879 affirmed their apprehensions. The assurance of protection after Chotteau's departure from America, and the growing demand and the advanced prices of wine at the turn of the decade, stimulated a new interest in grape culture that lasted until the middle 'eighties.

The depression of 1875, 1876, and 1877, followed by the tariff issue of the next two years, momentarily overshadowed the growing threat of the phylloxera. Although the disease had been known for some time, it had become particularly dangerous and more prevalent by the close of the 'seventies. The optimism of the wine men, in consequence of their recent tariff victory and their growing prosperity, was to be seriously undermined by this disease.

Chapter X
The Phylloxera

THE MOST SERIOUS BLOW to California viniculture during the nineteenth century was the appearance of the phylloxera. It not only destroyed many vineyards but it threatened the very foundations of the industry.[1] This disease was known to have existed in California before 1870, but grape growing was so prosperous that the vineyardists were indifferent to the threat inherent in the phylloxera.[2] By 1876 the increased virulence of the disease constituted a major threat to the future of wine culture in California.

Recent investigations by viticulturists and horticulturists have agreed that the phylloxera is not only indigenous on the native grape vines of the eastern United States but almost harmless to them.[3] The insect that caused the tremendous destruction in California is an "aphidlike form that lives upon the roots and sometimes upon the leaves" of the vines.[4] The phylloxera is a genus of insects belonging to the Aphididae family, which includes more than thirty species.[5] The most common member of the genus is the *Phylloxera Vastatrix*, more commonly known as the grape phylloxera.[6] The earliest description of this malady in California was made in 1876 by Professor Eugene W. Hilgard of the University of California College of Agriculture.

In most respects the Phylloxera resembles the common plant lice (*Aphis*), the main difference being that its wings lie flat, and overlap on the back, instead of being erected roof-fashion; and that the three-jointed antennae have the terminal joint much the long-

---

[1] For notes to chap. x, see pp. 193–196.

The California Wine Industry, 1830-1895

est. All are quite small, the perfect winged form of the Vine Louse being about one-twentieth of an inch in length. Its peculiar feature is the great varieties of forms which it is capable of assuming under different circumstances. Among them we distinguish two chief types, viz.: *the leaf-inhabiting* one or *Gall Louse*, and the *root-inhabiting* or *Root Louse*.[7]

A native of the eastern United States, the *Phylloxera Vastatrix* was accidentally carried to Europe from America between 1858 and 1863,[8] when many American native vines were being transplanted in Europe for grafting purposes. The result of these importations was to introduce the disease into every wine region of the world. The first European discovery of the insect was made in England in 1863.[9] Several years later it was recognized in France, and after 1869 it became the greatest menace facing the French vineyardists.

Although the phylloxera was native to American wild vines, nothing was known of its deadly effects on the *Vitis vinifera*. The former survived, but the latter did not.[10] The phylloxera was first observed in America in 1856 by Asa Fitch, State Entomologist of New York. He called it the *Pemphigus vitifolice*.[11] Since it did not harm the native vines of New York, no alarm or publicity was aroused by Fitch's discovery. Moreover, the infant status of the American (including the California) wine industry limited the interest in this discovery to a small group. In 1856 the phylloxera in America was an academic rather than a practical issue. It did not remain so for long.

It is impossible to determine the exact date when the disease first reached California. Hilgard maintained that the introduction of the phylloxera was coincident with the introduction of the European vines.[12] Other authorities claim that the disease first appeared in California around 1871.[13] The phylloxera was first definitely identified in a vineyard two miles north of the town of Sonoma in August, 1873.[14] The discovery was made by the Viticultural Club of Sonoma. To verify their observations and to assure proper identification of the disease, specimens of the insect were sent to C. V.

The Phylloxera

Riley, Entomologist of the United States Department of Agriculture, who identified the insect as the *Phylloxera Vastatrix*.[15]

With the advent of the highly susceptible *Vitis vinifera*, the phylloxera became a pest in California. It was not surprising then that the first traces of the disease should be found where the European vines flourished in great abundance— in the vineyards of the Buena Vista Vinicultural Society at Sonoma. Colonel Agoston Haraszthy began his large-scale planting of European grape vines in the latter 'fifties and early 'sixties. As early as 1860, decayed and dying vines were noticed in the vineyards of the estate. No microscopic examinations were made—no one suspected the presence of the disease.[16] Despite the appearance of the common symptoms of the phylloxera—"short growth, small and colorless grapes, early yellow leaves"—the failure of the vines was attributed to the inadaptability of the soil. After the discovery by the Viticultural Club of Sonoma in 1873, an organized system of vine examination was inaugurated in the hope of checking its spread. Every possible remedy known at the time was tried, but all control measures failed. The phylloxera and the depression of 1876 contributed to the failure of the Buena Vista Vinicultural Society.[17]

Since the pest thrived on the European varieties, the many imported vines in Sonoma and Napa counties made these areas the earliest hosts for the phylloxera. Between 1873 and 1879 more than 400,000 vines were dug up in Sonoma alone; Napa, Yolo, El Dorado, and Placer counties also suffered greatly.[18] The counties north of San Francisco Bay were the most seriously infested, but by 1890 the invasion had spread to southern California. Since wine grapes of Los Angeles and surrounding counties were being replaced by raisin and table varieties, the extent of the damage caused by the phylloxera there was never comparable to that in the northern regions of the state.[19]

The disease made slow, steady progress, but many growers refused to recognize the menace.[20] Not until the middle

The California Wine Industry, 1830–1895

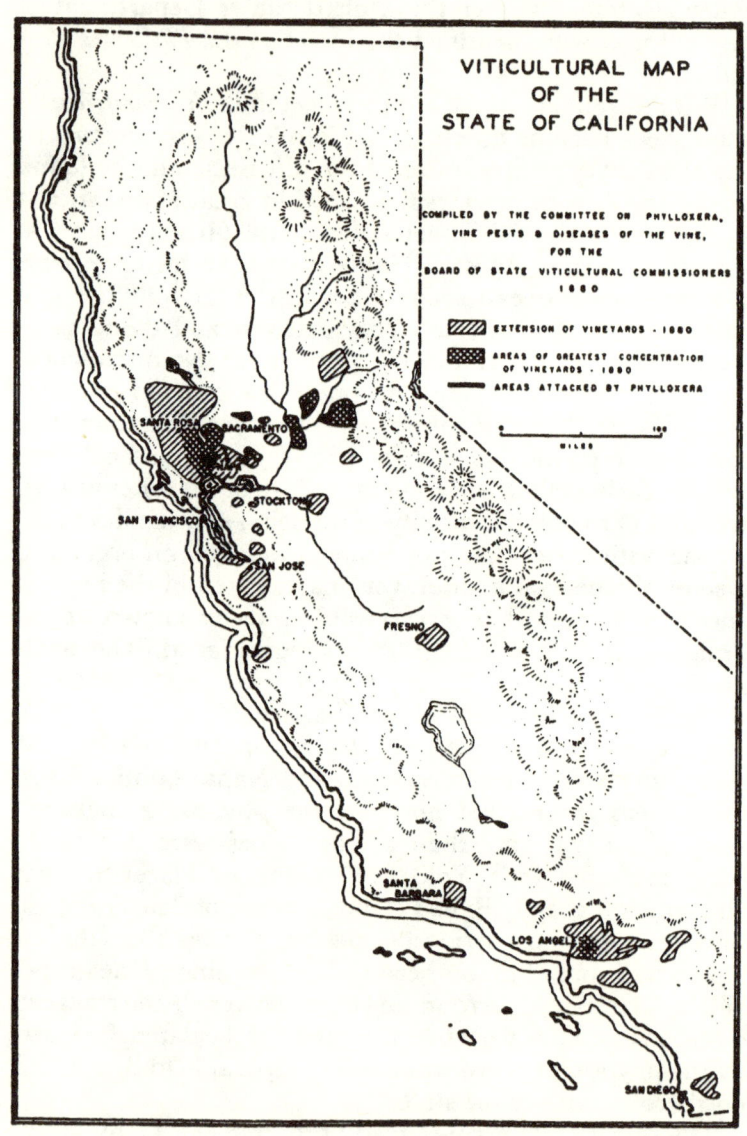

The Phylloxera

'eighties did the extent of the disease in California shock the vineyardists into action.[21] In many instances that action came too late.[22] The 1873 report of the California Wine Growers' Wine and Brandy Manufacturers' Association stated that good cultivation and proper care would prevent any and all diseases from attacking a vineyard.[23] Such statements only encouraged more indifference. As late as 1879 the State Vinicultural Society in its annual report was reluctant to admit that the phylloxera would spread outside of Sonoma County.[24]

The early indifference that Californians manifested toward the disease can be attributed in part to the relatively slow development and to the localized areas of infection during the early 'seventies. There were many reasons for this retarded expansion of the areas of infection. Most important, the winged form of the insect was quite rare during the early period. Thus infection was carried only by plows and other farm equipment.[25] The richness of the virgin soil of California supplied the plants with a high degree of resistance. Healthy vines were able to withstand the insect for a long period of time. However, this initial resistance ultimately broke down.[26] Hilgard maintained that in the

> ... dry atmosphere [of California] the swellings resulting from the bite of the phylloxera are not so quick to develop and spread over the surface of the roots, for ... the injury ... to the vines arises not so much from the amount of sap that it sucks from the roots or leaves, but mainly from the swellings that form where the insect inserted its sucking apparatus, and which start decay of the roots.[27]

When Hilgard began his campaign to instruct the vineyardists of the history and habits of the phylloxera in the middle 'seventies, he found most grape growers still indifferent. The leading wine men of the state planned no concerted action. In 1879 the *Alta California Almanac* wrote, "Nothing has been done ... to check the phylloxera, and whether they will do more damage, is a matter about which there is a difference of opinion."[28] Many wine men deliberately concealed the fact that their vineyards were infested and considered such a charge to be an insult.[29] This attitude seriously prevented early recognition and control measures. Writing in 1875 and 1876, Professor Hilgard says:

To my surprise, I could hear ... little about the phylloxera for a year or two ... ; nor could I obtain any definite information regarding its progress by correspondence. ...

It appears that the cause of this silence was twofold: First, the great depression of the wine interest, causing a feeling that the culture might as well be given up for something more profitable; second, that although the spread of the insect had continued steadily, yet it was so much slower than has been the case in Europe, ... that a great deal of incredulity and wild speculation as to the cause of the dying out of the vines had become current.[30]

During the years of depression, 1876 and 1877, the dejected condition of the industry and the unwillingness of most vintners to face the issue prevented any substantial precautionary or repressive measures from being taken. The price of wine fell so low that it was not unusual for the growers to destroy their own vines, thus removing the hosts.[31] Although the disease had not yet wrought havoc in California at this time, Hilgard alone warned the viticulturists of the state of the possible disastrous effects of the insect. As early as 1876 he requested legislative aid to enforce control measures. He also advised California grape growers to plant phylloxera-resistant vines.[32] Both programs were temporarily ignored, and Professor Hilgard was called an alarmist.

By 1880 the damage caused by the disease increased substantially. The demand for American wines had increased because of the decline in the production of French wines, brought about by the ravages of phylloxera in that country. It was therefore to the economic advantage of California growers to protect their steadily increasing markets. To protect and to extend further the demand of this enlarged market, it was necessary to increase the planting. However, the spread of the disease had a tendency to discourage momentarily any substantial increase in the acreage under cultivation after 1880.[33]

The Phylloxera

The dreaded insect now assumed the winged form and began to infest new areas.[34] The new boom in the industry had enlarged the area of infestation. It was not unlikely that the use of diseased vines to plant new areas contributed more to the spread of the infection than the biological traits of the insect itself.[35]

The advance of the disease was greatest among the old vines, whose lack of vitality made them the most susceptible.[36] Equally favorable to the growth and development of the disease was soil exhaustion. Shallow, black adobe soils, subject to shrinkage and cracking in summer, were also ideal habitats for the phylloxera. The dry seasons of 1882 and 1883 further contributed to the development of the pest in California.[37]

By the middle of the 'eighties there were four accepted and experimentally proved methods to combat the phylloxera: insecticides, submersion, planting vines in sand, and resistant vines.[38] Of the four methods, possibly only the last was practicable. The use of insecticides—bisulphide and sulfocarbonate of potassium—either injected or carried into the soil dissolved in water, killed the insect. This process was very expensive, had to be repeated annually, and, unless performed competently, destroyed the vines.[39] Many other insecticides were adaptable, but all were too costly and impractical.[40] Moreover, many valueless imitations appeared on the market, and the ordinary grower could not distinguish the good from the bad.

Submersion and planting in sand were equally impracticable. The former was possible only under very special conditions. Very few vineyardists could—or would—completely flood their vineyards under one or two feet of water for sixty days. Moreover, although the phylloxera would be destroyed, the vineyard would become susceptible to various fungous diseases. Submerged vineyards required heavy fertilization if they were to survive the inundation.[41] Planting vines in sand was equally difficult. To be phylloxera-proof, the soil must be at least 85 per cent silica. As in submersion, the vines planted in sand produced grapes of an inferior quality.[42]

The only practical defense against the phylloxera was the resistant vines. They had already proved successful in the struggle against the insect in France. The discovery of the resistant American vines was made by Europeans.[43] It soon became obvious to the continental grape growers that the *viniferas* could not survive the attack of the insect. They concluded that the only practicable remedy was to plant vines that would suffer little or nothing. The native American vines, which thrived in the forests of the eastern United States, flourished despite the phylloxera. The immediate answer was to plant these vines and then to graft the domestic *viniferas* upon them.[44] At first, bitter and costly failures accompanied the haphazard selection of native American vines. The first error was the failure to recognize the fact that there were as many native varieties as there were domestic ones. After careful study it was observed that eighteen native American varieties were not only immune to the phylloxera but—equally important—were adaptable for later grafts of *viniferas*.[45] Once the correct variety was selected, the *vinifera* that was grafted on the resistant vine produced *"heavier crops, sweeter and better matured grapes, of larger size, than the Vinifera would produce on the same soil were there no phylloxera at all."*[46] Although these advantages were substantial, the resistant vines required *"more care to get them started than the Viniferas."* This was one of the strongest arguments against the use of resistant stock.[47] Still, it was the only safe course to follow.

The French vineyardists accepted the resistants as the most certain as well as the cheapest and most practicable answer to their plight. The Californians hesitated and only reluctantly accepted and approved the planting of American resistant varieties. This attitude was incomprehensible to the suffering vineyardists of France. The outstanding French viticulturists looked to America—and specifically to California—as the one country where tradition advanced rather than retarded progress.[48] The reluctance with which Cali-

The Phylloxera

fornians accepted the resistants was beyond comprehension to the French.

Professor George Husmann, of Missouri and later of Napa County, California, was a leader in the development of phylloxera-resistant vines.[49] It is largely to his credit that the vinicultural industry of the state survived the disease.[50] The work of Husmann, Hilgard, and other leaders in this struggle was aimed at finding an adaptable resistant upon which to graft the domestic vines of California.[51] At first it was thought that the native *Vitis californica* would answer every purpose. Experience appeared to prove that this variety was useless as a general species. What was needed was a stock whose root was resistant to the phylloxera and at the same time adaptable to the soil and climate of the region and compatible with the *vinifera* that was to be grafted for the top.[52] Finding such a stock proved very difficult, because no single variety fulfilled all the requirements.

The first problem was to ascertain what native varieties were phylloxera-resistant. As far as was known, no vine was totally immune from attack. The real criterion was that the "resistant vine and its roots [would] not only outlive the attacks, but flourish and bear remunerative crops, under the same conditions which the more sensitive vines [would] succumb."[53] The California Agricultural Society immediately took upon itself the role of educating the grape growers on defense remedies. Dismissing submersion and insecticides as a "procrastination of destruction," the society devoted lengthy and erudite articles on resistants adaptable to California.[54] The work of this organization was laudable, but it failed to reach the general vineyardist. Too few growers read and studied the society's publications.

By 1880 the extent of the damage was too great for individual vineyardists to carry the burden alone. The greatest havoc was in the coast counties. Here the presence of the winged form of the insert and the less sandy soil of these areas facilitated the spread of the disease.[55] The vineyard area of California was rapidly decreasing, and few farmers ventured to plant vines near infected districts.[56] The loss to vineyardists was estimated at a thousand dollars a day. Many vineyards of Sonoma and Napa counties were totally destroyed, and the whole northern California industry was threatened.[57] In the face of this disaster very few resistant vines were planted. In part this was due to obstinacy and ignorance, but financial difficulty was also a factor. By 1893 half of the vineyards of Napa County were seriously infected and the others were at least mildly diseased.[58]

As early as 1875 the State Vinicultural Society recommended state aid to combat the phylloxera.[59] Wetmore, Husmann, Hilgard, and others were convinced that without a definite policy the individual growers could not and would not take definite preventive measures. The following year a bill "to save from destruction the Vineyards of California, and to extinguish the Phylloxera in said Vineyards," was introduced in the state senate.[60] The bill provided that experiments be conducted under the direction of the Professor of Agriculture of the University of California. This bill authorized inspection of vineyards suspected of being infected, and aimed to bring the disease out in the open and to fight it with all available resources. Although the bill appropriated only $10,000 for this herculean project, the idea behind it was sound. If the senate had enacted the measure instead of letting it die in legislative procedure, the work that was done later would have been greatly facilitated. As it was, the senate took no action and the disease continued to spread.

This legislative failure did not discourage the viniculturists of the state. Instead it made them even more militant in their demands for legislative aid. Between 1878 and 1880 the struggle to check the ravages of the phylloxera became involved with the fight for a state commission of viticulture. During this two-year period the control of the disease was left with the individual growers, supported and informed by the State Agricultural and State Vinicultural societies.

Although definite quarantine and control regulations were not put into effect until after the creation of the State Board

The Phylloxera

of Viticultural Commissioners in 1880, certain accomplishments must be noted. The discovery of the resistant vine was the most important contribution made toward checking the ravages of the phylloxera. It was upon this vine that the entire wine industry—both Californian and European—was saved. The classification of native species according to their adaptability to soil and climate and their compatibility to different European *vinifera* grafts inaugurated a new era in viticulture. It was not until the California grower imitated the French vineyardist in slowly transplanting his vineyard from domestic to resistant stock that the phylloxera was checked. A beginning was made before 1880; the period after the founding of the state board was devoted to the general realization of the project. While the disease was virulent until well into the 'nineties, the basis for the industry's transformation was established in the latter 'seventies. Neither in France nor in California has the insect ever been totally exterminated. However, both countries have succeeded in controlling and limiting its destruction.

There were California viticulturists who regarded the advent of the disease as a blessing in disguise.[61] In their opinion it had the effect of checking overproduction, with its attendant lower prices, and eliminating the mere speculators from the industry.[62] But it also brought disaster upon many sound and responsible wine men. If it was a blessing in disguise, it was an expensive one. There is no doubt that the industry as a whole had been hampered by the existence of many indifferent varieties (such as the Mission), from which inferior wines were made. The ravages of the phylloxera largely eliminated these varieties. However, it also destroyed some of the finest species. The elimination of the indifferent varieties resulted in the general enhancement of the quality of the California wines on the market, unfortunately with great financial loss and unnecessary waste.

Chapter XI
Founding of the State Board of Viticultural Commissioners, 1880

THE CREATION of the State Board of Viticultural Commissioners in April, 1880, was the culmination of a long fight for a state organization expressly devoted to the interests and the welfare of the California wine industry.[1] Since the creation of the California Wine Growers' Association in 1862, the need for a board of viticulturists that would command respect, could act with authority, and need not depend upon requisitions from individual growers for its funds was one of the most discussed subjects in viticultural circles. The earlier clubs, societies, and associations could only recommend legislation. They lacked funds as well as authority. By 1880 viticulture was certainly important enough and contributed enough revenue to the state to merit an organization entirely devoted to its welfare.

Several factors independent of the wishes of the wine men contributed to the creation of the State Board of Viticultural Commissioners in 1880. In spite of the efforts of the California viniculturists, and in spite of the optimistic statistics of the state's press, only a limited out-of-state market had been secured for California wines. The short crop of 1879, the exhausted supplies of old stock, and the sudden increased demand of 1880 made it difficult to meet the requirements of new markets. It was not surprising, therefore, that an awakened interest in vine planting should appear. The phyl-

---

[1] For notes to chap xi, see pp. 196–198.

State Board of Viticultural Commissioners

loxera was causing havoc in many districts; there was a woeful lack of knowledge as to what should be done to check the disease and increase the number of vines under cultivation; and there were but a few "acknowledged authorities to apply to for information."[2] Under these conditions the state legislature seriously considered the creation of a viticultural commission.

Arpad Haraszthy and Professor Eugene W. Hilgard outlined the requirements and necessities of the proposed board before the state legislature early in 1880.[3] Haraszthy requested a "small sum" to permit the organization to print and distribute the information the society collected. The experimental and scientific research was to be delegated to the University of California College of Agriculture. The latter organization, with funds appropriated by the legislature, was to make the soil analyses necessary to fight the phylloxera and to promote grape culture.[4] Hilgard estimated that the university would require $4,000 for two years to carry on practical experiments at the vineyards, to make scientific soil tests on the university campus, and to publish its findings.[5]

On April 19, 1880, Governor George C. Perkins signed the bill creating the State Board of Viticulture, with an annual appropriation of $10,000.[6] The nine commissioners of the board were appointed by the governor on the same day, and they at once set out to supplement the work of Hilgard and the college of agriculture.[7] The enabling act authorized the governor to make all the appointments, and in most cases able and practical viticulturists were selected for the honored positions.[8] The act of 1880 divided California into seven viticultural districts.[9] Each district had one representative, who was to collect and disseminate information, propose soil tests if necessary, and acquire annual statistics to be filed at Sacramento. Most officers and representatives of the State Board of Viticultural Commissioners were "hard-working, honest men, carefully trained in their chosen line, and with the interests of the vineyardists in their hearts."[10]

The California Wine Industry, 1830–1895

It became immediately apparent that the act of 1880 was not specific as to the functions of the board in the fight against the phylloxera. The following year a second act was passed to expand and define the duties of the State Board of Viticultural Commissioners.[11] The act of March 4, 1881, designated the board as a board of health for "grape pests and diseases and made it responsible for experiments on remedies."[12] The new legislation created the office of chief executive viticultural officer. He and the secretary of the State Board of Viticultural Commissioners were the only two officials with a definite salary. The executive officer was given power, subject to the board's approval, to prevent the spread of vine diseases by "declaring and enforcing rules and regulations in the nature of quarantine."[13] These "rules and regulations" were all-inclusive and ranged from recommendations to prohibitions against the importation into the state, or the distribution of infected vines within the state. The provisions of this act were the bases of future health and sanitary vine legislation. As such they form an important part in the state's development of agricultural quarantine legislation.

The act of 1881 provided for an advisory board of horticulture.[14] This board immediately began functioning as a state horticultural commission, and in 1883 its status was confirmed by the legislature. The horticultural commission was for two years under the direction and supervision of the State Board of Viticultural Commissioners. In 1883 the viticultural commission was allotted more functions, and the horticultural commission became an independent organization.[15] Although both commissions were primarily interested in checking diseases, the horticulturists' interests were too diverse to be under the control and guidance of viticulturists.

The work of the State Board of Viticultural Commissioners can be divided into four categories: to fight and control diseases; to perform practical experiments with wines and vines; to promote the raisin industry; and to further viticultural education.

State Board of Viticultural Commissioners

From the beginning, the fuctions of the board were broad enough to encompass everything pertaining to viticulture and viniculture. The act of 1880 did not distinguish or specify the duties of the State Board of Viticultural Commissioners and the college of agriculture. Although it delegated wide authority to the viticultural commission, it also provided the University of California with broad powers to carry on viticultural experiments.[16] Only a few wine men understood the confused language of the act, and its interpretation soon became an issue of bitter debate. The allocation of money among the two organizations was always a difficult problem. The college of agriculture was intended to carry on original researches in grape and wine diseases, but the State Board of Viticultural Commissioners was always reluctant to admit that fact.[17] The failure of the two laws to define the functions of the board and the college of agriculture contributed materially to the final dissolution of the State Board of Viticultural Commissioners in 1894.

The first task of the commissioners was to build a viticultural library. This was imperative, for there was a woeful lack of scientific knowledge in this field in California. The commission began by purchasing all the books, pamphlets, and monographs in English on wine making and grape growing;[18] then it purchased all those in French, German, Italian, and Spanish. By 1887 the State Board of Viticultural Commissioners' library consisted of more than four hundred volumes—undoubtedly it was one of the best wine libraries in America at the time.[19] The scientific data on all aspects of viticulture that California possesses today are a tribute to the work of this commission.[20] Chief Executive Viticultural Officer Charles A. Wetmore traveled throughout Europe and collected much valuable data that were used to improve the wine varieties and processes.[21]

The newly acquired information was used to conduct experiments with new vines, fertilizers, and soil analyses. A series of wine conventions sponsored by the State Board of Viticultural Commissioners attracted many growers who were interested in improving their crops. These conventions became centers of advanced viticultural studies.[22] The immediate effect of these educational conferences was to promote the planting of better grade vines and to discourage the practice of setting out only the abundant bearers, or what the French called *"cépages d'abondance."*[23] Within five years, largely as a result of the efforts of the State Board of Viticultural Commissioners, the number of superior varieties increased by 100,000 acres. Between 1880 and 1882 more than 40,000 vines were planted. Within four years the new vines planted and the necessary improvements to maintain them were valued at $15,000,000. Within the same period the operation of State Board of Viticultural Commissioners cost the state of California no more than $14,000.[24]

The attempt of the State Board of Viticultural Commissioners to check the ravages of the phylloxera was one of its most publicized activities. Its library supplied valuable data to identify the presence and habits of the phylloxera. Valuable translations were made from French works, and various experiments with supposed phylloxera remedies were conducted.[25] The State Board of Viticultural Commissioners accepted a program outlined by Arpad Haraszthy to fight the phylloxera and to promote sound grape culture. Haraszthy proposed that the State Board of Viticultural Commissioners foster the

... establishing of experimental vineyards, properly equipped and maintained in every prominent viticultural center of the State, for the sole purpose of ascertaining the adaptability of different vines to raise the best grapes, in the greatest abundance, with the least accidents or disease in the different localities.[26]

The same month in which the State Board of Viticultural Commissioners was founded, the legislature approved and the governor signed a bill "for the better protection of fruittrees and vines."[27] The bill empowered the board of supervisors in the different counties to appoint a commission to investigate infected vines and to condemn and have removed any infected vineyards.[28] This act was aimed to permit local

State Board of Viticultural Commissioners

and county governments to fight the phylloxera when it became a threat to the whole community. The law was soon tested in the state courts, and the following year it was declared unconstitutional by the Supreme Court of California. This judicial action placed the entire burden of phylloxera control upon the State Board of Viticultural Commissioners and the college of agriculture.

The legislature appropriated $3,000 to the university to "report on results, progress, and treatment of the phylloxera," and Professor Hilgard, with the assistance of the State Board of Viticultural Commissioners, began his struggle to curb the ravages of the insect.[29] The first work of the board was to appoint a special committee on vine pests. On July 23, 1880, members of this committee visited the infected vines of Sonoma County and conferred with Hilgard as to what steps were to be taken.[30] The committee recommended resistant vines as the best policy to check and guard against the disease.[31]

While the State Board of Viticultural Commissioners was busy disseminating information to growers, the college of agriculture was conducting experiments with various types of resistant vines. One of the first practical results of the experiments conducted at Berkeley was proof that the *Vitis californica* was "well adapted as a grafting stock for a large number of the varieties of *vitis vinifera*."[32] This was an important observation, since heretofore this inexpensive variety was regarded by many vineyardists as totally useless. At the same time Hilgard opened an experimental vineyard at Berkeley to try different methods of killing the insect.[33] He soon discovered that Berkeley was not the place to carry on such experiments. Berkeley was too far from the "real" vineyard areas of California, and a thorough attempt to check the disease could be carried out only by experienced men being constantly on the job.[34]

On the basis of Hilgard's experiments the State Board of Viticultural Commissioners, through the chief executive viticultural officer, proposed that experimental vineyard plots be located in Napa, Sonoma, Santa Clara, and San Joaquin counties. These two-acre plots were to be planted with all the known varieties of resistant vines. The selection of plots, the expense of planting, costs of upkeep, and the purchase of resistant vines were to be in charge of the chief executive viticultural officer.[35] This work was to become one of the most important functions of the commission. Before the work of the State Board of Viticultural Commissioners the phylloxera was thought to exist only in Sonoma and certain nearby counties. The district commissioners discovered the disease also in Napa, Solano, Yolo, El Dorado, and Placer counties.[36]

The district commissioners not only helped conquer plant pests but helped improve wine-making and grape-growing practices.[37] Their annual reports on the status of viticulture in their respective districts constitute a large portion of the source material for the history of California wine making and grape growing. The function of the commissions in each district was to inform the state of local needs and desires, to aid in organizing local viticultural clubs and societies, to enlist experienced viticulturists to instruct grape growers in pruning, planting, and making wine, and to hold viticultural meetings and fairs.[38] The Haraszthian and subsequent vine importations gave California one of the largest assortments of grape varieties in any country. To locate the most adaptable soils and climates for these varieties was the aim of the State Board of Viticultural Commissioners and its district commissioners.

Although the commission pleaded for general quarantine and control legislation against the phylloxera, it was only through the coöperation of the individual grape growers that a perfect quarantine could be enforced.[39] Wetmore, as chief executive viticultural officer of the State Board of Viticultural Commissioners, requested that the state pass necessary laws to govern the introduction of new vines from the eastern United States and Europe, supervise the distribution of vines in California, and protect the vineyardists against negligent

State Board of Viticultural Commissioners

growers.[40] In November, 1881, Wetmore issued his famous quarantine rules.[41] The rules aimed to prevent new infestation by regulating the importation of new vines and by disinfecting every vine imported into the state or transplanted from one district to another within the state.[42] These were control measures. The research to eliminate or nullify the effects of the disease were carried on by Professor Hilgard and his assistants at Berkeley.

Between 1880 and 1887 the Berkeley campus of the University of California became the most important oenological research center of the state. Here, at the university's experimental plot, Hilgard carried on a series of experiments with the phylloxera and its effects on different species of resistant vines. However, many growers refused to accept or acknowledge the value of Hilgard's labors. Indeed, a delegation of Livermore Valley vineyardists read a resolution at the 1887 State Board of Viticultural Commissioners convention demanding that the "public nuisance and danger" of Hilgard's work at Berkeley be stopped.[43] The Livermore vineyardists feared that Hilgard's experiments with the winged form of the phylloxera would infect the whole valley. Only after considerable debate was Hilgard able to save his experimental plot and continue his researches.

The founding of the State Board of Viticultural Commissioners and the work of Hilgard mark the last stage in the organized fight against the phylloxera. The use of resistant vines and careful quarantine regulations slowly reduced the ravages of the insect. The disease was virulent until the 'nineties, but the slow transformation of California vineyards from domestic to resistant stock reduced the infection.

While engrossed in its investigation of the phylloxera, the State Board of Viticultural Commissioners was faced, in 1884, with a new and perplexing problem. Anaheim, one of the major wine-producing districts of California was struck with a mysterious vine disease.[44] At first several growers believed it to be the phylloxera, but careful investigation soon proved this theory to be wrong.[45] The first record of the

Anaheim—or California—disease appeared in the Anaheim *Gazette* in 1885.[46] The grape growers and wine makers of the district were financially ruined by the loss of their only revenue-producing industry. The complete collapse of viticulture in Anaheim is indicated by the reports of the State Board of Viticultural Commissioners.[47] Between 1884 and 1894, 30,000 acres of vines, which were valued at approximately $20,000,000, were destroyed.[48]

In July, 1886, Professor Hilgard was summoned for aid. Hilgard and other viticulturists were unable to diagnose the disease.[49] In all the history of California agriculture there had never been a similar malady, nor one that caused such sudden destruction. The disease attacked all varieties of grapes—the wild vines not excepted.[50] At first it was thought that climate, the soil, or animal or vegetable parasites were its causes. All these theories soon proved untenable. It soon became apparent that national aid was necessary. The state board was severely criticized for its failure to discover the cause of the disease, and in 1887 the southern California vineyardists appealed to Washington.[51]

The national agriculturists were equally baffled. Several members of the United States Department of Agriculture and the famous French vineyardist and oenologist Professor P. Viala were sent to California to study the infection.[52] They not only failed to find a remedy but were unable to classify it. At the 1889 convention of the State Board of Viticultural Commissioners serious disagreement as to the type and source of the disease dominated all discussion of the scourge of Anaheim.[53] One scientist concluded his investigations by stating the cause to be either the "climate, soil, change of season or bacteria. . . ."[54] It is not surprising that the Anaheimers were beginning to doubt the abilities of many so-called authorities.

In 1889 the United States Department of Agriculture assigned Newton B. Pierce to the problem. Pierce was the first man to bring to California a specialized knowledge of plant diseases. Although he never succeeded in establishing the

State Board of Viticultural Commissioners

exact nature of the disease, the fact that it subsided after his arrival justified calling it Pierce's disease.[55] When the contagion began to subside after 1889, the whole Santa Ana Valley had been infected.[56] The exact classification of the disease that caused such destruction is still unknown. By 1890 the famous Anaheim vineyards had been replaced with fruit trees.[57]

Within one decade the State Board of Viticulture had demonstrated its ability to cope with practical viticultural problems. Although it failed to solve the Anaheim disease, it accomplished a great deal toward defeating the phylloxera in California. Certainly no organization had done more to distribute practical scientific and technical data among the wine men of California. For the first time in the state's history there now existed a body of distinguished authorities with a valuable collection of classified scientific information at the disposal of every wine grower in California. The next few years were to determine its efficacy in handling political, commercial, and economic matters.

Chapter XII
A Business Cycle, 1880-1895

THE YEAR 1880 was in many respects a momentous one for the wine men of California.[1] That year the State Board of Viticultural Commissioners was established; the legislature of California directed the Board of Regents of the University of California to establish courses in viticulture at the college of agriculture; and the long-debated California state pure-wine law was finally enacted.[2] Before 1880 the state's viticultural interests were in a condition of chaos.[3] Lack of knowledge, the need of systematization, and few "beaten paths to follow" distinguished the pre-1880 era from the post-1880 one.

By 1880 grape growing and wine making had achieved significance commercially as well as industrially, and California's leading agricultural industry was on the threshold of a new—the modern—era.[4] The first generation of viticulturists brought to California the choice *viniferas* of Europe, the viticultural experience of the Old World, and trained American wine makers.[5] The second generation was to end America's dependence upon Europe for *vin ordinaire* and to increase and improve the wine-making facilities of the state.[6]

Between 1880 and 1895 the wine industry experienced its second business cycle. The ravages of the phylloxera, the growing demand for California wines on the east coast,[7] and the optimism that followed the recovery from the depression of 1876 gave impetus to the urge to set out more vines

---

[1] For notes to chap. xii, see pp. 198–201.

A Business Cycle

and to produce more wine. In 1881 and 1882 the demand for grape cuttings was so great that it far exceeded the supply.[8] Between 1881 and 1883 Leland Stanford planted more than 1,000,000 vines at his famous Vina Vineyard in Tehama county.[9] To be sure, very few vineyardists increased their acreage to such an extent, but Stanford serves to illustrate the optimism of these boom years. Most California wine growers felt that the demand for cheap wine would so increase that it would never meet the supply. The increased demand of 1880 brought about a five-year period of expansion. Viticulture again promised to be the most remunerative industry in California.[10] The extent of new plantings increased so rapidly that by 1889 more than 130,000 acres of land were devoted exclusively to vineyard purposes.[11] The advanced prices of the early 'eighties were used by the press of California to promote viticulture still further and to extend grape growing in new regions.[12]

The valuable suggestions the State Board of Viticultural Commissioners and the University of California College of Agriculture proposed to the grape growers and the wine makers during those early years of prosperity were accepted only reluctantly—if at all. Apart from its technical and scientific investigations, the State Board of Viticultural Commissioners also attempted to compile and make available the viticultural knowledge of the Old World in such a manner as to be of practical value to the vineyardists of California.[13] To facilitate and augment the functions of the college of agriculture, Arpad Haraszthy urged the legislature to provide funds to create more experiment stations. Only through research, Haraszthy maintained, could California achieve and maintain the viticultural leadership its resources warranted.[14] Research was not to be limited to technical and scientific questions alone, but to commercial and industrial problems as well. During the prosperous years of the early 'eighties the State Board of Viticultural Commissioners attempted, by means of the protective tariff and through a campaign to produce better wines, to strengthen the American market. In order to achieve this end it was imperative that California produce a good sound wine.[15]

In spite of the educational contributions these two organizations made toward achieving the superior production of wines in California, and in spite of the already recognized superiority of the choicer varieties, the decline in wine production resulting from the depression of 1876 and the ravages of the phylloxera caused many vineyardists to continue to plant the more abundant bearers—the Mission and the Zinfandel. Arpad Haraszthy estimated that as late as 1880, 80 per cent of the vines planted were of the Mission variety. By 1890 this was no longer true. In that year Arpad Haraszthy estimated that 90 per cent of California's wine grapes were of the best foreign varieties.[16] This change was brought about by the severe depression of 1886. Two panics within a decade finally convinced the grape growers of California of the necessity to improve the quality of their wine by selecting their grape varieties more judiciously.

The educational policies of the State Board of Viticultural Commissioners in this period were not aimed solely at the grape growers and the wine makers, but also at educating the American people. The commissioners proposed to introduce good wines to a larger American public and at the same time hoped to cultivate an appreciative palate among the indiscriminate wine drinkers of the United States. On this subject Arpad Haraszthy succinctly presented the problem when he stated:[17]

The great obstacle to our success . . . is, that the average American is a whisky drinking, water drinking, coffee drinking, tea drinking, and consequently a dyspepsia inviting subject, who does not know the use or value of pure light wine taken at the proper time and in moderate quantities. The task before us lies in teaching our people how to drink wine, when to drink it and how much of it to drink.

The quality of California wines improved steadily after the depression of 1876. However, many Americans still did not know that California produced excellent European-type

A Business Cycle

wines.[18] Adulteration and false branding were not uncommon. By 1885 the wine men of California directed their attention toward producing high-grade wines.[19] Much of the fine wine produced between 1885 and 1900 was skillfully manufactured by trained wine makers from the choice varieties planted after the depressions of 1876 and 1886. The Thirty-five gold, silver, and bronze medals awarded to California wines at the Paris Exposition of 1889 attest to the improved quality. Equally profitable to California was the display at the Louisville Exposition of 1885.[20]

The improved quality of all varieties of wine—red, white, sweet, and sparkling—helped the wine trade, increased out-of-state shipments, and generally contributed to the new prosperity of the early 'eighties. The high prices paid for wine in 1881, 1882, and 1883 caused many growers to become manufacturers as well.[21] In many instances these small wine men produced the most excellent wine. The individual grower-manufacturer never seriously threatened the large merchants, but a new group of small, independent, individually operated cellars found a successful and remunerative home market.

The wine trade of 1880 showed a decided increase over that of the preceding years.[22] It also indicated the increased popularity of red and light, dry, white wines.[23] Before 1880 Mexico and Central America were the largest foreign consumers, but by the early 'eighties the Sandwich Islands, Europe, Japan, and British Columbia became substantial and continuous markets.[24] By 1890 California was Europe's most serious competitor for the South American market. In 1892 the Italian government attributed the decline of its South American export trade to the competition from the California vintners.[25] Apart from the improved quality of the wine itself, lowered freight rates and better service also materially aided the California export trade.[26] After 1882, rail shipments surpassed shipments by sea, and since that date the railroads have been the chief carriers of California wine. The San Francisco market became more and more an important outlet for fresh grapes. The growing number of Italian, French, and Spanish immigrants accounted for the prosperous grape market in New York, Boston, New Orleans, Philadelphia, Chicago, and other cosmopolitan centers.[27]

The advanced prices, the large export trade, and the general viticultural prosperity lasted until 1886. In that year a large and inferior crop caused a panic in prices, and once again the grape and wine growers were on the road to a new depression.[28] A major disaster was avoided by the small crop of 1885, but the following year a record crop was harvested. The depression that hit the California wine industry in 1886 was largely the result of the overabundant plantings of the previous five years.[29] Although there was a general improvement in the quality of California's wine varieties, a substantial amount of cheap, adulterated wine was still produced. Inexperienced growers, diseased vines, and the speculative element were still present. Each contributed toward bringing on the depression.[30] It should be noted that the increased planting of foreign varieties—the finer European wine grapes—which were not necessarily abundant bearers, did not become prevalent until after 1886.

The low prices and slow sales lasted well into the 'nineties. Superior wines were selling at 6 and 8 cents a gallon at the wineries, and the optimistic statements of Wetmore and Haraszthy were described as "overoptimistic prognostications." However, the second "bust" in the wine industry was not without beneficial results. The severity of the depression led the more enlightened growers and merchants to seriously consider the status of their industry. It remained for a foreigner, Guido Rossati, a representative of the Italian Ministry of Agriculture, to present the most cogent statement on the status of the California market. Rossati attributed the collapse of the industry in 1886 to the search for immediate profits; the failure to realize that grape culture, to be successful and remunerative, is a long-term investment; and that experience, skillful handling of wines, and proper aging are the true criteria of success.[31]

A Business Cycle

The annual conventions of the State Board of Viticultural Commissioners began to discuss seriously the problems facing the industry. One of the most important and immediate issues was the scarcity of labor. Chinese were used almost exclusively in the field; however, their vinicultural inexperience and the growing objection to their increasing numbers, limited their employment.[32] Moreover, if superior wines were to be manufactured, trained cellar personnel was necessary. The industry could no longer rely on a nomadic labor supply. The post-depression years found local, county, and state societies advertising throughout the United States and Europe for experienced agriculturists. Although the scarcity of experienced wine makers was a disadvantage, the transportation problem of the middle 'eighties was equally serious. The still relatively exorbitant steamer and railway rates retarded the expansion of successful markets for California wines.[33] The lack of competition in transportation and such practices as collecting rebates, rate favoritism of as much as 3½ to 5 cents a gallon to large shippers, and charging higher rates for a short haul than for a long one caused the railroads to become one of the important determining factors in the Continental wine trade. The railroads were not alone in showing favoritism; the Pacific Mail Steamship Company of San Francisco was also guilty of such practices.[34] The passage of the Interstate Commerce Act in 1887 gave the wine men only an element of relief. The discrimination in freight rates injured not only the growers but also the more vociferous, organized, and powerful group—the merchants.

The leading San Francisco wine merchants—Kohler and Frohling, Jacob Gundlach, Lachman and Jacobi, and Arpad Haraszthy and Company—attempted to stimulate the wine industry in general by securing new markets.[35] Between 1886 and 1894 these merchants industriously promoted various formulas to revive the wine trade. In 1887 the first shipment of California condensed must (the juice of the grapes before fermentation) was sent to London. This was the beginning

The California Wine Industry, 1830–1895

of a profitable trade, and attempts were made to introduce and popularize California must in Mexico.[36] Since must was not dutiable, it was hoped that a substantial traffic could be developed.

New outlets for wine, grapes, and brandy were found, but recovery did not follow rapidly. In 1888 a committee of wine men requested the financiers of California to put wine on the approved list of collaterals for loans, but no banker accepted the proposal.[37] Since the established banking houses of California refused to lend money on wine, a grape growers' and wine makers' bank, under the direction of vineyardists, was proposed.[38] Founded on the same principle as the Granger's Bank, the California institution had as its main objective to make advances to distressed vineyardists on wine as collateral. However, to insure competent management, there were to be three financiers on the board of directors. The establishment of this bank was prevented by difficulty in raising money and by a growing distrust between the wine merchants and the wine growers.

The wine crisis resulting from the panic of 1886 lasted well into the early 'nineties. The low prices and the slow sales of wine and grapes between 1886 and 1892 caused a serious schism within the ranks of the viticulturists themselves. The growers, unable to find a market for their wine, blamed the merchants for the general depression of the industry.[39] Many farmers found little comfort in the prognostications of the State Board of Viticultural Commissioners or in the economic and commercial statements of the merchants. The small grower, faced with financial ruin and unable to borrow on his wine, demanded action. The San Francisco newspapers, particularly the *Examiner*, published a series of articles listing the causes of the depression and proposing many remedies.[40] William Randolph Hearst had an immediate and personal interest in grape growing.

Seeking to promote positive action among the wine men, the *Examiner*, during July and August, 1889, determined to find the cause and the remedy for the wine panic. To secure

A Business Cycle

the views of the growers, the paper prepared and distributed a circular. The interest of the *Examiner* in the viticultural crisis is shown by the following letter.

July 8, 1889

Sir: The present depression in the wine trade, the low price obtainable by winemakers for a sound wine, and the heavy pressure on the storage capacity of a majority of winemakers, . . . seriously threaten one of the leading industries of the State, and call for special efforts on the part of all patriotic citizens to do all in their power to assist in placing the business of winemaking, which is of such vast importance to the State, on the best and firmest basis.

That the winemakers of the State are not receiving a fair compensation for their wine is admitted by all who have given the subject any consideration, but how best to bring about a fairer adjustment of the relations of producers, middlemen and consumers is something that seems very difficult to decide. Until it is decided a constant agitation of the question cannot but benefit the winemakers, and through them the entire State.

In order to arrive at a proper understanding of the situation it is necessary that the opinions of as many winemakers as possible on the situation and the best remedy therefor be secured. To facilitate the gathering of such information the *Examiner* will esteem it a favor if you will fill out the inclosed blank and return to this office at your earliest convenience. Respectfully,

W. R. Hearst[41]

For several days the *Examiner* printed the opinions of the growers who had responded to Hearst's letter. Most of the replies recommended distilling more brandy, planting fewer grapes, curing more raisins, and improving the general quality of the wine marketed. However, the most significant—and the one that caused the most controversy—was the reply of Professor Hilgard. Hilgard said that there was no general fault with California wine that could not be remedied by "judicious treatment and honorable means."[42] He endorsed coöperative brandy distilleries, and felt that district coöperative depots for labeling, bottling, and marketing wine would aid and hasten the industry's recovery. On this latter

The California Wine Industry, 1830–1895

point, however, Hilgard warned the growers and merchants of the necessity for expert knowledge and assistance. Hilgard blamed the California wine makers and the California wine merchants for the extended depression. He severely censured both groups for their emphasis upon "pretty bottles and beautiful labels" rather than upon an attempt to improve the quality of their wine.

Several days later the seventh state viticultural convention was held in San Francisco.[43] C. A. Wetmore, who had now become president of the State Board of Viticultural Commissioners, challenged the statements of Hilgard. With this verbal and journalistic encounter, the State Board of Viticultural Commissioners and Professor Hilgard parted ways. Wetmore censured Hearst for relying "upon the judgment of a college professor rather than the taste and experience of educated, practical men, connoisseurs in wine. . . ." The fight between Hilgard and Wetmore was carried on during the several days the convention was in session. Indeed, the debates, lectures, and discussions became so bitter and so acrimonious that the 1889 meeting of the State Board of Viticultural Commissioners convention was one of its most noted. Under such circumstances it was not surprising that little or no positive action was taken. There were the usual recommendations, petitions, and proposals, but actual accomplishments were few.

The depression continued, and the growers and merchants became increasingly more embittered. In 1892, Zinfandel grapes sold for $10 a ton in San Francisco, and Mission— if they could find a buyer—commanded no more than $5.[44] Another year at such prices would force a great many vineyardists into bankruptcy. Then France and other countries embarked on a protective tariff policy, which depressed the wine trade even further.[45] The *Pacific Wine Brewing and Spirit Review* epitomized the state of the California wine market as "absolutely flat."[46]

The State Board of Viticultural Commissioners had established a viticultural cellar and café in San Francisco with

A Business Cycle

the hope of creating a wine center. However, the expected meetings between buyers and sellers did not materialize. Although the viticultural display did the industry no harm, it did not promote trade or increase prices.

The continued depression caused many growers to question whether the State Board of Viticultural Commissioners had not already served its purpose. The first attacks against the policy and action of the commission were heard at this time. The opinion was voiced among wine men that if the State Board of Viticultural Commissioners could no longer aid them, there was no reason why the board should be continued.

As early as 1889 it had been suggested that the "concentration of the bulk of the wine of the State under a single management would secure innumerable advantages. . . ."[47] Such an organization could facilitate the blending, mixing, and handling of wine, and assure its uniform quality. The association would improve sales and promote trade, since it could assure quality and purity. Moreover, the system would aid the small grower who was unable to construct and maintain a large wine plant.[48] Such an association of producers could at least insure the growers a small profit for their labors. The next few years found the growers seriously discussing the possibilities of such a venture.

While the growers were searching for a solution the merchants were equally distressed by the depressed condition of the industry. In 1892 the principal dealers of the state formed the California Wine Association for their mutual protection[49] and to raise prices and stimulate trade. In 1894 the growers organized and formed the California Wine Makers' Corporation for a similar purpose.[50] The two organizations now attempted to revive the industry through coöperation.[51]

The corporation, by securing control of enough wine to determine its price, entered into a contract with the association by which the dealers agreed to purchase from the corporation four million gallons of wine annually. Since the

The California Wine Industry, 1830–1895

vineyardist could receive only 6 or 8 cents a gallon for his wine on the open market, the two groups formed a close alliance for the next few years. Between 1894 and 1896 the corporation sold all its wine to the association.[52] This happy relationship lasted until the close of the 1896 harvest. The continued ravages of the phylloxera and a severe frost in May of that year reduced the wine crop. Prices automatically began to rise, and the growers demanded more money for their wine. In the fall the corporation, without consulting the association, raised its price to 20 cents a gallon. The dealers refused to pay more than 15 or 18 cents, and the result was a deadlock.[53] The corporation, by a unanimous resolution, refused to sell its wine at less than 20 cents and prepared to store it in San Francisco.

This action brought on a wine war between the dealers and the producers, which resulted in a series of suits and countersuits. The struggle was carried on in both the courts and the wine market. The corporation now also became a distributor, and the association purchased as much wine as it could from independent growers. The fight lasted until the turn of the century, when advanced prices, improved trade, and a general prosperity caused the two organizations to settle their difficulties.

Material benefits were derived, however, from the discontent of the 'nineties.[54] The struggle between the producers and the dealers went beyond the economic depression. The difficult relationship between the two was as old as the industrial and commercial development of the industry itself. The merchants were the chief—and in some cases the only—outlet for the producers. Much of the strife arose from the infant status of the industry, but the dishonest and mercenary practices of many merchants were also important factors. The wine war of the 'nineties forced the growers to find new outlets for their products and caused them to remedy basic defects in production and distribution. It also finally convinced them that a good, sound, salable wine was the best insurance against low prices.

A Business Cycle

The difficulties in the industry were not confined to the struggle between the grower and the merchant. The issues at stake were basic and, as such, permeated every aspect of California viticulture. The prolonged depression of the 'nineties brought criticism upon the State Board of Viticultural Commissioners. One of the first serious attacks by wine growers came in 1893 from the Wine Growers' Union of Napa County,[55] which sent a resolution to the legislature requesting that the commission be abolished. Otherwise, the representatives of the county were to work to prevent the passage of appropriations for the board's support.[56] This attack was a reflection of the depressed condition of the industry. The Napa vintners censured the State Board of Viticultural Commissioners for its optimism and for its "authoritative announcement that over-production of wine need not be feared. . . ."

The lack of confidence in the work of the commission became more and more prevalent as the depression continued.[57] Although the board had done an excellent job in collecting viticultural literature and distributing the results of its findings on the phylloxera and other vine pests, the real experimental and scientific work originated at the college of agriculture. The financial bickering between the State Board of Viticultural Commissioners and Professor Hilgard over appropriations, legislative aid, and viticultural data reflected badly on the board. No one could ignore the valuable contribution Hilgard and his assistants had made to the wine industry of California. The excellent work of the University of California in all branches of agriculture was a serious threat to the existence of many of the recently founded agricultural boards and commissions,[58] which accomplished little to justify their appropriations from the state.

The crucial question in 1894 was whether the State Board of Viticultural Commissioners should be continued. The only justification for the board's continued existence was its work in distributing viticultural information and as a pressure group for the wine interests of California. The annual

The California Wine Industry, 1830–1895

convention of growers and merchants were interesting and beneficial but not indispensable. Many wine men seriously doubted whether the board was still useful. This doubt and the depression of the 'nineties facilitated the task of the advocates of governmental economy to justify the board's abolition.[59]

Between 1892 and 1895 the *Rural Californian* and other publications began a concentrated attack on useless boards and commissions.[60] The "horse racing agriculturist" and the "corner grocery viticulturist" who dominated these boards, according to the *Rural Californian*, did not justify the expense of supporting them. Throughout the year 1894, and especially during the November elections, the officers—past and present—of the State Board of Viticultural Commissioners tried to save their commission by defending its usefulness and attacking its enemies.[61] However, dissension within the ranks prevented unified action.

On March 27, 1895, the state legislature repealed the enabling act of the State Board of Viticultural Commissioners and turned over its functions, library, and records to the College of Agriculture of the University of California.[62] The viticulturists lamented the passing of the board and censured the wine men of the state as a body for not supporting it.[63] Toward Hilgard, and the University of California in general, their resentment knew no bounds. The former was attacked as a university politician, a "viticultural fraud"; the latter was the bête noire of the defunct commissioners.

By December, 1895, the State Board of Viticultural Commissioners was ready to deliver its effects to the Board of Regents of the University of California.[64] Once the transfer was completed, the professor of agriculture was placed in charge of viticultural research in California. Several years later the eminent viticulturist George Husmann stated that the viticultural work of the university was one of its most conspicuous accomplishments.[65] He saw no need for any new boards or commissions.

However, in 1895 the deposed commissioners proposed to

A Business Cycle

established a "college of viticulture," which was to be the worthy successor of the State Board of Viticultural Commissioners. The sponsors of this new institution were the so-called leaders and motivators of the old state board.[66] Such men as C. A. Wetmore, Arpad Haraszthy, Isaac De Turk, and others who had quarreled with Hilgard were the most vociferous in the fight for a new central body of wine men. They gave no credit to the university, for which they had only contempt; they wanted an institution independent of the state. The new "college of viticulture" was to be free from "political considerations" and from the "theorists and dreamers" who controlled the college of agriculture.[67] The new board was to have no capital, but was to handle all problems as they came up. The stated intention of its supporters was.

... to have a nucleus of a working body in San Francisco which can be ready for action whenever desired for matters of national and State legislation, for the collection of exhibits, and generally to undertake the work hitherto carried on by the State Viticultural Commission in its commercial relations. State aid will not be solicited.[68]

The college was incorporated under the state law that provided for establishing "colleges and seminaries of learning." The new "college of viticulture" may have given comfort to the deposed commissioners, but it did very little else. From 1895 to the present the college of agriculture, with its experimental stations, has been the great center of viticultural learning in California. The prosperity and vigor of the industry today attest to its success. Between 1880 and 1895 the California wine industry went through more than a business cycle. The prosperity of the early 'eighties and the depression that followed resulted in opening a new era for the viticulturists of the state. The recovery of the middle 'nineties marked the beginning of the new business, commercial, and large-scale industrial development of the industry. Before California viticulture was finally established commercially, the industry had to tackle certain national

The California Wine Industry, 1830–1895

problems. Tariff, taxation, and the fight for a pure-wine law were important problems to every vineyardist and wine maker of California. The years between 1880 and 1895 witnessed the transformation of viticultural ideas, institutions, conditions, and policies within the state itself; these same years witnessed also the formulation and enactment of national legislation aimed to satisfy many of the demands of the wine interests of California.

Chapter XIII
National Problems, 1880-1895

THE TECHNOLOGICAL and economic transformation of California viticulture between 1880 and 1895 cannot be explained without reference to basic national issues. The coöperation and support of the federal government was needed to promote grape culture and wine making. California viticulture was no longer a local industry with a local market; it had become a national industry with a world market. Once the wine maker became dependent upon foreign and out-of-state trade for his profits, he could no longer look only to Sacramento for aid and protection. The continued welfare of the vineyardists became interwoven with the other industrial and agricultural interests represented in Congress.

In February, 1880, a state legislative committee on the culture of the grape in California held a series of hearings to formulate a program of legislative aid to promote grape culture.[1] Such a meeting during the pre-depression' eighties indicates the growing importance of governmental aid—both federal and state—to agriculture. The California viniculturists demanded specific legislation aimed to satisfy the growers and merchants.

One of the results of the 1880 talks was the adoption by the State Board of Viticultural Commissioners of a set of resolutions informing Congress of the legislative aims of the California wine men.[2] The resolutions covered taxation, tariff protection, and the fight for the passage of an effective pure-wine law. These were the three major national issues

---

[1] For notes to chap. xiii, see pp. 201–203.

of importance to the wine men of the 'eighties and 'nineties. In March, 1883, a concurrent resolution of the California assembly instructed the state's congressmen and senators to urge Congress to enact a series of laws to promote and protect the culture of the grape in America.[3] This circular advocated relief from brandy and wine taxes and tariff protection, and also proposed that 10 per cent of the federal revenue collected from wines and spirits be paid back to the state in which the product was produced "in proportion to the quantities produced therein."[4] This scheme originated with C. A. Wetmore, and he proposed that the money paid back be used to promote viticulture.

Although the latter proposal was never seriously considered by the national legislators, the California wine men were able to arouse enough support for the measure to encourage other wine states to endorse it. Within three years (1886) the National Viticultural Association was organized at Washington.[5] Wetmore resigned from the State Board of Viticultural Commissioners to become its first president, and the national association prepared to

... organize the wine growers of the whole country into an imposing body that will be able to secure the passage of desirable legislation and look after the interests of the wine growers more effectively than can the present unrelated and independent state organizations.[6]

The tariff was a "matter of very serious import" to the wine men of California.[7] Most growers and merchants were committed to tariff protection. To them protection was not only gospel but an obligation. Arpad Haraszthy said:

A reduction of tariff on any article competing with American industry ... is a blow struck at us, at our homes. If we want protection for ourselves, then we should uphold every branch of American industry that we can encourage with our voices and protect with our votes.[8]

Between 1878 and 1879 the California wine men were able to prevent the passage of the proposed Chotteau trade treaty. Through vigilance, bargaining, and unified action

National Problems

they hoped to continue to secure protection for themselves.[9] Although Congress must levy all tariff rates, they are generally fixed—usually item by item—to meet as many local demands as possible. The wine men of California have worked continuously to have their specific demands met.

Shortly after 1880 the tariff once again became an active political issue. The election of 1880 gave the Republicans control of both the legislative and executive branches of the government, but tariff revision cut across party lines and presented serious problems. When the party leaders finally decided on action, each branch of Congress worked on a bill independent of the other. The result was chaos. The California wine men were opposed to any downward revisions that would allow European wines to compete with those of California. Every viticultural club, society, and local committee demanded protection. Their demands were specifically aimed to increase the duties on fortified wines,[10] because low rates on fortified wines meant the importation of "highly spirituous" wines that could be diluted and sold at very low prices.[11]

The final bill, passed in March, 1883, merited the name Ida M. Tarbell gave it—the "Mongrel Tariff." The wine men were displeased because it did not increase the rates on wine to 4 cents for every 1 per cent of alcohol over 10 per cent.[12] Equally distressing was the talk of further downward revisions. When President Grover Cleveland demanded a downward revision of the tariff two years later, the wine men of California prepared to fight for more protection and to vote Republican. The wine rates of the tariff act of 1883 were not determined by alcoholic strength, but the law was in every other respect protective.

Although the wine men were unable to increase the fortified-wine duties in 1883, they were able to prevent the passage of a proposed reciprocity treaty with Mexico. The State Board of Viticultural Commissioners went on record against all forms of reciprocity.[13] The proposed bill would have allowed reciprocal trade arrangements with Mexico. The wine

The California Wine Industry, 1830–1895

men joined forces with other protected American interests and defeated the bill.[14] J. de Barth Shorb, one of the commissioners of the state board, interpreted the proposed bill as the beginning of the destruction of the entire fruit industry of southern California.[15] Several other attempts at reciprocity with Mexico were made between 1883 and 1890, but coöperation and bargaining among the protected interests defeated all attempts to lower the tariff.[16]

Once the Mexican reciprocity issue had been defeated, the tariff, as an active and immediate issue, was overshadowed by the wine panic of 1886. Slow sales and declining prices caused the wine men to investigate local production problems. The fight over the Mills Bill found the wine men vociferously on the side of protection. In the election of 1888 they were a unit and a vested interest on the side of protection. It must be noted, however, that the tariff cut across party lines, and there were wine men who did favor a low tariff. Viticulturists who advocated a downward revision of the tariff were neither numerous nor popular.

The wine men were abundantly consoled and protected by the tariff act of 1890—the McKinley tariff.[17] The agricultural duties had the desired effect on the farmer vote, and the wine and brandy rates pleased the strongest advocates of protection.[18] C. A. Wetmore went to Washington and coöperated with the wine interests of the Atlantic coast and the liquor distillers of Kentucky.[19] The tariff act of 1890 protected American brandy and liquor distillers with a $2.50 duty a gallon.[20] Champagne and still wines were protected with equally high rates. Under the McKinley Act the wine and liquor industry of America had truly achieved protection.

The measure was popular with the interests it protected, but the Republicans received the most serious electoral defeat in their history in the congressional elections of 1890. With the election of Cleveland in 1892, tariff reform once again became an active political issue.

The Wilson Bill, Cleveland's hope for a real downward

National Problems

revision of the tariff, brought the California wine men to open hostility with the party he represented.[21] The California growers submitted long tracts and voiced pessimistic outcries over the proposed bill.[22] Petitions, resolutions, and memorials were written to Congress, to the House Committee on Finance, and to Sacramento. The proposed substitution of ad valorem for specific rates on wine and brandy caused the California growers to send C. A. Wetmore to Washington to prevent the passage of the bill.[23] The possible return to ad valorem rates was a serious threat to the wine men. Under no circumstances could they let this threat go by unchallenged.[24]

Once again the wine men successfully thwarted any real downward revision. Coöperating with the other lobbies that had descended upon Washington, the wine men were able to salvage many of the rates of the McKinley Act. Their greatest victory was the defeat of the proposal to return to ad valorem rates. In its final form, the Wilson-Gorman Act was so far removed from Cleveland's pledge of a downward revision that he called it a "piece of party perfidy."

The successful attack on the Wilson Bill was one of the major successes of the State Board of Viticultural Commissioners. Between 1880 and 1895 the wine men of California had assured themselves of protection and a monopoly of the American market in European-type wines. This was no small achievement. It reserved for California the whole American market. Imported wines were now definitely luxuries. Under the protective tariff acts of the 'eighties and 'nineties, the California wine industry expanded and grew prosperous.

At the same time that the industry fought for protection, it also clamored for relief from federal excise taxes. The wine production of California between 1880 and 1895 increased annually.[25] Not only did still-wine production increase, but the depressions of 1876 and 1886 caused increased production of sweet fortified wines. The manufacture of sweet wines necessitated the use of brandy, and brandy was taxed by the government. The wine men now demanded the use of tax-free brandy for the manufacture of sweet wines. Their campaign for a sweet-wine law was accompanied by demands for modification of the existing brandy laws.

In 1889, Los Angeles and other southern California counties formed the Protective Viticultural League[26] to "look after the interests of wine makers, especially with reference to the Internal Revenue Department." More simply stated, their purpose was to secure a revision of the brandy laws as well as the passage of a sweet-wine law that would allow the use of tax-free brandy.[27] J. de Barth Shorb, president of the newly created league, maintained that the 90-cent tax on spirits used to manufacture sweet wine was not only exorbitant but placed imported sweet wines in a favored position.

As early as 1885 an attempt was made to secure the passage of a similar sweet-wine law, but the bill never passed the Democratic House Committee on Ways and Means.[28] Between $7,000 and $8,000 were raised by California wine men in 1885 to pass such a law. The money was used to pay a "lobby" in Washington to promote the bill. In 1885 the Republican Senate succeeded in passing such a bill, but the Democratic House defeated it.[29] Attempted once again by the Fifty-first Congress, the sweet-wine law was then defeated in the House of Representatives. The wine men of California, already irritated with the Democratic Party's views on a low tariff, were outraged by its attitude on the sweet-wine law. The failure of the Democrats to pass this legislation made the wine men more and more inclined to support the Republican Party.

The efforts of the wine men were crowned with success in October 1890,[30] when the long-desired "Sweet-Wine Bill" was enacted as a part of the McKinley Tariff Act of that year.[31] C. A. Wetmore deserves credit for the final form of the bill. It was he who caused the bill to be framed with special reference to the needs and desires of the California wine men.[32] The law provided that only grape spirits could be used to fortify wines—truly a major victory. Only California produced enough grape brandy to use exclusively for fortification purposes. The other wine-producing states of America—notably Ohio and New York—were forced to use grain or other spirits. California sweet wines could now command substantial advantage. Isaac de Turk, president of the State Board of Viticultural Commissioners, understood the significance of this victory when he stated in his annual address:

> The greatest victory was in obtaining the exclusive use of grape spirits for fortifying. The commission has stood . . . almost alone among all organized bodies, in resisting all overtures permitting the use of corn spirit, wheat spirit, or any other spirit not produced from the grape. This is one of the most important features of the bill, and by maintaining this position from the first to last in the five years' struggle to secure the passage of the bill, a substantial advantage has been gained for the wine makers, and for the industry generally.[33]

The act of 1890 was exactly what the California men wanted. They could fortify their wines up to 24 per cent with tax-free grape brandy. This gave the California producers a great advantage over the wine manufacturers of the east coast.[34] It was too much to expect, however, that the Eastern producers would not challenge such favoritism. In 1894 the law was modified to allow the wine men east of the Rocky Mountains to use up to 10 per cent of cane and beet sugar to fortify their wines.[35]

This action did not invalidate the beneficial effects of the law on the sweet-wine production of California.[36] C. A. Wetmore and the Commissioner of Internal Revenue were responsible for the modified act of 1894. Conferences with the Eastern wine men found them amenable to Wetmore's proposal that only cane or beet sugar be used to fortify wines. The revision of 1894 was therefore mutually acceptable to both the Eastern and California wine men. The prohibition against the use of corn or other spirits served as a partial check against the production of spurious wines.[37]

The effect of the sweet-wine law on the production of

The California Wine Industry, 1830-1895

fortified wines was at once noticeable. California produced, according to one of the leading national trade periodicals, approximately 800,000 gallons of sweet wines in the 1890-1891 season.[38] The following season (1891-1892) the benefits of the use of tax-free grape brandy increased the total production of sweet wines to approximately 2,900,000 gallons.[39]

Assured of the use of tax-free grape brandy, the California wine men now attempted to promote a revision of the tax on the manufacture of commercial brandy.[40] As he was in the fight for a sweet-wine law, Wetmore was once again the moving spirit behind the demands for a revision of the tax on brandy and the bonding requirement. The California brandy distillers wanted more than a reduction in taxes the privilege of taking brandy out of bonded warehouses without paying the tax. They requested that the tax be paid only after the final sale. C. A. Wetmore presented these facts to to the Commissioner of Internal Revenue in May, 1894.[41] However, it was several years before any important action was taken on the matter. In this respect the hopes of the California wine men to secure any immediate major revision of the brandy laws failed.

While the industry was fighting for a protective tariff, a sweet-wine law, and a revision of the brandy regulations, the other great issue—a pure-wine law—was not ignored. Between 1880 and 1895 all four of these questions were prominent subjects of discussion. The meetings of the state board, the National Viticultural Association, and the sessions of local and county societies pondered each of these questions.

The depressions of 1876 and 1886 made the pure-wine issue an increasingly important one. If California was to secure a permanent domestic and foreign market for its product, the quality of its wine and brandy must be consistently good. This was a responsibility that did not rest entirely with the merchants and producers of California wine. Considerable damage to the vinicultural reputation of California was done by adulteration and false labeling on both the Atlantic and the Pacific coasts. As early as 1860 the wine men of Cali-

National Problems

fornia seriously considered state and federal regulations to curb these nefarious practices, but until the 'eighties very little had been accomplished toward this end.

In the early 'eighties it was difficult to find a glass of California wine under a California label.[42] A great many "foreign" wines, which sold in San Francisco restaurants and taverns from one to two dollars a bottle, were "doctored" California wines. Visitors and travelers on the Pacific coast could find a good glass of wine only at the wineries.[43] Many Californians could honestly say they never drank a glass of California wine; they drank it under foreign—French, German, or Spanish—labels.[44]

The leaders of California viniculture, aided and supported by the State Board of Viticultural Commissioners, outlined a program to curb adulteration and to promote honest labeling.[45] Wetmore suggested the creation of "a vigorous organization to boycott all hotels, restaurants, . . . which undertake to sell California products under false labels. . . ."[46] This was neither practical nor feasible. In 1886 the San Francisco *Chronicle* published an exposé of the wine situation in California.[47] This had some effect, and for a short time there was a minimum of adulteration. However, some form of legislative control was needed, and the Board of State Viticultural Commissioners recommended a federal antiadulteration law.[48]

In May, 1882, the State Board of Viticultural Commissioners opened its campaign for a federal pure-wine law. Thirteen hundred growers, wine makers, and merchants signed a petition demanding that Congress enact a pure-wine law.[49] Several New York wine merchants opposed such a law on the ground that it discriminated against their products, but the State Board of Viticultural Commissioners ignored these complaints. The following year the board appointed a commission of three to inform the federal government on the extent of adulteration of wine in America. The three delegates requested that the

. . . machinery of the internal revenue system . . . be utilized to protect the public against imposition and high prices by requiring that all wines sold in this country under a name or brand indicating a foreign origin should bear a stamp representing the full amount of the duty on imported wines.[50]

Haraszthy believed that the depression in California wines could be alleviated by national legislation heavily taxing all adulterations. He maintained that pure California wine could not compete against the cheap, "doctored" wine, and that the Eastern market for California wines would disappear if the counterfeiters were not heavily taxed.

The great problem in writing a pure-wine law was in determining what constituted an adulteration.[51] Such a law must be specific and must define its terminology. A general, national pure-wine law drawn up without reference to the practical problems of wine making would be useless. To achieve the desired results, the law must be written with specific reference to the practical prolems of production. On this subject there was a marked difference of opinion between the Ohio and the California wine makers.

The question of what constituted falsification differed markedly among the California and the Ohio producers.[52] The California growers would allow only the use of grape brandy to fortify wines. The Ohio vintners, since they produced little or no grape brandy suitable for fortification purposes, demanded that they be allowed to fortify with spirits. Other differences arose over the use of sugar, water, and coloring matter in the manufacture of various wines. Before a national pure-wine bill could be passed, these differences must be reconciled.[53] Nothing could be accomplished without the support and the good will of the Eastern vintners.

In May, 1886, a convention of wine growers was held in Washington. Wetmore represented California at this national convention, the purpose of which was to organize societies throughout the United States to work for a national pure-wine law.[54] After a series of meetings, consultations, and plenary sessions, the convention of American vintners drew up a national bill. The different wine groups had

National Problems

worked for more than a year to define adulterations and to work out the details of action. The final bill was supported by the United States Department of Agriculture and the Bureau of Internal Revenue.[55]

The proposed law allowed the Eastern vintners to use sugar in fortifying wine but not to "stretch" the wine by adding water and sugar. This provision, in itself a loophole, had to be incorporated to placate the Eastern wine men. A prohibitive tax was placed on all adulterations; moreover, all adulterated wine had to be clearly labeled. This requirement was the most effective part of the bill. Wetmore was satisfied with the bill and advocated that the State Board of Viticultural Commissioners and the wine men of California support it wholeheartedly.[56]

The bill was introduced in Congress in the fall of 1886 but failed to receive enough support to insure its passage.[57] There were many reasons why the wine men failed to secure the passage of a national pure-wine law. Most important was the fact that the proposed legislation did not receive the wholehearted support of the industry. Many vintners doubted the necessity of such a law and were unwilling to fight for its passage. Equally important was the opposition of the wine merchants, importers, and other powerful interests.[58]

The failure to secure the passage of this bill left the wine men of America totally unprotected. The State Board of Viticultural Commissioners attempted to find a partial remedy for the situation in securing the passage of a state pure-wine law. But, having exhausted its funds in the attempt to secure the passage of the national law, the state board could now only recommend that the state pass a law protecting the manufacturers of pure wine.[59] Thus, although its campaign for a state law was much more limited, the final results were much more gratifying.

In March, 1887, the state legislature passed an act "to prohibit the sophistication and adulteration of wine. . . ."[60] The act defined pure wine and prohibited the use of any materials "intended as substitutes for grapes, or any part of

The California Wine Industry, 1830–1895

grapes." The act also required the state controller to furnish labels guaranteeing the purity of the article. Each bottle, case, demijohn, or barrel must have such a label clearly affixed.[61] This latter provision was to cause serious difficulties among the producers and merchants.

As soon as the law was enacted, enforcement difficulties arose.[62] The act made provision for neither printing the stamps nor for a state analyst to analyze the samples. Both functions fell to the state board. The board was not equipped to carry on these added burdens, and the enforcement of the law rested upon the diligence, scrutiny, and good faith of the merchants and producers.[63] The attorney-general of California, G. A. Johnson, indicated the difficulties the enforcement of such a law would present when he stated that analytic tests of all wine transactions would be necessary to prevent all adulterations.

The law immediately encountered the stubborn opposition of the dealers.[64] This was in many ways expected, because the law was drafted, sponsored, and supported by the growers. The burden of securing stamps and guaranteeing purity presented distribution problems not easily surmountable. Every major San Francisco merchant opposed the law. In many respects it was an affront to the honesty and integrity of every California wine dealer. The wine merchants did not let the law go unchallenged. In August, 1887, the dealers drew up a circular requesting every producer to make a chemical analysis of each shipment of wine. The merchants refused to accept any wine without having a representative of the producer sample, check, seal, and analyze the wine on its arrival.[65]

Such a procedure was not only inconvenient but expensive. 1887 was a depression year, and the producer was fortunate if he could find a buyer. To enforce the spirit as well as the letter of the new law was hardly conducive to business. It is true that many of the charges of adulteration made against the dealers were not difficult to substantiate; however, it was the wine merchants whose enterprise and

National Problems

energy opened new markets. The attitude of the San Francisco merchants was therefore not unjustifiable. For more than a decade the producers distrusted them; now the dealers doubted their honesty in the future. Charles Bundschu, one of California's outstanding wine merchants, presented the most intelligent opinion on the new law at the fifth state viticultural convention.

I suppose it has been framed to protect our industry, and if it accomplishes this object we all must willingly submit to the evident hardships it provides in the stamp clause. I can only remind you, gentlemen, that if it should interfere in the free development of trade and commerce the merchant will not be the only one to suffer....[66]

It soon became evident that the pure-wine law interfered "in the free development of trade and commerce." *Bonfort's Wine and Spirit Circular* said the law attempted to make the legislature carry on the wine business.[67] The effect of the act upon the wine transactions was immediately apparent. The demand of the merchants for guarantees from the producers caused the wine trade to lag. However, within a short time the constitutionality of the law was challenged.

Henry Kohler, of the old and renowned firm of Kohler and Van Bergen, was the first merchant arrested for violating the pure-wine act.[68] The San Francisco Wine Dealers' Association accepted "with satisfaction the opportunity ... to test the constitutionality of the law" and assumed all obligations in the case of the state *vs.* Henry Kohler.

The notoriety given this case caused the demand for wine stamps to cease almost entirely. Unstamped bottles and packages were sold with little or no regard for the new law.[69] Both the growers and the merchants were waiting for the opinion of the California Supreme Court. In November, 1887, eight months after the passage of the pure-wine law, the court nullified section 8 of the act of March, 1887. This was the section interpreted by the State Board of Viticultural Commissioners to require growers and merchants to affix pure-wine stamps on all packages, bottles, and con-

The California Wine Industry, 1830–1895

tainers.⁷⁰ The supreme court held that the word "desired," as used in section 8 of the California Pure Wine Act in speaking of stamping wines, was "expressive merely of a legislative wish or suggestion. . . ."⁷¹ The court held that the stamping of wines was therefore not obligatory. This verdict left the dealers free to stamp their wines or not as they saw fit.

It was not difficult to foresee what course the merchants would follow. For all practical purposes the decision of the California Supreme Court invalidated the entire law. Once the stamping requirement was abolished, there was no one to say whether the wine was pure or not. The demand for stamps fell off almost entirely. A few dealers attached pure-wine stamps on individual bottles,⁷² but this was more for advertising than to guarantee purity.

The act of March, 1887, was drafted and sponsored by the State Board of Viticultural Commissioners, and its invalidation by the court was a serious defeat for the commissioners.

Several attempts were made to formulate other state laws, but by 1890 the State Board of Viticultural Commissioners determined that the purity of California wines could be protected only by the passage of a national wine law.⁷³ Consequently, once again the old struggle was renewed. A national convention of wine growers representing the producers of every wine state of the United States was held in Washington.⁷⁴ The National Viticultural Association attempted to secure Congressional action. However, their work and that of the California wine men was not to be successful for another fifteen years. Not until the passage of the Pure Food and Drug Acts in 1906 was there an effective national antiadulteration law. The act of 1906, which became effective January 1, 1907, applied to goods shipped in foreign or interstate commerce, and protected the California vintners ainst adulteration and misbranding.

The struggle of the California wine men for national aid and protection between 1880 and 1895 met with both success and failure. The protective tariffs of the 'eighties and

National Problems

'nineties stimulated the growth and development of the industry. The passage of the Sweet Wine Law of October, 1890, gave added impetus to the production of fortified wines and opened new markets for exploitation. Although the industry failed to secure a national pure-wine law or a major revision of the brandy regulations, the experience the California growers and merchants gained in participating in national politics was to serve them well in the future.

Epilogue

BY 1895 THE California wine industry was well established. Between that date and the passage of the Eighteenth Amendment the vineyardists of California produced better grapes and superior wines than at any time in the past. The structure of the industry, however, did not change materially. California viticulture had become established in the years between 1830 and 1895. The next twenty years were devoted to growth, expansion, and increased commercialization.

In 1895 there were still a few vineyardists whose lifetime had covered the entire span of effort, progress, and hard-learned lessons. From the first commercial beginnings of the 'thirties in Los Angeles County, grape growing and wine making had spread, by 1895, to nearly every county in the state. At the turn of the century California's eight wine districts had become world-famous. This transformation from the pastoral to the industrial state was one of the great agricultural achievements of nineteenth-century California.

The *viniferas* had been brought to California at the time of the establishment of the Spanish missions, but the commercial development of the industry dates only from the late 'thirties and early 'forties. The pioneer viticulturists Jean Louis Vignes and William Wolfskill were two of the first commercial vintners of Los Angeles. Their success awakened an interest in this branch of agriculture, but it was not until the gold rush that the demand for wine increased to such an extent that viticulture became one of the most profitable agricultural pursuits in California.

Many of those who failed to find their El Dorado at the "diggings" turned to grape growing and wine making. These speculators did very little for California's wine reputation or for the progress of viticulture. It was not until the advent

---

[1] For notes to epilogue, see pp. 203–204.

Epilogue

of Colonel Agoston Haraszthy de Mokesa that real progress was made toward scientific grape growing and wine making. California owes a great debt to Haraszthy. This colorful Hungarian is responsible for propagating the choice varieties of European *viniferas* in California. Before he came to California the Mission was almost the exclusive wine variety of the state. The limited use Vignes made of European vines was experimental; Haraszthy laid the basis for making the Zinfandel, the Malvoisie, and many other varieties commercially and viniculturally important.

The growing wine fever of the 'fifties and 'sixties penetrated every county of the state. Grape culture became one of the most popular agricultural pursuits in California, and in 1862 the state legislature took a mild interest in promoting the cultivation of the vine in California. After 1860, the state—and then the nation—became vitally interested in the welfare of the California grape growers and wine makers. By 1880, viticulture became important enough to warrant a special commission. In that year the State Board of Viticultural Commissioners was established. During its fifteen years of existence the board did notable work in fighting the phylloxera, in trying to find the cause and to curb the ravages of Pierce's disease, and in attempting to secure favorable tax laws, protective tariffs, and a national pure-wine law. Not all its efforts were successful, but, in its failure to secure a national pure-wine law and a revision of the brandy regulations, the board and the industry gained experience.

Between 1880 and 1895 the last stages of nineteenth-century industrial and commercial development were accomplished. Recovering from the ruins of two major depressions within ten years and surviving the ravages of the phylloxera, the California wine industry emerged, by 1895, one of the most important branches of commercial agriculture in the state. The economic vicissitudes of these fifteen years caused both the grower and the merchant to strike out on new paths, to endeavor to correct defects in their system, and to produce a consistently better wine.

The California Wine Industry, 1830–1895

When Congress passed, in 1890, an act providing for an exhibition, to be held in 1892, "to commemorate the progress of the nation in art, industry, and agriculture," California prepared to exhibit not only the resources of its mineral empire but the progress of its viticulture. The remarkable transformation that California grape growing and wine making had experienced within six decades was displayed before the world at Chicago in 1893.

At the annual meeting of the State Viticultural Convention held in San Francisco on May 18, 1892, the plans and preparations for a California wine exhibit at Chicago were discussed.[1] The following year the legislature authorized the governor "to prepare, or have prepared, a volume expository of the resources of the state of California for the purpose of distribution at the World's Columbian Exposition at Chicago."[2] This volume aimed to inform the visitors at the "White City" of the agricultural, mineral, and industrial developments of the state. The wine men did not feel this was adequate, and in order to assure their industry more space and greater notoriety at Chicago they appointed a committee, representing the major viticultural districts of California,[3] to prepare a suitable wine program for the Chicago exposition.[4]

After serious deliberation upon the amount of money that was to be appropriated for the display of California wines at Chicago, the committee presented its tentative program before the viticulturists of California at their annual convention. The committee recommended and the State Board of Viticultural Commissioners accepted the committee's proposed plans. The state board organized and collected the exhibits, and the committee was delegated to carry on the practical work at Chicago.

Both the European and California wine displays at Chicago were under the immediate supervision of the Spanish viticulturist and diplomat Enrique Dupuy de Lôme. Within five years de Lôme was to become more famous for his description of President McKinley than for his vinicultural

Epilogue

erudition. The California wine exhibit at Chicago included a general display in the horticulture building and a concentrated display in the national building for purposes of competition and awards. The viticultural exhibit of California was all-inclusive. Many of the major growers and merchants participated and displayed their products. Every kind of vine, grape, wine, and every method and process of manufacture was exhibited at Chicago.[5] The purpose of the California wine exhibit was not to achieve individual recognition in the form of gold, silver, or bronze medals, although many individual wineries did so. The real value of such an exhibit was the opportunity to make America conscious of California wines and conscious of California as the wine land of America. In this respect the California wine exhibit was only a partial success.

A great tribute, however, was paid to the business acumen of the California growers and merchants by the Italian agriculturist Guido Rossati.[6] The big show of wine at Chicago, Rossati maintained, not only increased the consumption of California wines on the east coast but indicated the high degree of commercial development of California viticulture.

The display was sufficiently varied, extensive, and in some respects effective, but the system of making awards and the lack of general sampling facilities were material handicaps.[7] Moreover, several of the wine jurors were not competent judges. To secure the critical reports of the French, British, and other European wine experts, C. A. Wetmore visited Chicago in 1893.

Wetmore was able to secure a critical report of California wines by three distinguished European wine experts —Charles F. Oldham of Oldham, Grierson and Co., London wine merchants; E. Dubois, a member of the International Wine Jury; and François Gos, French Commissioner of Viticulture to the United States.[8] Oldham outlined the progress of California viticulture within the past fifty years and stated that California was rapidly "taking its place as one of the principal wine producing countries of the world."

The California Wine Industry, 1830–1895

The wines Oldham sampled at Chicago were not only of excellent quality but fine examples of superior manfacturing.[9] Dubois was equally impressed by the vintages of California, and he praised all wines deserving praise and recognition. However, he did not fail to point out the dishonesty in calling California brandy "cognac."[10] He also pointed out the proved fallacies that some California growers continued to practice: faulty choice of grapes, incorrect training of vines, and too rapid fermentation.

Of greater value was the report of Commissioner Gos. Gos was appointed and instructed by the French government to make a special study of California wines.[11] Gos's mission was to report to the French government, not only the quality of the current vintages of California, but

> ... to examine everything connected with their production, beginning with the setting out of the vines. Then we hope to follow every successive step in their culture, and all the processes to which the juice is subjected until it is ready for marketing.[12]

The published results of Commissioner Gos's tour of vineyards complimented the California wine men on their progress, their business acumen, and on their excellent wines. He further stated:

> The people of France and of Europe have not the slightest conception of the magnitude of the wine industry in California nor of the rapid progress you have made in the quality of your wines. Such methods as you have developed here I never saw before, and while your wines have not yet all the characteristics of "*grand vin*," yet you have accomplished so much in that direction that I am positive you will soon be making as fine wines as the world can boast.[13]

Although the reports of Oldham and Gos were particularly gratifying to the California wine men, the State Board of Viticultural Commissioners was not too pleased with the management and arrangement of the California exhibit at Chicago. The display did not represent the state as a whole. The final result was a series of individual displays emphasizing individuality. The exhibit failed to create a conscious-

Epilogue

ness of California as the wine land of America.[14] In many cases it was a display of labels since many firms, instead of sending wine, sent empty labeled bottles. By awarding the exclusive privilege of determining the prices of wine and brandy to the various concessionaires at the fair, the state board destroyed any real opportunity it had to prove that California produced good cheap wine. The action of the state board placed the reputation as well as the price of California wines in the hands of the concessionaires.

Unsatisfied with the general outcome of the Chicago exposition, the State Board of Viticultural Commissioners prepared to hold a midwinter international wine exposition in San Francisco in 1894[15] to advertise California as a wine state and a producer of good, cheap wines, a purpose not sufficiently accomplished at Chicago.

If the Chicago exposition had failed to prove that the majority of California wines were *vini sani* (sound wines) rather than *vini fini* (fine wines), it did not fail to show the progress of grape growing and wine making in California within the past fifty years.[16] The viticultural advances were not only visible in the quality and diversity of the wine produced, but also in the techniques of production and in the perfection of cooperage and viticultural equipment. By 1895 California could boast nearly every variety of wine grape well adapted and well cultivated.

By the turn of the century California was well on its way toward becoming the wine land of America. Between 1895 and 1918 the California wine industry manufactured more and better wine, increased its sales, and captured new export markets. The 6,000,000 southern European immigrants who entered the United States between 1901 and 1915 increased the consumption of wine, and many of these also added their skill and knowledge to the development and specialization of this California industry. The years of industrial and commercial progress between 1830 and 1895 were the results of the experience and erudition of Europe, the agricultural wealth of California, and the commercial

The California Wine Industry, 1830-1895

enterprise and energy of America. These three elements were largely responsible for making viniculture one of the most important and remunerative branches of California's commercial agriculture.

The significant and substantial achievements of the formative years made for steady progress in the early part of the twentieth century. Between 1900 and 1915, when local prohibition movements began to gain momentum, the California wine industry experienced a gradual increase in both grape acreage and wine production. Greater capital and an increase in the number of persons employed in the industry was followed by improved methods of national distribution and more efficient trade practices. Profits and consumption in this period varied with the fluctuations of the business cycle and the price of the article. Wine was still a luxury and far from being or immediately becoming a national beverage. By 1915, viticulture was sufficiently developed industrially to survive thirteen years of national prohibition.

The National Prohibition Enforcement Act was ratified by the necessary thirty-six states in January, 1919, but it did not become law until January 16, 1920. The effects of the growing prohibitionist campaign on the California wine industry, however, had been felt several years earlier. In 1912 California produced 50,000,000 gallons of wine; by 1919 wine production had dropped to 27,000,000 gallons. Prohibition seriously curtailed the production of wine, but at the same time there was a marked increase in winegrape shipments.

Prohibition and the immediate postwar depression of 1920 caused a brief depression in the wine industry. By 1922, however, the business cycle was already registering an upward trend. The return of prosperity, confusion over the interpretation of the various prohibition requirements relating to home production of nonalcoholic fruit juices, and the increase in the home production of wine led to a marked expansion in fresh-grape sales and shipment. Prohibition tended to increase the price of wine grapes throughout the

Epilogue

United States to unprecedented levels, which in turn increased the value of grape lands, caused new capital to be attracted to grape growing, and stimulated the urge to plant more vines. As in earlier periods of expansion, the unscrupulous as well as the scrupulous were attracted to viticulture. Many who were interested only in immediate profits planted grapes in areas totally unsuited for successful viticulture. The expansion in vine acreage was also accompanied by poor selection of varieties and careless packing and shipment practices. Such activities soon disorganized and demoralized the whole industry. California viticulture lacked stability throughout the prohibition era.

After the repeal of the Eighteenth Amendment the wine industry was faced with serious problems that were not easily surmountable and that demanded the active aid of the federal and state government. The immediate post-repeal demand for wine was great, and the supply was low. The problems of readjusting supply, demand, and prices were not completely solved until 1938. Many of the pre-prohibition wine facilities of the state—wineries, cooperage, and equipment—were either badly in need of repair or nonexistent. Viniculture was sorely in need of capital, and once again a number of unscrupulous investors entered the industry and seriously damaged the reputation of California wines. The profit seekers produced poor wines, falsified labels, and generally subscribed to all kinds of unethical business practices. The result of such activities was to cause the intervention of the Federal Alcohol Control Administration. Bad wines caused the whole industry to suffer. This led to the next problem—underconsumption rather than overproduction. The aim of the industry was to increase consumption through better wine varieties. In order to achieve this end, the marketing facilities had to be improved. This was a long and difficult task since it involved both federal and state excise taxes and control legislation.

In 1934 the Wine Institute was organized. This nonprofit corporation worked to establish wine standards, to

The California Wine Industry, 1830-1895

increase wine consumption by advertising it as a food product, to widen distribution by attempting to lower excise taxes and simplify control legislation, and to advance the sale and consumption of wine throughout the United States. In 1934 the Federal Alcohol Control Administration was set up under the National Recovery Administration to set up standards of competition and to promote stability within the industry. In December, 1934, the Board of Public Health of the State of California also came to the industry's aid when it established standards of quality for wine. A substantial improvement in the quality of wine produced, higher consumer income, lower selling prices, simplification of federal and state control legislation, as well as a reduction in federal and state excise taxes, all caused a new upward trend in both production and profits in 1939. By 1940 the industry was operating on a more stable basis than at any time since repeal.

World War II and the uncertainties of the postwar years obviated that stability, accentuated old problems, and created new ones. During the war years Eastern liquor interests acquired several of the state's major wineries. It is impossible, at this time, to determine to what extent these changes in equity will affect not only individual policy and management but the whole industry. The increased demand for grapes and wine during and immediately following the war made it impossible to achieve any real equilibrium in the production of wine, raisin, and table grapes. These three branches of viticulture are interdependent, and any instability in one of them immediately affects prices and profits in the other two. Although this remains a fundamental problem, the tariff, revenue, and control legislation still require serious consideration. To attempt to reconcile these issues in terms of state and national requirements alone is no longer possible. The interests of the wine industry today must be determined and considered in terms of the international commitments of the United States. Faced by these problems, the California wine men today are striving to achieve a new stability and to establish sound postwar norms.

NOTES

NOTES TO PROLOGUE

¹ Wine Institute Bulletin, *Thirteenth Annual Wine Industry Statistical Survey*, Pt. III, 1. (For complete citations, see Bibliography.)
² *Ibid.*
³ *Ibid.*, pp. 1–2.
⁴ J. Arthaud, *De la vigne et ses produits*, p. 260.
⁵ John F. Allen, *A Practical Treatise on the Culture and Treatment of the Grape Vine in the United States*, p. 9; Arthaud, *op. cit.*, p. 278.
⁶ Herbert B. Leggett, "The Early History of Wine Production in California," (M.A. thesis, University of California, 1939), pp. 1–10, *passim;* Guido Rossati, *Relazione di un viaggio d'istruzione negli Stati Uniti d'America*, pp. 144–145; Frank Schoonmaker and Tom Marvel, *American Wines*, pp. 61–62; George Husmann, *Grape Culture and Wine Making in California*, p. 15.
⁷ The exact date of the introduction of the vine into California is still a matter of dispute. Although there is no conclusive evidence to determine the exact date, the various sources agree that it was between 1769 and 1771. Hubert H. Bancroft believes vineyards were planted in the first permanent Spanish settlements between 1769 and 1773.
⁸ George A. Pettit, "The University and California Wines," *California Monthly*, XXXII (Jan., 1934), 18–19; Andrew W. M'Kee, "The Grape and Wine Culture of California," *United States Patent Office Reports, Agriculture*, 1858, p. 338; Newton B. Pierce, *Grape Diseases on the Pacific Coast*, pp. 24–25.
⁹ Pettit, *op. cit.*, pp. 18–19; M'Kee, *op. cit.*, p. 339. The Spanish priests also brought the White Muscatel to California. Since it was not an abundant bearer, it was never extensively cultivated.
¹⁰ Good accounts of the early period are to be found in: Leggett, *op. cit.*, pp. 14–36; Schoonmaker and Marvel, *op. cit.*, chap. iv; Morton P. Shand, *A Book of Other Wines than French*, pp. 147–150; Idwal Jones, *Vines in the Sun: A Journey Through the California Vineyards*, contains interesting accounts of various wine districts and personalities. Also valuable are the accounts in the Sacramento *Bee*, August 30, 1935, p. 2; San Francisco *Examiner*, April 6, 1890, pp. 37–49. This issue of the *Examiner* covered the viticultural industry of California in detail.
¹¹ Tom Gregory, *History of Sonoma County*, p. 30; Hubert H. Bancroft, *History of California*, VII, 46; Horatio F. Stoll, "Pioneer Winemakers of the Historic Sonoma District," *Wines and Vines*, XVIII (May, 1937), 5; San Francisco *Merchant*, July 20, 1888, pp. 113–114.
¹² *Report of the California State Board of Agriculture*, 1911, p. 183.
¹³ Bancroft, *op. cit.*, VII, 46.
¹⁴ Alfred Robinson, *Life in California*, pp. 45, 52.
¹⁵ "High Spots in Napa's History," *Wine Review*, II (Aug., 1934), 14. George

Notes

C. Yount, the first white settler in Napa County, planted a vineyard in about 1835 from cuttings he received from the Spanish priests. San Francisco *Merchant*, July 20, 1888, pp. 113–114.

[16] Bancroft, *op. cit.*, II, 757.

[17] Leggett, *op. cit.*, p. 33.

[18] Alexander Forbes, *California: A History of Upper and Lower California from Their First Discovery to the Present Time*, p. 264.

[19] "California as a Vineland," *Atlantic Monthly*, XIII (May, 1864), 601. The period from 1771 to 1840 or 1850 has been characterized as the mission period of California wines; however, a more precise delineation would end the mission domination of California viticulture in the early 'thirties. At this time individual enterprises were initiated that marked the beginnings of the commercial period. These early efforts were on a very limited scale, but they opened a new era—an era in which viticulture was to emerge from a domestic pursuit to an industrial and commercial one.

[20] John S. Hittell, *Resources of California* (1st ed., 1863), p. 193.

[21] Forbes, *op. cit.*, p. 173.

[22] *Revue Viticole: annales de la viticulture et de l'oenologie françaises et étrangères*, I (1859), 60–61. (Hereafter cited as *Revue Viticole*.)

NOTES TO CHAPTER I
JEAN LOUIS VIGNES, WILLIAM WOLFSKILL, AND THE BEGINNINGS OF COMMERCIAL VINICULTURE, 1830–1848

[1] Forbes, *California*, p. 264.

[2] Vignes MS (This citation refers to a folder of miscellaneous manuscript notes in the Bancroft Library of the University of California entitled, "Jean Louis Vignes.") William Heath Davis, *Seventy-five Years in California*, p. 120, states that Vignes arrived with him at Monterey in 1831 on the bark *Louisa* from Boston; however, other evidence indicates that Vignes arrived in 1829. See also: Vicente P. Gomez, "Lo que sabe sobra cosas de California." MS in the Bancroft Library, (1876), p. 124; Daniel Levy, *Les Français en Californie* p. 64.

[3] Irving McKee, "Jean Louis Vignes: California's First Professional Wine Grower," *Wine Review*, XVI (July and Sept., 1948), 12, 18; Jones, *Vines in the Sun*, p. 212. Though the evidence does not agree on the exact date of Vignes' birth, it can be assumed that he was born sometime between 1779 and 1783; on July 15, 1831, he applied for his *carta de segundad*, stating his age as forty-eight and his occupation as cooper and distiller.

[4] *Alta California*, February 2, 1862; Bancroft, *History of California*, VII, 46.

[5] Vignes MS; California Wine Advisory Board, *The Wine Industry*, Wine Handbook Series, no. 1, p. 7. (Hereafter cited as *Wine Handbook*.)

Notes

⁶ Davis, *op. cit.*, pp. 120–121; Jones, *op. cit.*, p. 212. Although Vignes is credited with being the first person to bring foreign grape cuttings to California, there is no evidence on what specific varieties he introduced.

⁷ Davis, *op. cit.*, p. 121; Vignes MS.

⁸ Vignes MS. There is some question whether Jean M. Vignes was the first relative to emigrate to California.

⁹ McKee, *op. cit.*, p. 18; Pierre Sansevain to Arpad Haraszthy. Copy of a letter, dated June 22, 1886, in the Bancroft Library, "The Haraszthy Family," pp. 46–48. (Hereafter cited as Haraszthy MS.)

¹⁰ *Ibid.*

¹¹ *Wine Handbook*, p. 7.

¹² Horatio F. Stoll, "Development of the California Wine Industry," *Argonaut*, CXII (March 16, 1934), p. 112.

¹³ Davis, *op. cit.*, p. 120.

¹⁴ W. H. Emory, *Notes of a Military Reconnoissance from Fort Leavenworth in Missouri to San Diego in California.* . . . U. S. 30th Cong., 1st sess., S. Ex. Doc. 7, p. 122.

¹⁵ Haraszthy MS, p. 47.

¹⁶ Vignes MS; John S. McGroarty, ed., *History of Los Angeles County*, I, 31.

¹⁷ *Southern Californian*, April 11, 1855, in "Hayes' Scraps, Los Angeles," V, 21.

¹⁸ Rockwell D. Hunt., ed., *California and Californians*, III, 117–118, contains a brief biographical sketch of William Wolfskill.

¹⁹ H. D. Barrows, "William Wolfskill, the Pioneer," *Annual Publications of the Historical Society of California*, V (1902), 287–294.

²⁰ Other important biographical data on Wolfskill are in the following: *Cozzens' Wine Press*, January 20, 1859, p. 60; "Hayes' Scraps, Agriculture," pp. 266–267; *Southern Vineyard* (Los Angeles), December 10, 1859. Use of the files of this newspaper was made possible through the courtesy of the Henry E. Huntington Library and Art Gallery, San Marino, California.

²¹ Hunt, ed., *op. cit.*, II, 141; George L. Camp, ed., "The Chronicles of George C. Yount," *California Historical Society Quarterly*, II (April, 1923), 37.

²² Barrows, *op. cit.*, V, 291; *Cozzens' Wine Press*, January 20, 1859, p. 60.

²³ *Alta California* (San Francisco), December 20, 1858; *Cozzens' Wine Press*, January 20, 1859, p. 60.

²⁴ *Ibid.*; Barrows, *op. cit.*, pp. 292–293. Shortly before Wolfskill's death (Los Angeles, October 3, 1866) his son-in-law, H. D. Barrows, the southern California historian, recorded the Kentuckian's adventures. Barrows later published them in the *Wilmington* (California) *Journal*, October 29, 1866. The Barrows article in the *Annual Publications of the Historical Society of California* is an abridged form of the earlier article.

²⁵ There is some doubt whether Wolfskill or Vignes was the first to plant oranges in California. The active period of these two pioneers is almost synchronous, hence it is difficult to determine exact dates of planting specific fruit trees. In such a case as this, however, the establishment of definite dates

Notes

is of little consequence in the general perspective of California's horticultural development, for the activities of both men were unequaled in this period.

[26] *California Farmer and Journal of Useful Sciences*, August 17, 1854, p. 4. (Hereafter cited as the *California Farmer*.)

[27] Harris Newmark, *Sixty Years in Southern California, 1853–1913* (2d. rev. ed.), p. 199.

[28] Edwin Bryant, *What I Saw in California*, p. 412.

[29] *Ibid.*

[30] Leggett, *op. cit.*, p. 44.

[31] McKee, *op. cit.*, p. 18.

[32] Rossati, *op. cit.*, p. 146; U. S. Tariff Commission, *Grapes, Raisins and Wines, a Survey of World Production*, Annual Reports, 2d. ser., no. 134, p. 369; U. S. Census Office, *Seventh Census*, 1850, p. 174.

[33] Bryant, *op. cit.*, p. 412.

[34] *California Star* (San Francisco), October 30, 1847.

[35] San Francisco *Herald*, May 9, 1856.

[36] Monterey *Sentinel*, March 26, 1856, in "Hayes' Scraps, Agriculture," p. 213.

[37] Bryant, *op. cit.*, pp. 303–304.

[38] Jacob D. Stillman, *Seeking the Golden Fleece, a Record of Pioneer Life*, p. 129.

[39] Leggett, *op. cit.*, p. 44.

[40] Rossati, *op. cit.*, p. 146.

NOTES TO CHAPTER II
THE PRE-HARASZTHIAN 'FIFTIES

[1] Rossati, *Relazione di un viaggio d'istruzione negli Stati Uniti d'America*, p. 146.

[2] U. S. Tariff Commission, *Grapes, Raisins and Wine*, p. 224.

[3] Robert G. Cleland and Osgood Hardy, *March of Industry*, p. 48; Schoonmaker and Marvel, *American Wines*, p. 62.

[4] W. H. Murray, *Builders of a Great City, San Francisco's Representative Men, the City, Its History and Commerce*, I, 28.

[5] Benjamin Greenleaf, *The California Almanac for 1849*, p. 22.

[6] Jesse B. Schilling, "Brief Economic History of the California Wine-Growing Industry," p. 2. A mimeographed outline of the main developments in the wine industry issued by the Wine Institute, San Francisco.

[7] George Husmann, "The Present Condition of Grape Culture in California," *Yearbook of the United States Department of Agriculture*, 1898, p. 551; for general historical sketches of the period 1850–1860 written by prominent California wine men see also: Arpad Haraszthy, "Wine Making in California," *Overland Monthly*, VII, o.s. (Dec., 1871), 489–497. This is the first of a series of four articles with the general title "Wine Making in California." The first

Notes

article has for its subtitle, "Early Difficulties," and covers the period from ca. 1850–ca. 1865. Charles A. Wetmore, prominent wine man of the 'seventies, 'eighties, and 'nineties, discusses the problems facing the young industry in an article in the San Francisco *Merchant*, November 7, 1884, pp. 17–20.

[8] Eugene W. Hilgard, "The Agriculture and Soils of California," *United States Department of Agriculture Reports*, 1878, p. 504.

[9] San Francisco *Herald*, May 9, 1856.

[10] Bancroft, *History of California*, VII, 47; *Southern Vineyard*, October 16, 1858; Peter J. Delay, *History of Yuba and Sutter Counties*, p. 241.

[11] Bancroft, *op. cit.*, VII, 47.

[12] C. A. Menefee, *History and Descriptive Sketch Book of Napa, Sonoma, Lake and Mendocino*, p. 202.

[13] Bancroft, *op. cit.*, VII, 47.

[14] Menefee, *op. cit.*, pp. 234–235.

[15] *California Farmer*, September 12, 1856, 58.

[16] Horace Greeley, *An Overland Journey from New York to San Francisco in the Summer of 1859*, p. 329.

[17] Cleland and Hardy, *op. cit.*, p. 47; *Cozzens' Wine Press*, July 20, 1857, p. 110.

[18] Bancroft, *op. cit.*, VII, 47.

[19] *Ibid.*, VII, 43–44.

[20] *Cozzens' Wine Press*, July 20, 1857, p. 111.

[21] *Official Report of the California State Agricultural Society's Third Annual Fair and Cattle Show*, p. 30.

[22] *Ibid.*

[23] *California Rural Home Journal* (San Francisco), February 15, 1865, p. 6.

[24] *California Farmer*, October 19, 1855, pp. 124–125.

[25] Newmark, *Sixty Years in Southern California*, p. 25; *Alta California*, August 19, 1857.

[26] Hittell, *Resources of California* (1st. ed.), p. 201.

[27] Keller, "Grapes and Wines of Los Angeles," *United States Patent Office Reports, Agriculture*, 1858, p. 346.

[28] Agoston Haraszthy, *Grape Culture, Wines, and Wine Making: with Notes upon Agriculture and Horticulture*, pp. 151–152. This is the official account of Haraszthy's tour of Europe as a member of the Committee on Grape Culture of the California State Legislature.

[29] *California Farmer*, September 5, 1856, p. 50.

[30] See below, notes 38 and 39.

[31] Los Angeles *Star*, April 3, 1852.

[32] Keller, *op. cit.*, p. 348.

[33] Bancroft, *op. cit.*, VII, 46.

[34] *Southern Vineyard*, October 2, 1858.

[35] Los Angeles *Star*, April 7, 1855, in "Hayes' Agricultural Scraps," p. 209; Hippolyte Ferry, *Description de la Nouvelle Californie*, p. 277. Ferry not only spoke of the quantity of the Los Angeles wine produce but for its quality as well.

Notes

[36] "Bancroft Scraps, Agriculture," IV, 717; *California State Register*, 1859, p. 243.

[37] M'Kee, "The Grape and Wine Culture of California," *United States Patent Office Reports, Agriculture*, 1858, p. 343.

[38] According to the *California State Register*, 1859, p. 243, the number of vines under cultivation in Los Angeles County for 1856 was 726,000; for 1857 it dropped to 600,000; and in 1858 it increased to 1,650,000.

[39] The specific figures cited by different sources vary on the exact number of vines under cultivation for the years 1856–1858. The *California State Register*, 1859, p. 243 cites the following: for 1856, 1,540,134; for 1857, 2,265,062; for 1858, 3,954,548. The *Transactions* of the California State Agricultural Society, 1859, p. 343 cites the following: for 1856, 1,442,491; for 1857, 2,048,241; and for 1858, 4,090,717.

[40] *California Farmer*, January 25, 1861, p. 161.

[41] Charles Kohler MS. A folder of miscellaneous manuscript material in the Bancroft Library of the University of California.

[42] *Southern Vineyard*, November 20, 1858.

[43] *California Farmer*, December 17, 1858, p. 156; *Southern Vineyard*, December 4, 1858.

[44] McGroarty, ed., *History of Los Angeles County*, I, 193.

[45] Keller, *op. cit.*, p. 338.

[46] Leo Laliman, *Vignes et Vins Étrangerès, Cépages et Vins Américains*, p. 45 in the University of California Library pamphlet collection "Pamphlets on Wine," Vol. VIII, No. 2; C. Ladrey, "Faits pour servir à l'histoire de la vigne en Californie," *Revue Viticole*, III (1861), 214.

[47] *Revue Viticole*, I (1859), 126.

[48] Russell B. Blowers MSS. This is an uncatalogued collection of several boxes of miscellaneous manuscript material including ledgers, journals, day books, expense accounts, bank pass book, letters, and general business correspondence of a prominent raisin and grape pioneer. This collection is in the Bancroft Library of the University of California.

[49] *History of Napa and Lake Counties*, p. 203.

[50] Irving McKee, "Vallejo: Pioneer Sonoma Wine Grower," pp. 4–5. MS copy at Wine Institute, San Francisco.

[51] Husmann, *Grape Culture and Wine Making in California*, p. 16; California State Agricultural Society, *Transactions*, 1859, p. 302.

[52] Hilgard, *op. cit.*, p. 504.

[53] "Wines and Vineyards in California," *California Mail Bag*, I (July, 1871), ix.

[54] U. S. Dept. Agric., *Yearbook*, 1898, pp. 551–552.

[55] *Revue Viticole*, II (1860), 64.

[56] *Southern Vineyard*, December 22, 1859.

[57] *Revue Viticole*, IV (1862), 463–464.

[58] *Cozzens' Wine Press*, July 20, 1857, p. 111.

Notes

⁵⁹ Bancroft, *op. cit.*, VII, 49.
⁶⁰ M'Kee, *op. cit.*, p. 342; The *Revue Viticole*, I (1859), 62, called the "Sparkling California" of the Sansevain Bros., a fine wine; San Francisco *Evening Bulletin*, May 2, 1857.
⁶¹ M'Kee, *op. cit.*, p. 342.
⁶² Murray, *op. cit.*, I, 29.
⁶³ *Alta California*, March, 1855, in "Hayes' Agricultural Scraps," p. 201.
⁶⁴ Walter Colton, *Three Years in California*, pp. 355–356; McGroarty, ed., *op. cit.*, I, 248; Leggett, *op. cit.*, p. 45.
⁶⁵ Los Angeles *Star*, April 3, 1852.
⁶⁶ McGroarty, ed., *op. cit.*, I, 178.
⁶⁷ Los Angeles *Star*, January 15, 1853.
⁶⁸ *Southern Vineyard*, October 2, 1858.
⁶⁹ Leggett, *op. cit.*, p. 59.
⁷⁰ Keller, *op. cit.*, p. 347.
⁷¹ "Hayes' Scraps, Agriculture," p. 198.
⁷² *California Farmer*, September 5, 1856, p. 50.
⁷³ *Ibid.*, February 18, 1863, p. 178.

NOTES TO CHAPTER III

CHARLES KOHLER, PIONEER WINE MERCHANT

[1] San Francisco *Merchant*, April 29, 1887, pp. 1–2.
[2] Charles Kohler MS Notes (1886) in the Bancroft Library of the University of California, Berkeley. A folder of various manuscript notes on the life and activities of Charles Kohler with several pages about Agoston Haraszthy as well as California viniculture generally.
[3] San Francisco *Merchant*, April 29, 1887, pp. 1–2.
[4] Kohler MS, p. 1.
[5] Charles Kohler, "Wine Production in California," MS (1878), p. 3. This manuscript is also in the Bancroft Library; it is a detailed account of the activities of this pioneer in grape growing and wine making in California with notes and comments on various viticultural personalities during Kohler's lifetime.
[6] San Francisco *Merchant*, April 29, 1887, pp. 1–2.
[7] Board of State Viticultural Commissioners, *Viticulture and Viniculture in California*, pp. 10–14.
[8] Kohler, "Wine Production in California," MS, p. 3.
[9] Kohler MS, p. 2.
[10] Bancroft, *History of California*, VII, 48–49; *Alta California*, October 13, 1862; "California as a Vineland," *Atlantic Monthly*, XIII (May, 1864), 603–604.

Notes

[11] Leggett, "The Early History of Wine Production in California," p. 47.

[12] *Alta California*, October 13, 1862; San Francisco *Merchant*, April 29, 1887, pp. 1–2.

[13] *California Farmer*, October 3, 1856, p. 84.

[14] Since there is no other evidence to substantiate these foreign shipments, they should be accepted with great caution.

[15] Kohler MS, p. 6.

[16] Kohler, "Wine Production in California," MS, p. 5.

[17] *Alta California*, September 23, 1862.

[18] *Ibid.*, November 8, 1857, p. 2.

[19] *Cozzens' Wine Press*, January 20, 1859, p. 60; M'Kee, "The Grape and Wine Culture of California," *United States Patent Office Reports, Agriculture*, 1858, p. 343.

[20] *San Francisco Directory . . . 1860*, p. 42.

[21] *San Francisco Directory . . . 1861*, p. 42.

[22] *California Farmer*, January 25, 1861, p. 161.

[23] *Alta California*, October 13, 1862.

[24] *Ibid.*

[25] *Ibid.*

[26] Kohler, "Wine Production in California," MS, p. 8.

[27] *Ibid.*, p. 7.

[28] *Ibid.*, pp. 7–8.

[29] *Ibid.*, p. 9.

[30] *Ibid.*, p. 10.

[31] Kohler MS, p. 8.

[32] *Alta California*, October 13, 1862; Kohler MS, p. 8; *San Francisco Directory . . . 1864*, pp. 40–41.

[33] *Alta California*, October 13, 1862; Kohler MS, p. 8; *San Francisco Directory . . . 1864*, pp. 40–41.

[34] *Alta California*, October 13, 1862; Kohler MS, p. 8; *San Francisco Directory . . . 1864*, pp. 40–41.

[35] Kohler MS, p. 10.

[36] *Ibid.*, pp. 9–12.

[37] *Alta California*, October 13, 1862.

[38] C. Ladrey, "Faits pour servir à l'histoire de la vigne en Californie," *Revue Viticole*, III (1861), 214. Ladrey establishes 1856 as the date of the first successful wine house in California and credits Kohler and Frohling with this date, but he sets 1857 as the date of the Sansevain firm.

[39] Pierre Sansevain to Arpad Haraszthy. Copy of a letter dated June 22, 1886, in Haraszthy MS.

[40] *Bonfort's Wine and Spirit Circular*, June 10, 1890, p. 87.

[41] Kohler MS, p. 5.

[42] *Ibid.* Contains a series of accounts by his contemporaries of the work and contributions of the Kohler firm to California viticulture.

Notes

NOTES TO CHAPTER IV
THE AGE OF HARASZTHY

[1] Schoonmaker and Marvel, *American Wines*, p. 64; Murray, *Builders of a Great City*, I, 29.

[2] Haraszthy MS, p. 2, in the Bancroft Library, University of California, Berkeley. This is a detailed account of Agoston Haraszthy by his son and later prominent viniculturist of California. It also contains valuable material on general California viticulture. For other material on Agoston Haraszthy's activities, see also: Hubert H. Bancroft, *History of California*, VII; *Dictionary of American Biography*, VIII; Tom Gregory, *History of Sonoma County;* W. E. Smyth, *History of San Diego;* C. A. Menefee, *History and Descriptive Sketch Book of Napa, Sonoma, Lake and Mendocino;* an important and informative obituary article is in the *Alta California*, August 27, 1869; Rockwell D. Hunt, ed., *California and Californians*, III, has an interesting biographical sketch. Paul Fredericksen of Oakland, California, is writing a full-length biography of Agoston Haraszthy. A series of articles by him appeared in *Wines and Vines*, June–October incl., 1947.

[3] Paul Fredericksen, "Haraszthy Comes to California," *Wines and Vines*, XXVIII (June, 1947), 25.

[4] Haraszthy MS, p. 2.

[5] *American Wine Press and Mineral Water News*, December 15, 1900, p. 25.

[6] Haraszthy MS, p. 4.

[7] Frona Eunice Wait, *Wines and Vines of California*, p. 91.

[8] Horatio F. Stoll, "Agoston Haraszthy's Eventful Career," *Wines and Vines*, XVIII (Jan., 1937), 16–17.

[9] Haraszthy MS, p. 6.

[10] Herbert Leggett, "The Early History of Wine Production in California," p. 61; Fredericksen, *op. cit.*, p. 26.

[11] John S. Hittell, *The Commerce and Industries of the Pacific Coast*, pp. 245–246.

[12] Idwal Jones, "He Planted the Zinfandel," *Westways* XXXIV (Sept., 1942), 12–13; Wait, *op. cit.*, p. 91.

[13] Haraszthy MS, p. 7.

[14] Fredericksen, *op. cit.*, pp. 26, 42.

[15] Paul Fredericksen, "Haraszthy's Busy Last Years," *Wines and Vines*, XXVIII (Oct., 1947), 22; Bancroft, *History of California*, VII, 44. The exact origin of the Zinfandel as well as the exact date of its introduction into California are not certain. Although Haraszthy seriously propagated and cultivated this variety, there is no conclusive evidence to substantiate the popular claim that he is responsible for its introduction. Charles A. Wetmore, *Ampelography of California*, p. 10, maintains, "it is . . . certain that it was in this State long before Colonel Haraszthy visited Europe as State Viticultural Commissioner" in 1861.

Notes

[16] Hittell, *Commerce and Industries*, p. 246.

[17] Haraszthy's account of his work at the United States Mint is discussed in a letter he wrote to Major Jacob R. Snyder dated San Francisco, June 10, 1857. A copy of this letter is in: California Historical Records Survey, *Calendar of the Major Jacob Rink Snyder Collection of the Society of California Pioneers*, pp. 64–65.

[18] *Horticultural Review and Botanical Magazine*, IV (1854), 309.

[19] Paul Fredericksen, "Haraszthy in San Francisco and San Mateo," *Wines and Vines*, XXVIII (July, 1947), 15.

[20] *Idem*, "Haraszthy's Early Years in Sonoma," *Wines and Vines*, XXVIII (August, 1947), 17.

[21] San Francisco *Merchant*, July 20, 1888, pp. 113–114; Wait, *op. cit.*, p. 92; Hittell, *Commerce and Industries*, p. 246.

[22] M'Kee, "The Grape and Wine Culture of California," *U. S. Patent Office Reports, Agriculture*, 1858, pp. 343–344; Leggett, *op. cit.*, pp. 65–66.

[23] Fredericksen, "Haraszthy's Early Years in Sonoma," *op. cit.*, pp. 17–18; Hunt, ed., *op. cit.*, III, 526.

[24] *Alta California*, October 8, 1859, in "Hayes' Agricultural Scraps," p. 373.

[25] H. M. Butterfield, "The Builders of California's Grape and Raisin Industry," *Blue Anchor*, XV (Febr., 1938), 3.

[26] Gregory, *History of Sonoma County*, p. 142.

[27] Anonymous, *Grape Culture in California*, in the Bancroft Library pamphlet collection "Pamphlet Box of Materials on California Viticulture and Wine Making." *Annual Reports of the Chief Executive Officer to the Board of State Viticultural Commissioners*, II, 38. Owing to lack of funds as well as the increased work of this officer, the second report covers the years 1882–1883 and 1883–1884. As a result of several printings and the different series of the various reports of this commission, it is at times difficult to find specific items. To facilitate reference to these reports see: Adelaide R. Hasse, *Index of Economic Materials in the Documents of the States of the United States, California*.

[28] San Francisco *Merchant*, July 20, 1888, pp. 113–114.

[29] *Ibid.*

[30] Board of State Viticultural Commissioners, *Report to Governor Waterman, 1888*, in the University of California Library collection "University of California Papers on Wine."

[31] *Transactions of the State Agricultural Society*, 1859, pp. 298–299; Los Angeles *Star*, February 15, 1855, in "Hayes' Agricultural Scraps," p. 202.

[32] Husmann, *Grape Culture and Wine Making in California*, p. 17.

[33] *Alta California*, April 26, 1858.

[34] *California Farmer*, December 2, 1859, p. 132.

[35] *California Wine, Wool and Stock Journal*, I (June, 1863), 107; Hittell, *Resources* (1st. ed.), p. 196.

[36] Fredericksen, "Haraszthy's Early Years in Sonoma," *op. cit.*, pp. 17–18.

[37] *Ibid.*; *Report of the State Board of Agriculture*, 1911, p. 185; Alberta Snell,

Notes

"Viticulture in California, 1870–1900, a Chapter in the Economic History of California," (M.A. thesis, University of California, Berkeley, 1929), p. 4.

[38] *California Farmer*, September 7, 1860, p. 12.
[39] Fredericksen, "Haraszthy's Early Years in Sonoma," *op. cit.*, p. 18.
[40] *Southern Vineyard*, October 11, 1859.
[41] Horatio F. Stoll, "California's Important Grape Industry," in *California Grape Grower*, p. 3.
[42] *California Farmer*, December 24, 1858, p. 164; Leggett, *op. cit.*, p. 67.
[43] *Alta California*, August 22, 1860; *Southern Vineyard*, August 2, 1859.
[44] *California Farmer*, June 27, 1855, p. 28; January 11, 1855, p. 12; February 22, 1855, p. 58; November 7, 1856, p. 113; Leggett, *op. cit.*, p. 68.

[45] C. Ladrey, "Faits pour servir à l'histoire de la vigne en Californie," *Revue Viticole*, III (1861), 215; Leo Laliman, *Vignes et Vins Étrangères, Cépages et Vins Américains*, VIII, 45, in the University of California collection "Pamphlets on Wines"; "Hayes' Agricultural Scraps," p. 260, contains clippings with statistics showing the decrease of wine imports into California.

[46] California, Appendix to Assembly Journals, *An Act to Provide for the Better Encouragement of the Culture of the Vine and the Olive*, sess. 12, doc. 15, (1861), pp. 7–8; *California Farmer*, March 25, 1859, p. 60; Leggett, *op. cit.*, p. 50; Bancroft, *op. cit.*, VII, 47.

[47] *Statutes of California* (1859), p. 213.
[48] *Alta California Almanac and Book of Facts*, 1879, p. 83.
[49] In 1868 Haraszthy went to Nicaragua and started a sugar plantation. On July 6, 1869, he disappeared. It is generally believed that he drowned while crossing a river on his plantation; his body was never recovered.
[50] Idwal Jones, "He Planted the Zinfandel," *Westways*, XXXIV (Sept., 1942), 12.
[51] *Cozzens' Wine Press*, May 20, 1856, p. 94.
[52] Murray, *op. cit.*, I, 28.
[53] "Wine-making in California," *Harper's Monthly*, XXIX (June, 1864), 22.

NOTES TO CHAPTER V

THE COMMITTEE ON THE IMPROVEMENT OF THE GRAPE VINE IN CALIFORNIA

[1] *Alta California*, February 15, 1861.
[2] "Bancroft Scraps, Agriculture," IV, 734; California, *Appendices to the Journals of the Assembly*, sess. 12, doc. 15 (1861), pp. 9–10. The title of this series varies. California, *Journal of the Assembly*, sess. 12 (1861), p. 253.
[3] *San Francisco Merchant*, April 20, 1888, pp. 113–114; Arpad Haraszthy, *Report to Governor Waterman*, pp. 1–2, in Eugene W. Hilgard, "University

Notes

Papers." This is a miscellaneous bound collection of papers relating to the viticultural work of Professor Hilgard.

[4] Paul Fredericksen, "Haraszthy's Mission to Europe," *Wines and Vines*, XXXVIII (Sept., 1947), 17.

[5] *California Farmer*, June 7, 1861, p. 118.

[6] Celeste Murphy, *People of the Pueblo*, p. 277, contains the text of Secretary Seward's letter to the consuls of the United States regarding Haraszthy's trip.

[7] Agoston Haraszthy, *Grape Culture, Wines and Wine Making: with Notes upon Agriculture and Horticulture*, p. xv.

[8] *Revue Viticole*, III (1861), 691–692.

[9] Leggett, "The Early History of Wine Production in California," p. 75.

[10] Haraszthy, *op. cit.*, p. xvi.

[11] *Ibid.*

[12] Murray, *Builders of a Great City*, I, 29; Gregory, *History of Sonoma County*, p. 142; Hittell, *Commerce and Industries*, p. 247.

[13] San Francisco Chamber of Commerce, *Franco-American Commerce: Statements and Arguments in behalf of American Industries against the proposed Franco-American Treaty*, p. 13 (hereafter cited as *Franco-American Commerce*). A complete list of the Haraszthian importations is in: Board of State Viticultural Commissioners, *First Annual Report* (2d. ed., 1881), pp. 184–188.

[14] Haraszthy, *op. cit.*, p. xx.

[15] Letter of Agoston Haraszthy to Governor Downey, dated Buena Vista ranch, February 8, 1862, in California, *Appendices to the Journals of the Legislature*, sess. 13, doc. 13 (1862), p. 29; *California Farmer*, February 21, 1862, p. 154.

[16] Haraszthy, *op. cit.*, pp. xviii-xxiii.

[17] *Ibid.*, p. xxi.

[18] *California Farmer*, February 21, 1862, p. 156.

[19] Walton E. Bean, "James Warren and the Beginnings of Agricultural Institutions in California," *Pacific Historical Review*, XIII (Dec., 1944), 361–375, is an account of Warren's position.

[20] *Sacramento Union*, April 10, 1862.

[21] California, *Appendices to the Journals of the Legislature*, sess. 13, doc. 13 (1862), p. 29.

[22] *Sacramento Union*, February 17, 1862.

[23] *Ibid.*

[24] *California Farmer*, April 11, 1862, p. 17; Leggett, *op. cit.*, p. 75.

[25] *Sacramento Union*, April 10, 1862; *California Farmer*, April 11, 1862, p. 17.

[26] Fredericksen, *op. cit.*, pp. 17–18.

[27] Haraszthy MS, pp. 8–9. Subsequent legislatures have tried to rectify the state's indebtedness, but the heirs of Colonel Haraszthy have constantly refused to accept any remuneration.

[28] *Ibid.*, p. 10.

[29] Board of State Viticultural Commissioners, *Viticulture and Viniculture in*

Notes

California, p. 16; Charles A. Wetmore, *Treatise on Wine Production and Special Reports on Wine Examination, the Tariff, and the Internal Revenue Taxes, and Chemical Analyses*, p. 30. This monograph is in: Board of State Viticultural Commissioners, *Annual Report of the Board of State Viticultural Commissioners, 1893–1894*, Appendix B (hereafter cited as Wetmore, *Treatise*).

[30] California, *Appendices to the Journals of the Legislature*, sess. 13, doc. 13, (1862) p. 25.

[31] *California Farmer*, March 15, 1861, p. 17, contains a complete text of Commissioner Warner's report.

[32] California, *Appendices to the Journals of the Legislature*, sess. 13, doc. 13, (1862), pp. 12–13.

[33] *Ibid.*

NOTES TO CHAPTER VI
THE ANAHEIM COÖPERATIVE AND THE SONOMA CORPORATION

[1] Charles Kohler, "Wine Production in California," MS, (1878), p. 6: Charles Kohler, MS, p. 4; Vincent P. Carosso, "Anaheim, California: A Nineteenth Century Experiment in Commercial Viniculture," *Bulletin of the Business Historical Society*, XXIII (June, 1949), 78–86.

[2] Lucile E. Dickson, "The Founding and Early History of Anaheim, California," *Annual Publications of the Historical Society of Southern California*, XI (1919), 27; Major Ben C. Truman, *Semi-Tropical California*, pp. 145–150; *Alta California*, February 21, 1857.

[3] *Los Angeles Star*, June 2, 1855, in "Hayes' Agricultural Scraps," p. 211.

[4] Hallock F. Raup, *The German Colonization of Anaheim, California*, University of California Publications in Geography, VI (1932), pp. 123–146; Charles Nordhoff, *The Communistic Societies of the United States*, p. 362.

[5] "Bancroft Scraps, Agriculture," IV, 748.

[6] "Bancroft Scraps, Counties," II, 470.

[7] Dickson, *op. cit.*, pp. 29–30 states: "of all the trades and professions represented not one was a farmer and only one knew anything about wine-making." Raup, *op. cit.*, p. 123, after careful investigation of the manuscript material of the Anaheim Water Company and records in the Anaheim City Hall, states: "Grape-growing and wine-making were unfamiliar occupations to them. They were almost wholly ignorant of agricultural practice, especially in a land that was deficient in rainfall." On the basis of the evidence alone, it is impossible to accept Kohler's statement, since eyewitness accounts and newspaper articles do not corroborate Kohler's claim.

[8] Harris Newmark, *Sixty Years in California*, p. 213.

[9] *Alta California*, September 28, 1865; Dickson, *op. cit.*, p. 27; "Bancroft

Notes

Scraps, Agriculture," IV, 748. The sources differ slightly as to exact acreage of the tract and exact cost per acre. The two average figures are 1,165 acres and 1,200 acres, whereas the cost figure per acre varies between two dollars and two dollars and eight cents. The consensus is 1,200 acres at two dollars.

[10] Cronise, *Natural Wealth of California*, p. 107; "Bancroft Scraps, Counties," II, 470.

[11] Raup, *op. cit.*, p. 13.

[12] "Bancroft Scraps, Counties," II, 470; Sacramento *Union*, February 10, 1858.

[13] Bentham Fabian, *The Agricultural Lands of California*, p. 8.

[14] Nordhoff, *op. cit.*, p. 362.

[15] Raup, *op. cit.*, p. 129.

[16] *Alta California*, September 28, 1865; Raup, *op. cit.*, p. 129.

[17] *Southern Vineyard*, April 8, 1858; "Bancroft Scraps, Counties," II, 470.

[18] *Alta California*, December 21, 1857.

[19] Newmark, *op. cit.*, pp. 212–213; *Anaheim, Southern California, Its History, Climate, Soil, and Advantages. . . .* , Vol. III in the Bancroft Library collection "Orange County Pamphlets."

[20] Richard Melrose, ed., *Anaheim: The Garden Spot of California*, p. 10, Vol. III in the Bancroft Library collection "Los Angeles County Pamphlets."

[21] *Alta California*, September 28, 1865.

[22] *Revue Viticole*, I (1859), 192.

[23] Sacramento *Union*, March 19, 1859; San Francisco *Evening Bulletin*, February 5, 1858.

[24] *Southern Vineyard*, December 22, 1859, contains an itemized account of the expenses of the Society between September, 1857, and September, 1859.

[25] Dickson, *op. cit.*, p. 30; *California Farmer*, December 23, 1859, p. 153; "Hayes' Agricultural Scraps," pp. 274–275; Sacramento *Union*, March 19, 1859.

[26] "Bancroft Scraps, Counties," II, 483; Nordhoff, *op. cit.*, p. 363; Raup, *op. cit.*, p. 131.

[27] *California Farmer*, December 23, 1859, p. 153; Raup, *op. cit.*, p. 131.

[28] Nordhoff, *op. cit.*, p. 159.

[29] *California Farmer*, December 23, 1859, p. 153; Melrose, ed., *op. cit.*, p. 11; "Bancroft Scraps, Counties," II, 483.

[30] Raup, *op. cit.*, p. 131.

[31] "Bancroft Scraps, Agriculture," IV, 748; *Southern Vineyard*, December 22, 1859; *Alta California*, September 28, 1865, estimates the vintage of 1861 at 75,000 gallons.

[32] Dickson, *op. cit.*, p. 32.

[33] Melrose, ed., *op. cit.*, p. 11.

[34] "Bancroft Scraps, Counties," II, 470.

[35] John F. Carr, *Anaheim: Its People and Its Products*, p. 3, in the Bancroft Library collection: "Wines and Viniculture in California." For wine-produc-

Notes

tion statistics between 1860 and 1869 see, *Alta California*, September 28, 1865; and "Bancroft Scraps, Counties," II, 483; I, 363, 393.

[36] Dickson, *op. cit.*, p. 31; Newmark, *op. cit.*, p. 309; Raup, *op. cit.*, p. 129.

[37] Newmark, *op. cit.*, p. 213.

[38] Dickson, *op. cit.*, pp. 31–32; Raup, *op. cit.*, p. 130.

[39] The following statistics give an indication of Anaheim's growth. From the original 1,200 acres of 1857, the community, by 1874, embraced 3,200 acres; the value of the land in the latter year approximated $500 per acre; and in 1870 the community produced 400,000 gallons of wine and 10,000 gallons of brandy.

[40] Haraszthy MS, p. 12; Wait, *Wines and Vines of California*, p. 94; Gregory, *History of Sonoma County*, p. 143.

[41] *Revue Viticole*, II (1860), 62.

[42] Paul Fredericksen, "Haraszthy's Busy Last Years," *Wines and Vines*, XXVIII (Oct., 1947), 22; *Statutes of California*, (1863), p. 324; Buena Vista Vinicultural Society, *Reports of the Board of Trustees and Officers*, p. 4.

[43] *California Wine, Wool and Stock Journal*, I (April, 1863), 60; "Wine-Making in California," *Harper's Monthly*, XXIX (June, 1864), 22–23; *Alta California*, September 21, 1863.

[44] "By-Laws and Prospectus of the Buena Vista Vinicultural Society," p. 5, in *The California Miscellany: Being a Repository of Reports, Pamphlets, etc.*, (1860–1866), Vol. X.

[45] *California Wine, Wool and Stock Journal*, I (May, 1863), 79; "By-Laws and Prospectus....," pp. 15–16.

[46] *Alta California*, September 21, 1863, contains an itemized account of the vines, fruit trees, and other resources of the B. V. V. S. as of 1863, as well as estimated expenditures, profits, and production for a ten-year period.

[47] Fredericksen, "One Hundred Years of American Champagne," *Wine Review*, XV (July, 1947), 14.

[48] Haraszthy MS., pp. 25–26; Wait, *op. cit.*, p. 94.

[49] *Monthly Reports of the United States Department of Agriculture*, 1868, p. 283, cites the following statistics as the champagne produce of the B. V. V. S.

    1863: 9,000 bottles (total failure)
    1864: 72,000 bottles (sold *ca.* 550 dozen; remainder disposed)
    1865: 42,000 bottles (too rapid fermentation resulted in 50 per cent failure)
    1866: 40,000 bottles
    1867: 90,000 bottles (expected entirely good results)

[50] *Report of the Board of Trustees and Officers of the Buena Vista Vinicultural Society*, 1866, p. 10 in the Bancroft Library collection "Wines and Viniculture in California"; *Alta California*, July 28, 1863; Fredericksen, "Haraszthy's Busy Last Years," *Wines and Vines*, XXIII (Oct., 1947), 22.

[51] *Hunt's Merchants' Magazine*, LVIII (1868), 387; H. D. Dunn, "California:

Notes

Her Agricultural Resources," *Report of the United States Department of Agriculture*, 1866, p. 607.

[52] Direzione Generale dell'Agricoltura, *Notizie e Studi sulla Agricoltura, produzione, e commercio del vino in Italia e all'estero*, p. 322; Haraszthy MS, p. 26.

[53] "By-Laws and Prospectus . . . ," p. 17; *Alta California*, July 28, 1863.

[54] *Report of the B. V. V. S.*, 1864, p. 5.

[55] *Report of the U. S. Dept. Agric.*, 1869, p. 447; *Report of the B. V. V. S.*, 1864, p. 7.

[56] *Report of the B. V. V. S.*, 1864, p. 7.

[57] *Report of the Board of Trustees and Officers of the Buena Vista Vinicultural Society*, 1865, p. 6 in the Bancroft Library collection: "Wines and Viniculture in California."

[58] Samuel J. Bowles, *Across the Continent* . . . . , p. 284.

[59] *Report of the B. V. V. S.*, 1866, pp. 7–8.

[60] *Alta California*, February 21, 1865.

[61] *Ibid.*, February 2, 1869.

NOTES TO CHAPTER VII
INDUSTRIAL DEVELOPMENT AND ORGANIZATION, 1860–1870

[1] Charles F. Oldham, "California Wines," *Journal of the Society of Arts*, XLII (Febr. 2, 1894), 195-196; Schoonmaker and Marvel, *American Wines*, p. 29; Bancroft, *History of California*, VII, 40.

[2] "Bancroft Scraps, Agriculture," I, 125; Leggett, "The Early History of Wine Production in California," p. 59; *California Wine, Wool and Stock Journal*, I (April, 1863), 56.

[3] John H. Carmany, *A Review of the Year 1866. Compiled from the Mercantile Gazette and Prices Current*, p. 20.

[4] United States Census Office, *Eighth Census of the United States*, II, 35; John S. Hittell, *Resources of California* (6th. ed.), p. 251.

[5] *Sacramento Bee*, August 30, 1945; Schoonmaker and Marvel, *op. cit.*, p. 62; Thomas Hyatt, *Handbook of Grape Culture* (2d ed., 1876), p. 21.

[6] *The Weekly Oregonian*, March 12, 1864; C. Ladrey, "Faits pour servir à l'histoire de la vigne en Californie," *Revue Viticole*, III (1861), 16; H. D. Dunn, "California: Her Agricultural Resources," *Report of the United States Commissioner of Agriculture*, 1866, p. 608.

[7] *California Rural Home Journal*, January 15, 1866, p. 137, typifies the new approach toward advertising the California wine potential. To refute Eastern journals and to allay any doubts as to the grape and wine produce of California, this journal presents a series of statistical tables noting the production and value of wine between 1850 and 1860.

Notes

[8] Bentham Fabian, *The Agricultural Lands of California*, p. 8; Samuel Bowles, *Our New West*, p. 437.

[9] *California Wine, Wool and Stock Journal*, I (July, 1863), 119; For the viticultural investment of California in this period, see also: *California Farmer*, January 16, 1863, p. 146; "Bancroft Scraps, Agriculture," IV, 776; State Board of Agriculture, *Report of the State Board of Agriculture*, p. 198.

[10] California, *Appendices to the Journals of the Legislature*, sess. 13, doc. 27 (1862), p. 3; Hittell, *Resources of California* (1st. ed.), p. 197; Fabian, *op. cit.*, p. 8; Hyatt, *op. cit.*, pp. 36–37.

[11] Hyatt, *op. cit.*, pp. 20–21.

[12] Dunn, *op. cit.*, p. 604.

[13] Leggett, *op. cit.*, p. 80; Arpad Haraszthy, *Report to Governor Waterman*, p. 1; Anonymous, *My Vineyard at Lake View*, p. 66; *American Yearbook and National Register for 1869*, p. 292.

[14] Bancroft, *op. cit.*, VII, 47; Leggett, *op. cit.*, pp. 60–61; Dunn, *op. cit.*, p. 606; *Pacific Coast Almanac*, 1869, p. 63.

[15] Hittell, *Resources of California* (1st. ed.), p. 200; *San Francisco Directory for the Year 1869*, p. 51.

[16] *Alta California Almanac*, 1868–1870, p. 51.

[17] Leggett, *op. cit.*, p. 92; *Pacific Coast Almanac*, 1869, pp. 64–65.

[18] Bowles, *op. cit.*, p. 437; *Hunt's Merchants' Magazine*, LVIII (1868), 387–388.

[19] "Bancroft Scraps, Agriculture," IV, 735; Fabian, *op. cit.*, p. 9; *California Farmer*, November 16, 1860, p. 89.

[20] Bowles, *Across the Continent*, p. 285.

[21] Bureau of Labor Statistics, *First Biennial Report of the California Bureau of Labor Statistics*, 1883–1884 p. 179, contains good statistical tables on production, value, exports of wine, etc. See also *Transactions of the State Agricultural Society*, 1863, p. 265; 1864–1865, p. 382; *California Farmer*, January 20, 1865, p. 1.

[22] *California Wine, Wool and Stock Journal*, I (Febr., 1863), 28–29.

[23] J. S. Silver, "The Vineyards of California," *Overland*, I (Oct., 1868), 307–308; U. S. Dept. Agric., *Monthly Reports*, 1868, p. 282.

[24] *San Francisco Directory for 1861*, p. 42.

[25] California Bureau of Labor Statistics, *First Biennial Report*, 1883–1884, p. 179.

[26] *Pacific Coast Almanac*, 1870, p. 58.

[27] *California Rural Home Journal*, February 15, 1865, p. 6; *Transactions of the State Agricultural Society*, 1868–1869, p. 268; *Appendix to the Journal of Legislature*, sess. 13, doc. 27 (1862), p. 3.

[28] *Alta California*, November 18, 1862; *California Farmer*, January 2, 1863, p. 129.

[29] Claude B. Hutchins, ed., *California Agriculture*, p. 37.

[30] "Bancroft Scraps, State Fairs," p. 25.

Notes

[31] *California Wine, Wool and Stock Journal*, I (Febr. 18, 1863), 22.

[32] *California Farmer*, August 14, 1860, p. 4; *Alta California*, May 31, 1865.

[33] Carmany, *op. cit.*, p. 20; David W. C. Nesfield, *The Vine Land of the West*, p. 7; *Alta California*, December 30, 1862; *Franco-American Commerce*, p. 14.

[34] For complete texts of the memorial to Congress and the resolutions of the December, 1862, Wine Growers' Association, see: *California Wine, Wool and Stock Journal*, I (Jan., 1863), 3–5; *California Farmer*, December 12, 1862, p. 105; "Bancroft Scraps, Agriculture," IV, 738; *Alta California*, December 10, 1862.

[35] *Appendix to the Journals of the Legislature*, sess. 21, doc. 23 (1866), p. 4; Hyatt, *op. cit.*, p. 29.

[36] U. S. Dept. Agric., *Special Reports*, 1868, p. 282. The details and organization of the California wine men who fought to lower the wine and brandy tax are in: *California Wine, Wool and Stock Journal*, I (Jan., 1863), 2–6; (Febr., 1863), 22; "California as a Vineland," *Atlantic Monthly*, XIII (May, 1864), 600–604.

[37] "Bancroft Scraps, Agriculture," IV, 717.

[38] California Bureau of Labor Statistics, *First Biennial Report*, 1883–1884, p. 178; U. S. Dept. Agric., *Monthly Reports*, 1868, p. 282.

[39] *Pacific Coast Almanac*, 1870, p. 59.

[40] For a detailed discussion of the various memorials, resolutions, debates, etc., see: U. S. Congress. House of Representatives, *Resolution of the State of California, in relation to the tax on native wines*, 38th. Cong., 1st. sess., H. Misc. Doc., 7 (1863); "Bancroft Scraps, Agriculture," IV, 717; *Appendix to the Journals of the Legislature*, sess. 14, doc. 25 (1863), pp. 5–8.

[41] "Bancroft Scraps, Agriculture," IV, 756; *Letter from J. Ross Browne to the Committee on Finance of the Senate in Relation to the Proposed Tax on Native Wines*, (1866), pp. 2–8, in the Bancroft Library collection "Wines and Viniculture in California"; *California Farmer*, July 26, 1866, p. 17; *Alta California*, October 17, 1866; Carmany, *op. cit.*, p. 20.

[42] "Bancroft Scraps, Agriculture," IV, 763; Carmany, *op. cit.*, pp. 20–21; *Alta California*, November 2, 1866.

[43] "Bancroft Scraps, Agriculture," IV, 759; "Bancroft Scraps, Counties," II, 763–764.

[44] *Constitution of the California Wine Growers' Association* (1866), p. 5, in Bancroft Library collection "Wines and Viniculture in California."

[45] "Bancroft Scraps, Agriculture," IV, 756; *Letter from J. Ross Browne*, p. 2.

[46] "Bancroft Scraps, Agriculture," IV, 756.

[47] Alberta Snell, "Viticulture in California, 1870–1890, a Chapter in the Economic History of California," p. 8; Sacramento *Union*, February 24, 1872, estimates 253,643 gallons of brandy produced in 1868, whereas the U. S. Dept. Agric., *Monthly Reports*, 1868, pp. 280–281, estimates the total yield for that year at about 400,000 gallons.

[48] *Constitution of the California Wine Growers' Association*, pp. 5–10.

Notes

⁴⁹ *Alta California*, December 12, 1862; *California Farmer*, December 18, 1862, p. 114.
⁵⁰ *California Wine, Wool and Stock Journal*, I (Jan., 1863), 4.
⁵¹ *California Farmer*, December 18, 1862, p. 114.
⁵² The statistics for the period 1868–1869 are approximately as follows:

    Sonoma County   Los Angeles County
    1868, 2,865,427 gals.   1868, 3,838,000 gals.
    1869, 4,182,279 gals.   1869, 3,925,000 gals.

Pacific Coast Almanac, 1869, p. 65; *Alta California Almanac*, 1870, pp. 58–59; *Alta California*, January 11, 1870.

NOTES TO CHAPTER VIII
PROSPERITY, DEPRESSION, AND RECOVERY, 1868–1878

¹ California, *Appendices to the Journals of the Legislature*, sess. 18 (1870), III, 268.
² San Francisco *Bulletin*, June 17, 1870, in "Bancroft Scraps, Agriculture," I, 142.
³ Charles Kohler, "Wine Production in California," MS, p. 20; "Bancroft Scraps, Agriculture," IV, 847.
⁴ *Report of the State Board of Agriculture*, 1911, p. 198; *Transactions of the State Agricultural Society*, 1870–1871, pp. 502–503.
⁵ *Alta California Almanac*, 1871, pp. 88–89.
⁶ *Report of the State Board of Agriculture*, 1911, p. 185.
⁷ Bush and Company, *Illustrated Descriptive Catalogue of American Grape Vines* (3d. ed., 1895), pp. 6–7; "California's Most Important Juice Grape Varieties," p. 10, in the *California Grape Grower*. One of the most important varieties introduced in the 'seventies was the Spanish Mataro.
⁸ "Bancroft Scraps, Agriculture," I, 137; Charles Nordhoff, *California for Health, Pleasure, and Residence* (new ed., 1882), p. 218.
⁹ Henry Viztelly, *The Wines of the World Characterized and Analyzed*, p. 163; "Bancroft Scraps, Agriculture," IV, 855. These figures should be accepted with great caution, since there is wide disagreement as to the exact amount of wine exported as well as to the meaning of the term "exported." Most of the statistical evidence available does not distinguish between total exports to foreign countries and exports to other parts of the United States.
¹⁰ *Grape Culturist*, II (July, 1870), 178.
¹¹ Kohler, MS, pp. 10–12.
¹² *Grape Culturist*, II (July, 1870), 178, lists the major merchants in San Francisco and includes the types and amounts of wines shipped out of the state January–July, 1870.
¹³ *Alta California Almanac*, 1871, p. 113.

Notes

¹⁴ *Ibid.*, 1878, p. 50.
¹⁵ Nordhoff, *op. cit.*, p. 219.
¹⁶ *Alta California Almanac*, 1874, p. 57.
¹⁷ Horatio F. Stoll, "California's Important Grape Industry," in *California Grape Grower*, p. 19.
¹⁸ Nordhoff, *op. cit.*, p. 220.
¹⁹ "Bancroft Scraps, Agriculture," I, 137.
²⁰ Bancroft, *History of California*, VII, 47; George Husmann, *American Grape-Growing and Wine-Making*, p. 162.
²¹ Virginia E. Thickens, "Pioneer Agricultural Colonies of Fresno County," *California Historical Society Quarterly*, XV (March and June, 1946), 30–32.
²² *By-Laws of the Eisen Vineyard Company and Prospectus; Addressed to the Board of Directors and Stockholders by E. T. Eisen, President*, pp. 5–6 (hereafter cited as *Eisen By-Laws and Prospectus*).
²³ *Alta California*, September 18, 1871.
²⁴ Hittell, *Resources* (6th ed.), p. 255.
²⁵ *Alta California*, February 15, 1871.
²⁶ Stephen Powers, *Afoot and Alone: A Walk from Sea to Sea by the Southern Route*, pp. 274–275.
²⁷ Nordhoff, *op. cit.*, p. 218.
²⁸ "Viniculture and Wine-Making in California," *California Mail Bag*, I (June, 1871), vii–viii.
²⁹ Robert Lambart Price, *The Two Americas; An Account of Sport and Travel*, p. 196.
³⁰ Sacramento *Union*, March 4, 1870.
³¹ "Bancroft Scraps, Agriculture," IV, 845.
³² *Transactions of the California State Agricultural Society*, 1870–1871, p. 483.
³³ Sacramento *Union*, February 24, 1872; *Transactions of the California State Agricultural Society*, 1870–1871, p. 483.
³⁴ *Transactions of the California State Agricultural Society*, 1870–1871, pp. 484–485.
³⁵ San Francisco *Call*, December 20, 1872.
³⁶ Petaluma *Crescent*, January 31, 1872; Folsom *Telegraph*, January 20, 1872. The Fence Law afforded the vineyardists and orchardists protection from grazing animals.
³⁷ *Statutes of California*, 1871–1872, pp. 203–204, 241, 384, 412, 510, 563–566, 685–689, 700.
³⁸ *Appendices to the Journals of the Legislature*, sess. 18 (1870), III, 268.
³⁹ Gouverneur William Morris and H. C. Bennett, *An Essay on the Manufacturing Interests of California. . . .*, p. 39, contains a list of the cost of labor in California by county; John Codman, *The Round Trip*, p. 65; Nordhoff, *op. cit.*, pp. 219–220.
⁴⁰ *Alta California Almanac*, 1871, p. 81.
⁴¹ *Report of the Committee on the Culture of the Grape, on the Cultivation of the*

Notes

Grape, and the Production of Wines and Brandies in California, p. 6, in the Bancroft Library collection "Pamphlets on California Viticulture."

[42] Hugh Quigley, *The Irish Race in California and on the Pacific Coast*, p. 134.

[43] Codman, *op. cit.*, p. 66.

[44] Arpad Haraszthy, *Report to Governor Waterman . . . 1888*, p. 2; State Board of Viticultural Commissioners. *Report of the Sixth Viticultural Convention*, 1888, p. 10; Rossati, *Relazione di un viaggio d'istruzione negli Stati Uniti d'America*, p. 147.

[45] Hyatt, *Handbook of Grape Culture*, (2d. ed.), p. 18a.

[46] *A Review of the Commercial, Financial, and the Mining Interests of the State of California and the entire Pacific Coast* . . . 1876, p. 53, in the Bancroft Library collection "California Pamphlets."

[47] *Alta California Almanac*, 1874, p. 57; 1871, p. 51.

[48] San Francisco *Call*, November 24, 1875.

[49] *Appendices to the Journals of the Legislature*, sess. 18, (1870), III, 271.

[50] U. S. Commissioner of Agriculture, *Report of the Climatic and Agricultural Features and the Agricultural Practice and Needs of the Arid Regions of the Pacific Slope* . . . , p. 101. This report is in the series: U. S. Dept. Agric., *Special Reports*, Report No. 20 (hereafter cited as *Special Report* No. 20).

[51] Claude B. Hutchins, ed., *California Agriculture*, p. 206; *Alta California Almanac*, 1874, p. 58; Quigley, *op. cit.*, p. 136.

[52] George Husmann, "The Present Condition of Grape Culture in California," U. S. Dept. Agric., *Yearbook*, 1898, pp. 552–553; Snell, *op. cit.*, pp. 11–12.

[53] Henry Lachman, "Early California Wine Industry," in *Official Report of the Session of the International Congress of Viticulture at the Panama-Pacific International Exposition*, p. 29.

[54] Quigley, *op. cit.*, p. 136.

[55] Price, *op. cit.*, p. 234.

[56] Sacramento *Union*, August 23, 1869; San Francisco *Call*, May 8, 1870.

[57] "Bancroft Scraps, Agriculture," IV, 821.

[58] Snell, *op. cit.*, p. 9.

[59] *History of Napa and Lake Counties*, pp. 204–205.

[60] *Appendices to the Journals of the Assembly and Senate of California*, sess. 23, doc. 16 (1880), p. 7; *Special Report* No. 20, pp. 100–101.

[61] Husmann, *American Grape-Growing and Wine-Making*, p. 171.

[62] Idwal Jones, "Lords among the Vintners," *Westways*, XXVII (Sept., 1935), 26; *Alta California Almanac*, 1879, p. 85; Husmann, *op. cit.*, p. 173; "Bancroft Scraps, Agriculture," II, 257.

[63] "Bancroft Scraps, Agriculture," II, 383.

[64] *Alta California*, September 18, 1875.

[65] Edward Roberts, "California Wine-Making," *Harper's Weekly*, March 9, 1889, p. 197.

[66] *Ibid.*

Notes

⁶⁷ Charles Joly, *Note sur un pied de vigne en Californie*, p. 1. This is a pamphlet in Charles Joly, *Mélanges*.

⁶⁸ San Francisco *Call*, September 15, 1875.

⁶⁹ George Husmann, "Grape, Raisin, and Wine Production in the United States," *U. S. Dept. Agric. Yearbook*, 1902, p. 418.

⁷⁰ Hutchins, *op. cit.*, p. 206; Haraszthy, *Report to Governor Waterman . . . 1888*, p. 2.

⁷¹ The mildew is a "thin, whitish growth produced on organic matter and on plants by fungi" which causes discoloration and prevents proper growth and maturing.

⁷² "Bancroft Scraps, Agriculture," II, 365; *Alta California Almanac*, 1880, p. 67.

⁷³ Bancroft, *History of California*, VII, 47.

⁷⁴ Snell, *op. cit.*, p. 17; Haraszthy, *Report to Governor Waterman . . . 1888*, p. 2.

⁷⁵ Wait, *Wines and Vines of California*, p. 10.

⁷⁶ State Board of Viticultural Commissioners, *Second Annual Report of the Board of State Viticultural Commissioners*, 1881, p. 19; *Alta California Almanac*, 1881, p. 64 gives the wine and brandy figures for 1876–1879.

⁷⁷ Husmann, *American Grape-Growing and Wine-Making*, p. 172; *Report of the Annual Meeting of the State Vinicultural Society*, p. 5, lists the imports of French wine into the United States, 1868–1877.

⁷⁸ Husmann, *op. cit.*, p. 172.

⁷⁹ *Report of the State Vinicultural Society*, 1879, p. 7. To instruct the wine men of the different types of wine grapes the Society sponsored the publication of Hannah Millard, *Grapes and Grape Vines of California*.

⁸⁰ Haraszthy MS, p. 29.

⁸¹ *Report of the State Vinicultural Society*, 1879, p. 4.

⁸² Direzione Generale dell'Agricoltura, *Notizie e Studii sulla Agricoltura, produzione e commercio del vino in Italia e all'estero*, p. 322; San Francisco *Examiner*, April 6, 1890, pp. 2–3, contains a special section on the history of California wines; George Husmann, "The Present Condition of Grape Culture in California," *U. S. Dept. Agric. Yearbook*, 1898, p. 553.

⁸³ *Franco-American Commerce*, p. 57.

⁸⁴ "Bancroft Scraps, Agriculture," IV, 891.

⁸⁵ *Special Report* No. 20, p. 109.

⁸⁶ *Ibid.*, pp. 111–112.

NOTES TO CHAPTER IX
TARIFF RECIPROCITY, 1875–1879

¹ U. S. Tariff Commission, *Grapes, Raisins, and Wines; A Survey of World Production*, p. 314 in U. S. Tariff Commission, *Annual Report*, 2d. series, no. 134. (Hereafter cited as *Report* No. 134.)

² *Ibid.*

Notes

[3] *California Farmer*, February 24, 1870, p. 42.
[4] *Report of the State Vinicultural Society*, 1879, p. 2.
[5] "Bancroft Scraps, Agriculture," IV, 879.
[6] *Report of the State Vinicultural Society*, 1879, p. 2; *California Farmer*, June 12, 1879, p. 81.
[7] *Franco-American Commerce*, pp. 156–158.
[8] *Ibid.*
[9] *Report of the State Vinicultural Society*, 1879, p. 3.
[10] *Ibid.*
[11] *Ibid.*, p. 3.
[12] "Bancroft Scraps, Agriculture," IV, 889–890.
[13] Senate, *Resolution of Senator Sargent*, 45th Cong., 3d. sess., S. Misc. Doc. 61 (1879).
[14] "Bancroft Scraps, Agriculture," IV, 892.
[15] *Ibid.*, IV, 889.
[16] *Report of the State Vinicultural Society*, 1879, p. 3.
[17] *Franco-American Commerce*, p. 10; *Report of the State Vinicultural Society*, 1879, p. 3. The three resolutions requested all California Congressmen to "use their utmost effort to defeat any such treaty." Moreover, a committee was appointed to inform and submit all necessary statistics to the "various Chambers of Commerce throughout the country." The purpose of this action was to show the injurious effects of such a treaty, were it enacted.
[18] *Franco-American Commerce* is a compilation of all the speeches, motions, resolutions, and the like of the California wine men during the fight over the proposed reciprocity treaty with France.
[19] "Bancroft Scraps, Agriculture," IV, 893.
[20] *Report of the State Vinicultural Society*, 1879, p. 2.
[21] *Congressional Record*, 45th Cong., 2d. sess., February 13–March 25, 1878, pp. 1322, 1624, 1998; *ibid.*, 45th Cong., 3d sess., December 2, 1878–February 3, 1879, p. 153 contains a petition from the Legislature of the State of California to the United States Senate explaining the future effects of such a treaty. See also pages 227 and 419 for petitions referred to the Ways and Means Committee and the Finance Committee of the House of Representatives.
[22] *Franco-American Commerce*, pp. 202–211.
[23] *Ibid.*, pp. 159–202 contains a detailed discussion and statistical tables on the status and development of the California wine industry.

NOTES TO CHAPTER X
THE PHYLLOXERA

[1] Bancroft, *History of California*, VII, 47.
[2] Snell, "Viticulture in California, 1870–1900, a Chapter in the Economic History of California," p. 29; Cleland and Osgood, *March of Industry*, p. 82.

Notes

[3] Hutchins, ed., *California Agriculture*, p. 242; H. J. Quayle, "Grape Insects in California," in *Official Report of the Session of the International Congress of Viticulture*, p. 174; California Agricultural Experiment Station. *Report of the Viticultural Work during the Seasons 1883–1884, 1885 and 1886, 1887–1889, 1887–1893*, p. 375. A collection of reports and documents by Professor Eugene W. Hilgard of the University of California.

[4] Hutchins, *op. cit.*, p. 242.

[5] The literature on the phylloxera is voluminous. Most of the valuable historical and technical data is in French. The best works in English, as well as in most other foreign languages, are either translations or condensations from the French. An important guide to this material is Battista Grassi, *Contributo alla conoscenza delle fillosserine ed in particolare della fillossera della vite.*

[6] A. D. Imms, "Phylloxera," *Encyclopaedia Britannica* (14th ed., 1945), XVII, 855.

[7] Eugene W. Hilgard, "Lecture on the Phylloxera," in *Agricultural Experiment Station Bulletins*, No. 23, (1876), p. 3. The report cited was the first publication in California on plant pests and plant diseases.

[8] Arthur P. Hayne, *Resistant Vines: Their Selection, Adaptation, and Grafting*, p. 9. Copies are also available in the *Agricultural Experiment Station Bulletins*, and as an Appendix to the *Report of the California State Board of Viticultural Commissioners.*

[9] Imms, *op. cit.*, p. 855.

[10] *Report of Viticultural Work . . . 1887–1893*, p. 375; Hayne, *op. cit.*, p. 9.

[11] Hilgard, "Lecture on the Phylloxera," p. 1.

[12] *Special Report* No. 20, p. 156.

[13] *Ibid.*, p. 155; Snell, *op. cit.*, p. 29; Hutchins, *op. cit.*, p. 243.

[14] *Special Report* No. 20, p. 155.

[15] *Ibid.*

[16] *Ibid.*, pp. 155–156.

[17] *Alta California Almanac*, 1879, p. 84.

[18] California Wine Advisory Board, *Wine Handbook Number One*, p. 11; *Alta California Almanac*, 1879, p. 84; *Alta California*, September 12, 1878; George Husmann, "Resistant Vines," in *Official Report of the Session of the International Congress of Viticulture*, p. 44; Wait, *Wines and Vines*, p. 104.

[19] George Husmann, "Grape Investigations in the Vinifera Regions of the United States in U. S. Dept. Agric. Bureau of Plant Industry, *Bulletin* 172, pp. 10–11.

[20] Board of State Viticultural Commissioners, *Annual Report of Isaac de Turk, Commissioner for the Sonoma District*, p. 3. In the Bancroft Library collection "Pamphlet Box of Material on California Viticulture and Wine-making."

[21] Board of State Viticultural Commissioners, *Fourth Annual Report*, 1889–1890, p. 22.

[22] *Special Report* No. 20, p. 156; George Husmann, "Present Condition of Grape Culture in California," in *U. S. Dept. Agric. Yearbook*, 1898, p. 554.

Notes

[23] *Transactions of the State Agricultural Society*, 1873, p. 714.
[24] *Report of the State Vinicultural Society*, 1879, p. 4.
[25] *Report of the Viticultural Work . . . 1887–1893*, p. 378.
[26] *Ibid.*
[27] *Ibid.*, p. 378.
[28] *Alta California Almanac*, 1879, p. 84; *Special Report* No. 20, p. 156.
[29] *Report of Viticultural Work . . . 1887–1893*, p. 377.
[30] *Special Report* No. 20, p. 155.
[31] *Ibid.*, p. 155; *Report of Viticultural Work . . . 1887–1893*, p. 377.
[32] Hilgard, *op. cit.*, pp. 18–20; Board of State Viticultural Commissioners, *Report of the Fifth Annual State Convention*, pp. 4–11.
[33] *Alta California*, November 29, 1880.
[34] *Alta California Almanac*, 1881, p. 63.
[35] R. L. Nougaret, "Phylloxera in California," in *Official Report of the Session of the International Congress of Viticulture*, p. 181. Nougaret believes the phylloxera was brought to California from its native habitat on the eastern coast of the United States rather than from Europe. He also maintains that there is greater danger of introducing the pest from rooted American vines than from *vinifera* cuttings.
[36] A. Drioton, *All About the Phylloxera*, p. 7. In the University of California Pamphlet collection "Pamphlets on California Viticulture."
[37] Board of State Viticultural Commissioners, *Second Annual Report of the Chief Executive Viticultural Officer*, p. 7.
[38] Hayne, *op. cit.*, p. 10.
[39] *Ibid.*
[40] George Husmann, *Grape Culture and Wine Making in California*, p. 42; *Agricultural Experiment Station Bulletins*, esp. Vols. III and XVIII; *Bonfort's Wine and Spirit Circular*, January 10, 1888, p. 100, cites other inventions and remedies for the phylloxera, all impractical and costly.
[41] Hayne, *op. cit.*, p. 12.
[42] *Ibid.*, pp. 12–13.
[43] *Ibid.*, p. 14.
[44] Hutchins, *op. cit.*, p. 244.
[45] Hayne, *op. cit.*, p. 14, lists the native American varieties adaptable for California.
[46] *Ibid.*, p. 13.
[47] *Ibid.*
[48] Marguerite Fitz-James, *Grande culture de la vigne américaine, 1881–1883*, I, 51.
[49] Schoonmaker and Marvel, *American Wines*, p. 66.
[50] Eugene W. Hilgard, *Report of Viticultural Work . . . 1885–1886*, p. 139. *Transactions of the State Agricultural Society*, 1882, p. 162, contains an important discussion by Professor Husmann on resistant vines.
[51] Jerome Landfield, *California—America's Vineyard*, p. 1, a popular pamphlet

Notes

which also credits Luther Burbank, famed horticulturist of Santa Rosa, California, as an active participant in the fight against the phylloxera.

[52] Hutchins, *op. cit.*, p. 244.

[53] Hilgard, *Report of Viticultural Work . . . 1885–1886*, p. 140; *Bonfort's Wine and Spirit Circular*, January 10, 1888, p. 116; Newton B. Pierce, "Grape Diseases on the Pacific Coast," in *U. S. Dept. Agric. Farmer's Bulletin*, No. 30, p. 7.

[54] *Transactions of the State Agricultural Society*, 1882, pp. 158–166, contains an article on "Phylloxera-Proof Vines." The three species best adapted to California according to the Society's investigations were: (1) the *Vitis Aestivalis*, (2) the *Vitis Riparis*, and (3) the *Vitis Rupestris*. This article is a typical example of the educational literature published by the Agricultural Society; Charles Joly, "Note sur la viticulture en Californie," in *Mélanges*, II, 2–3, maintains that the resistant variety is the only accepted and certain remedy for the disease in France. Moreover, he asserts that the resistant is the only hope for the future of California viticulture.

[55] Quayle, *op. cit.*, p. 174.

[56] Wetmore, *Treatise on Wine Production*, p. 56.

[57] Murphy, *The People of the Pueblo*, pp. 234–235.

[58] State Board of Viticultural Commissioners, *Report of E. C. Priber, Commissioner for Napa County*, introduction.

[59] *Alta California*, September 18, 1875.

[60] *Appendix to the Journals of the Legislature*, sess. 21, doc., 26 (1876) pp. 3–5.

[61] George Husmann, *Grape Culture and Wine Making in California*, p. 43; Fitz-James, *Grande Culture de la vigne américaine, 1881–1883*, I, 18, refutes the idea that the phylloxera was a "blessing in disguise." The financial loss was too great to have aided anyone or the state in general. Furthermore, good wine is made by good wine makers not by good grapes alone.

[62] Cleland and Hardy, *March of Industry*, p. 82.

NOTES TO CHAPTER XI

FOUNDING OF THE STATE BOARD OF VITICULTURAL COMMISSIONERS, 1880

[1] Wait, *Wines and Vines*, p. 37; Edward R. Emerson, *The Story of the Vine*, p. 229.

[2] Arpad Haraszthy, *Report to Governor Waterman*, p. 3.

[3] *Appendices to the Journals of the Assembly and the Senate*, sess. 23, doc. 16 (1880), p. 7.

[4] *Ibid.*

[5] *Appendices to the Journals of the Assembly and the Senate*, sess. 23, doc. 16 (1880), p. 10.

[6] A complete text of the Act of 1880 is to be found in: State Board of Viti-

Notes

cultural Commissioners, *First Annual Report*, pp. 5–8; *Special Report* No. 20, pp. 158–160; Haraszthy, *op. cit.*, p. 3.

[7] Hutchins, *California Agriculture*, p. 243; Wait, *op. cit.*, p. 37.

[8] Wait, *op. cit.*, pp. 89–90, lists the original officers and the first district commissioners and contains a list of the standing committees of the S. B. V. C. See also: *Alta California*, May 27, 1880.

[9] *Special Report* No. 20, pp. 160–161.

[10] Emerson, *op. cit.*, p. 230.

[11] For a copy of the complete text of the Act of 1881 see: *Special Report* No. 20, pp. 160–161.

[12] Hutchins, *op. cit.*, pp. 245–246.

[13] *Special Report* No. 20, pp. 160–161.

[14] Hutchins, *op. cit.*, p. 246.

[15] Haraszthy, *op. cit.*, p. 5.

[16] Hilgard, *Report of Viticultural Work during the Seasons 1883–1884, 1884–1885*, p. 11, in University of California Pamphlet collection: "Pamphlets on Wine."

[17] *Notizie e Studi sulla Agricoltura*, p. 322.

[18] Haraszthy, *op. cit.*, p. 27.

[19] When the State Board of Viticultural Commissioners was abolished in 1894, the University of California inherited a valuable collection of books, monographs, and periodicals on grape growing and wine making. Through the efforts of Professor Hilgard and other viticulturists the Berkeley and Davis libraries of the university today contain extensive viticultural collections.

[20] Rossati, *Relazione di un viaggio d'Istruzione negli Stati Uniti d'America*, p. 147. This is one of a series of publications issued by the Ministero di Agricoltura, Industria, e Commercio.

[21] Snell, "California Viticulture, 1870–1900, a Chapter in the Economic History of California," p. 18.

[22] *Notizie e Studi* . . . , p. 325; Haraszthy, *op. cit.*, p. 24.

[23] Rossati, *op. cit.*, p. 147.

[24] *Bonfort's Wine and Spirit Circular*, August 25, 1882, p. 129; The San Francisco *Examiner*, April 6, 1890, carries an interesting article of the work of the S. B. V. C. from the time of its founding.

[25] Haraszthy, *op. cit.*, p. 25.

[26] *Ibid.*, pp. 24–25.

[27] *Statutes of California*, sess. 23 (1880), pp. 36–37.

[28] Hilgard, *Report of Viticultural Work . . . 1883–1884, 1884–1885*, p. 206.

[29] Hutchins, *op. cit.*, p. 243.

[30] *Alta California*, July 24, 1880.

[31] *First Annual Report of the Chief Executive Viticultural Officer*, 1881, p. viii; Board of State Viticultural Commissioners, *Recommendations on the Phylloxera*, in University of California pamphlet collection: "Pamphlets on Wines," Vol. I, no. 16, p. 7.

[32] *Bonfort's Wine and Spirit Circular*, August 25, 1883, p. 159.

Notes

[33] Hilgard, *Report of Viticultural Work . . . 1883–1884, 1884–1885,* pp. 205–210.
[34] *Ibid.,* pp. 206–207.
[35] *Fifth Annual Report of the California State Board of Viticultural Commissioners,* 1891–1892, p. 264.
[36] S. B. V. C., *First Annual Report,* p. 10.
[37] Wine Advisory Board, *Wine Handbook Number One,* p. 11.
[38] S. B. V. C., *First Annual Report,* pp. 163–164.
[39] *First Annual Report of the Chief Executive Viticultural Officer,* 1881, p. xxv.
[40] S. B. V. C., *First Annual Report,* p. 63.
[41] Complete texts of the quarantine rules are to be found in: *Special Report* No. 20, pp. 166–168; *First Annual Report of the Chief Executive Viticultural Officer,* 1881, pp. xxiii–xxv.
[42] *Special Report* No. 20, pp. 166–168.
[43] S. B. V. C., *Fifth Viticultural Convention,* 1887, p. 23.
[44] Lucille E. Dickson, "The Founding and Early History of Anaheim, California," p. 31, in *Annual Publications of the Historical Society of Southern California,* Vol. XI; Hallock F. Raup, *The German Colonization of Anaheim, California* (Berkeley, 1932), p. 136.
[45] Husmann, *Grape Investigations in the Vinifera Regions of the United States,* pp. 9–10.
[46] Wine Advisory Board, *Wine Handbook Number One,* p. 11.
[47] Raup, *op. cit.,* p. 136.
[48] Snell, *op. cit.,* pp. 27–29; Newton B. Pierce, *Grape Diseases on the Pacific Coast,* pp. 60–61.
[49] Hutchins, *op. cit.,* p. 266.
[50] San Francisco *Examiner,* August 8, 1889.
[51] Hutchins, *op. cit.,* pp. 266–267.
[52] *Bonfort's Wine and Spirit Circular,* January 10, 1888, p. 116; San Francisco *Call,* August 17, 1889; Hutchins, *op. cit.,* pp. 266–267.
[53] San Francisco *Call,* August 17, 1889.
[54] San Francisco *Examiner,* August 17, 1889.
[55] Hutchins, *op. cit.,* p. 267.
[56] Pierce, *op. cit.,* pp. 60–61.
[57] Raup, *op. cit.,* p. 137.

NOTES TO CHAPTER XII
A BUSINESS CYCLE, 1880–1895

[1] Sacramento *Bee,* August 30, 1935.
[2] See Chapter xiii for the passage of the California pure-wine law.
[3] Charles F. Oldham, "California Wines," *Journal of the Society of Arts,* XLII (Febr., 1894), 196–197.

Notes

[4] *Bonfort's Wine and Spirit Circular*, July 25, 1883, p. 122.

[5] W. H. Murray, *Builders of a Great City*, I, 31.

[6] R. G. Sneath, "Wine, Brandy and Olive Oil," *Overland Monthly*, XIV, n. s. (Aug., 1889), 175–179; Snell, "Viticulture in California, 1870–1900," pp. 20–21; *Sacramento Bee*, August 30, 1935.

[7] S. B. V. C., *Report of the Sixth Annual Convention*, 1888, p. 10; L. J. Rose, "Fruit Growing in Southern California," MS (ca. 1875–1880), p. 8; Letter from L. J. Rose to John S. Hittell dated San Gabriel, California, June 29, 1881, in the same MS collection of the Bancroft Library.

[8] *Special Report* No. 20, p. 101; John S. Hittell, *Commerce and Industries of the Pacific Coast*, p. 242.

[9] *Bonfort's Wine and Spirit Circular*, August 10, 1884, p. 141.

[10] George Husmann, "The Present Condition of Grape Culture in California," *U. S. Dept. Agric. Yearbook*, 1898, p. 553.

[11] *California Fruit Grower*, Aug. 17, 1889, p. 20.

[12] *Alta California*, November 29, 1880; Morris M. Estee, *Address delivered by Morris M. Estee at the opening of the Twenty-second Industrial Exhibition of the Mechanics Institute*, pp. 1–12; *Appendices to the Journals of the Assembly*, sess. 23 (1880), p. 4.

[13] *First Annual Report of the Chief Executive Viticultural Officer*, 1881, p. vii; *Bonfort's Wine and Spirit Circular*, July 10, 1885, p. 109; George A. Pettit, "The University and California Wines," *California Monthly*, XXXII (Jan., 1934), 20.

[14] Haraszthy MS, p. 25.

[15] S. B. V. C., *Third Viticultural Convention*, 1884, p. 140; *Proceedings of the California Pure Food Congress*, p. 42, in the Bancroft Library collection "California Commerce," Vol. I, no. 16.

[16] S. B. V. C., Report of the *Sixth Annual Convention*, 1888, p. 11; for the status of the industry by counties see *Special Report* No. 20, pp. 44–49; Arpad Haraszthy, *Report to Governor Waterman*, 1888, p. 11; "From 1769 to Prohibition," *California Magazine of Pacific Business*, XXVII (Oct., 1937), 46; Oldham, *op. cit.*, p. 196; *Alta California*, November 29, 1880.

[17] Haraszthy MS, p. 26.

[18] *Bonfort's Wine and Spirit Circular*, April 10, 1885, p. 260; L. J. Rose, MS, (1886), p. 6, in the Bancroft Library of the University of California.

[19] Snell, *op. cit.*, pp. 24–25; Charles A. Wetmore, *Treatise on Wine Production*, pp. 5–6.

[20] Husmann, *op. cit.*, p. 557; S. B. V. C., *Fourth Viticultural Convention*, 1886, pp. 24–25.

[21] Guido Rossati, *Relazione di un viaggio d'istruzione negli Stati Uniti d'America*, pp. 148–149.

[22] *Alta California*, November 29, 1880.

[23] Hittell, *op. cit.*, p. 749.

[24] Wait, *Wines and Vines of California*, pp. 39–40; George Husmann, *Grape Culture and Wine Making in California*, pp. 358–359.

Notes

[25] Estee, *Address* . . . 1887, p. 8; *Notizie e Studi sulla Agricoltura*, pp. 320–321.

[26] *Bonfort's Wine and Spirit Circular*, December 23, 1886, p. 96.

[27] Haraszthy, *Report to Governor Waterman*, 1888, p. 13; Jesse Schilling Blout, "A Brief Economic History of the California Wine-Growing Industry," p. 1. Mimeographed MS at the California Wine Institute in San Francisco; H. F. Stoll, "California's Important Grape Industry," in *California Grape Grower*, p. 19; Charles Carpy & Co. MS (1887), p. 4.

[28] Husmann, *op. cit.*, p. 19; Snell, *op. cit.*, p. 22.

[29] *Notizie e Studi*, p. 325.

[30] *California Fruit Grower*, III (July 13, 1889), 4; Snell, *op. cit.*, p. 23.

[31] Rossati, *op. cit.*, p. 147.

[32] *Bonfort's Wine and Spirit Circular*, August 10, 1888, p. 162; Heath, "Valley of Vineyards," *Californian*, II (Sept., 1880), 218.

[33] *Sacramento Bee*, January 23, 1885; Lachman and Jacobi, "Data Regarding California's Wine Industry," MS in the Bancroft Library. (See p. 5 for data on the California wine scene of the 'eighties.)

[34] San Francisco *Merchant*, April 27, 1883, pp. 58–59; *California Fruit Grower*, December 22, 1888, p. 8; *Bonfort's Wine and Spirit Circular*, December 25, 1888, p. 93.

[35] *Ibid.* September 14, 1883, p. 464.

[36] *Bonfort's Wine and Spirit Circular*, February 10, 1888, p. 169; July 10, 1888, p. 111.

[37] *California Fruit News*, August 25, 1888, p. 4.

[38] *Bonfort's Wine and Spirit Circular*, February 25, 1888, p. 191.

[39] San Francisco *Call*, August 18, 1889; *Bonfort's Wine and Spirit Circular*, August 25, 1889, p. 205.

[40] San Francisco *Examiner*, July 25, 1889; July 26, 1889; July 31, 1889; August 8, 1889. Nearly every issue between July 23, 1889, and August 18, 1889, had an article or an editorial on the California wine crisis.

[41] San Francisco *Examiner*, August 8, 1889.

[42] *Ibid.*

[43] *Ibid.*, August 16, 1889, pp. 4–5.

[44] San Francisco *Call*, October 8, 1892.

[45] S. B. V. C., *Sixth Annual Report*, 1893–1894, p. 7.

[46] *Pacific Wine, Brewing and Spirit Review*, January 26, 1891, p. 8.

[47] Sneath, *op. cit.*, pp. 176–178.

[48] *Ibid.*

[49] George Husmann, "Grape, Raisin, and Wine Production in the United States," p. 416, in *U. S. Dept. Agric. Yearbook*, 1902.

[50] *American Wine Press*, April 5, 1897, p. 4.

[51] *Western Broker*, May 15, 1891, p. 13.

[52] *American Wine Press*, April 5, 1897, p. 4.

[53] *Ibid.*

Notes

[54] *Bonfort's Wine and Spirit Circular*, July 25, 1891, p. 221.
[55] *California Fruit Grower*, February 18, 1893, p. 124.
[56] San Francisco *Call*, February 9, 1893.
[57] *Bonfort's Wine and Spirit Circular*, April 25, 1888, p. 285.
[58] *American Wine Press*, April 5, 1897, p. 5.
[59] *Rural Californian*, April, 1895, p. 196.
[60] *Ibid.*, November, 1894, p. 595.
[61] *Pacific Wine, Brewing and Spirit Review*, February 7, 1895, pp. 24-25.
[62] *Statutes of California*, 1895, p. 235; *American Wine Press*, April 5, 1897, p. 5.
[63] *Pacific Wine, Brewing and Spirit Review*, March 21, 1895, p. 13.
[64] S. B. V. C., "Minutes of the Executive Committee of the Board of State Viticultural Commissioners, June 10, 1889-December 23, 1895," MS, (1895), Bancroft Library, University of California.
[65] *American Wine Press*, November 15, 1902, p. 24.
[66] *Pacific Wine, Brewing and Spirit Review*, April 6, 1895, p. 18.
[67] *Ibid.*
[68] *Ibid.*, December 9, 1895, p. 12.

NOTES TO CHAPTER XIII
NATIONAL PROBLEMS, 1880-1895

[1] *Appendices to the Journals of the Assembly and Senate*, sess. 23, doc. 16 (1880), p. 3.
[2] *Bonfort's Wine and Spirit Circular*, January 10, 1883, p. 92.
[3] *Statutes of California*, 1883, pp. 398-399.
[4] *Ibid.*
[5] San Francisco *Merchant*, August 17, 1886, p. 147.
[6] *Bonfort's Wine and Spirit Circular*, January 25, 1887, p. 157.
[7] S. B. V. C., *Report of the Sixth Viticultural Convention*, 1887, pp. 12-15; Lachman and Jacobi, "Data Regarding California's Wine Industry," MS (1888), p. 5.
[8] Haraszthy, *Report to Governor Waterman*, 1888, p. 28.
[9] *Bonfort's Wine and Spirit Circular*, September 25, 1882, p. 162.
[10] *Ibid.*, April 10, 1883, p. 199.
[11] *Ibid.*, April 10, 1883, p. 200.
[12] San Francisco *Merchant*, August 15, 1884, p. 268.
[13] S. B. V. C., *Second Annual Report of the Chief Executive Viticultural Officer*, 1882-1884, pp. 21-22.
[14] James M. Callahan, *American Foreign Policy in Mexican Relations*, pp. 432-433.
[15] S. B. V. C., *Report of the Third Viticultural Convention*, 1884, pp. 40-41.
[16] Callahan, *op. cit.*, p. 433.

Notes

[17] *Sixth Annual Report of the S. B. V. C.*, 1893, pp. 76–80.
[18] Wetmore, *Treatise*, p. 60.
[19] S. B. V. C., *Sixth Annual Report*, 1893, pp. 76–80.
[20] *Ibid.;* Wetmore, *op. cit.*, p. 60.
[21] Wetmore, *op. cit.*, p. 62.
[22] *California Fruit Grower*, January 13, 1894, p. 32.
[23] *Ibid.*, January 27, 1894, p. 62; S. B. V. C., *Sixth Annual Report*, 1893–1894, pp. 68–69.
[24] Stephen M. White, *Products of Viticulture affected by the Tariff and Internal Revenue Laws*, p. 32. Pamphlet in the Bancroft Library collection "Wines and Viniculture in California."
[25] In 1884 California produced approximately 11,000,000 gallons of wine, by 1894 the total wine production of the state approximated 18,000,000 gallons.
[26] *Bonfort's Wine and Spirit Circular*, December 10, 1889, p. 87.
[27] *Ibid.*, May 25, 1882, p. 23.
[28] *A Comparison of the Records of the Two Parties made in the Interest of the Sweet Wine Men of California*, Vol. XXX, no. 8 in the Bancroft Library collection "California Pamphlets."
[29] *Ibid.*
[30] S. B. V. C., *Fourth Annual Report*, 1889–1890, pp. 76–80.
[31] Complete text of the Sweet Wine Law is to be found in *Sixth Annual Report of the S. B. V. C.*, 1893–1894, pp. 71–74.
[32] *Bonfort's Wine and Spirit Circular*, October 25, 1890, p. 147; *Notizie e Studi sulla Agricoltura, produzione, e commercio del vino in Italia e all'estero*, p. 324.
[33] S. B. V. C., *Fourth Annual Report*, 1889–1890, p. 23.
[34] *American Wine Press*, March 1, 1897, p. 11; *San Francisco Call*, December 9, 1890.
[35] *American Wine Press*, March 1, 1897, p. 11.
[36] Wetmore, *op. cit.*, p. 63.
[37] *Ibid.*
[38] *Bonfort's Wine and Spirit Circular*, June 25, 1891, p. 143.
[39] S. B. V. C., *Fifth Annual Report*, 1891–1892, p. 14.
[40] Wetmore, *op. cit.*, pp. 64–68.
[41] *Ibid.*
[42] *Bonfort's Wine and Spirit Circular*, March 10, 1885, p. 215.
[43] *Special Report* No. 20, p. 99.
[44] Robert Louis Stevenson, *Silverado Squatters*, pp. 38–39; Murray, *Builders of a Great City*, I, 30.
[45] *Alta California*, August 11, 1880.
[46] *Bonfort's Wine and Spirit Circular*, January 25, 1884, p. 126.
[47] Henry Lachman, "Early California Wine Industry," in *Official Report of the Session of the International Congress of Viticulture*, p. 29.

Notes

⁴⁸ *Second Annual Report of the Chief Executive Viticultural Officer*, 1882–1884, pp. 19–20.
⁴⁹ *Bonfort's Wine and Spirit Circular*, June 10, 1882, p. 80; S. B. V. C., *Report of the Third Annual Viticultural Convention*, 1884, pp. 158–159.
⁵⁰ *Bonfort's Wine and Spirit Circular*, January 25, 1884, p. 126.
⁵¹ University of California, *Agricultural Experiment Station Bulletins*, Vol. I, no. 65, p. 142; S. B. V. C., *Report of the Third Annual Viticultural Convention*, 1884, pp. 32–33.
⁵² *Bonfort's Wine and Spirit Circular*, September 10, 1887, pp. 233–234.
⁵³ S. B. V. C., *Report of the Fourth Viticultural Convention*, 1886, pp. 104–105.
⁵⁴ *Ibid.*, p. 105.
⁵⁵ *Ibid.*, pp. 105–106.
⁵⁶ *Ibid.*
⁵⁷ *Idem, Report of the Fifth Viticultural Convention*, 1887, p. 2.
⁵⁸ *Idem, Report of the Fourth Viticultural Convention*, 1886, p. 109.
⁵⁹ Haraszthy, *op. cit.*, p. 6.
⁶⁰ *Statutes of California*, 1887, pp. 46–50.
⁶¹ *Ibid.*; S. B. V. C. *Third Annual Report*, 1887, app. II, pp. 97–102.
⁶² S. B. V. C., *Third Annual Report*, 1887. Appendix II constitutes the report of the Chief Executive Viticultural Officer for the year 1887.
⁶³ *Ibid.*, App. II, p. 99.
⁶⁴ *Bonfort's Wine and Spirit Circular*, August, 1887, p. 146.
⁶⁵ *Ibid.*
⁶⁶ S. B. V. C., *Report of the Fifth Viticultural Convention*, 1887, p. 38.
⁶⁷ *Bonfort's Wine and Spirit Circular*, July 10, 1887, p. 117.
⁶⁸ *Ibid.*, August, 1887, p. 146.
⁶⁹ *Ibid.*
⁷⁰ S. B. V. C., *Third Annual Report*, 1887, p. 71.
⁷¹ *Bonfort's Wine and Spirit Circular*, November 23, 1887, p. 36.
⁷² *Ibid.*, March 23, 1888, p. 241.
⁷³ S. B. V. C., *Third Annual Report*, 1887, p. 71.
⁷⁴ San Francisco *Examiner*, April 6, 1890.

NOTES TO EPILOGUE

¹ San Francisco *Call*, May 19, 1893.
² *Statutes of California*, 1893, p. 149; *The Resources of California*, in the Bancroft Library pamphlet collection "California Miscellany." See n.s. Vol. I, no. 11, p. 129.
³ "Transactions of the Eighth Viticultural Convention," in S. B. V. C., *Fifth Annual Report*, 1891–1892, p. 129.
⁴ *Idem, Fifth Annual Report*, 1891–1892, pp. 109–113.

Notes

⁵ *Idem*, "Transactions of the Eighth Viticultural Convention, p. 86.
⁶ *Notizie e Studi*, p. 320.
⁷ Wetmore, *Treatise*, p. 43.
⁸ San Francisco *Call*, December 15, 1893; October 10, 1893; Wetmore, *op. cit.*, p. 50.
⁹ Wetmore, *op. cit.*, p. 58.
¹⁰ *Ibid.*, pp. 44-45.
¹¹ San Francisco *Call*, October 10, 1893.
¹² *Ibid.*
¹³ *Ibid.*, October 17, 1893.
¹⁴ S. B. V. C., *Sixth Annual Report*, 1893-1894, pp. 8-9.
¹⁵ *Ibid.*, pp. 79-80.
¹⁶ Rossati, *Relazione di un viaggio d'istruzione negli Stati Uniti d'America*, p. 149.

BIBLIOGRAPHY

BIBLIOGRAPHY

BIBLIOGRAPHIES, GUIDES, AND INDEXES

Abbott, M. J. "California: An Index to Some Unofficial Sources of Agricultural Statistics," in *Agricultural Economic Bibliographies*, Vol. XXXI, p. 5. Washington, 1930. Useful guide to materials for the twentieth century.

Agricultural Index. 10 vols., New York, 1919-1945. Useful guide to periodical literature.

"Bibliography of Wines, Spirits and Beer," in *Bonfort's Wine and Spirit Circular*, January 10, 1894, pp. 288-291. An unannotated list of books and articles dealing with the "manufacture, sale and consumption of wine, spirits, and beer."

Blankenhorn, Adolph. *Bibliotheca Oenologica.* Heidelburg, 1875. Works cited are largely in French, German, and Italian. Primarily a list of technical books and articles.

Bunje, E. T. H., J. H. Irish, R. Hagin, and M. Flaherty. "Cultural Contributions of California: California Viticulture" Section 1. MS in possession of the Giannini Foundation, University of California. A valuable annotated list of books on various aspects of California viticulture.

Cowan, R. E., and R. G. Cowan. *A Bibliography of the History of California, 1500-1930.* 3 vols., San Francisco, 1933. An unannotated author bibliography.

Edward, Everett. *A Bibliography of the History of Agriculture in the United States.* Washington, 1930. The section on California has excellent references with concise annotations.

Grassi, Battista. *Contributo alla conoscenza delle fillosserine ed in particolare della fillossera della vite.* Rome, 1912. An excellent bibliography on vine diseases, especially on the phylloxera.

Hasse, Adelaide R. *Index of Economic Materials in the Documents of the States of the United States: California* (Washington, 1907). The sections on grape culture, viticulture, and conventions are valuable for their precise citations.

Lacy, Mary C. "California: An Index to the Official State Sources of Agricultural Statistics," in *Agricultural Economics Bibliography.* Vol. XXXI, p. 1. Washington, 1930. Particularly valuable for the period 1918-1930.

Schenley Library Bibliography. New York, 1946. Stresses the more popular works.

Schmidt, Louis B. *Topical Studies and References on the Economic History of American Agriculture.* Rev. ed., Philadelphia, 1923.

Simon, Andre L. *Bibliotheca Vinaria. A bibliography of books and pamphlets dealing with viticulture, wine-making, distillation, the management, sale, taxation, use and abuse of wines and spirits.* London, 1913.

United States Commissioner of Agriculture. *A General Index of the Agricultural*

Bibliography

Reports of the Patent Office . . . 1837 to 1861, and of the Department of Agriculture . . . 1862 to 1876. Washington, 1879.

United States Department of Agriculture. *Bulletin Number Six.* Washington, 1902. "A list of the publications of the United States Department of Agriculture from 1840 to 1901."

United States Department of Commerce. *A Bibliography of the History of Agriculture in the United States.* Washington, 1930.

University of California. College of Agriculture. Agricultural Experiment Station. *Report of the Viticultural Work during the Seasons, 1887–1893* . . . . Sacramento, 1896.

———. *Report of the College of Agriculture and the Agricultural Experimental Station . . . July 1, 1917 to July 30, 1918.* Berkeley, 1918. Pp. 119–139 contain a "General Index to the Annual Report, Bulletins, Circulars of the California Agricultural Experiment Station, 1887–1918." This is the only printed index to these works.

Wine Institute. *Selective Bibliography of Wine Books.* San Francisco, 1944. Primarily a list of popular books.

MANUSCRIPTS

Blowers, Russell B. Several boxes of letters, pamphlet, and account books of an early California viticulturist and member of the State Board of Viticultural Commissioners.

California Board of State Viticultural Commissioners. "Minutes of the Executive Committee . . . June 10, 1889–December 23, 1895."

———. "Minutes of Meetings, May 24, 1880–December 9, 1895."

Carpy, Charles & Co. Notes. An important account of the California wine business during the 'eighties by one of the large wine manufacturers of the Pacific coast.

Daggett, Stuart. "Miscellaneous Notes on California Railroads." Contains incidental material on California viticulture.

Eggers, George H. "The Wine Industry in California."

Gomez, Vicente P. "Lo que sabe sobra cosas de California."

Haraszthy, Arpad. "The Haraszthy Family." By the son of Colonel Agoston Haraszthy.

Hayes, Benjamin I. "Notes on California Affairs."

Hittell, John S. "Commerce and Industries of the Pacific Coast." A collection of miscellaneous letters written by California vineyardists to Hittell.

Kohler, Charles. Notes.

———. "Wine Production in California."

Lachman, Abraham, and Jacob Jacobi. "Data Regarding California's Wine Industry."

Rose, L. J. Notes. Biographical sketch.

———. "Fruit-Growing in Southern California."

Bibliography

Vignes, Jean Louis. Notes. Notes of researchers and editors working on Bancroft's *History of California*.
Warren, J. L. Ten boxes of miscellaneous notes, letters, and articles.

UNPUBLISHED WORKS AND THESES

Blout, Jesse S. "A Brief Economic History of the California Wine-Growing Industry." Mimeographed history distributed by the Wine Institute of California, with special emphasis on the post-prohibition period.
Clark, Selden. "California's Wine Industry and Its Financing." Thesis, Graduate School of Banking of Rutgers University. New Brunswick, 1941.
Finch, John R. "Early Wine Growers of California: Historical Figures in the Building of California's Wine Empire in the Years 1769 to 1900. . . . "
Leggett, Herbert B. "The Early History of Wine Production in California." M. A. thesis, University of California, Berkeley, 1939. Special emphasis is placed on the early Spanish period.
Snell, Alberta. "Viticulture in California, 1870–1900, a Chapter in the Economic History of California." M. A. thesis, University of California, Berkeley, 1929.

PAMPHLET AND SCRAPBOOK COLLECTIONS

"Bancroft Scraps." 113 vols. in 121. The most useful volumes are those entitled: "California Agriculture," "California Counties," and "State Fairs." A collection of newspaper clippings and pamphlets.
California Agricultural Experiment Station. "Pamphlets on Viticulture, 1897–1911." Data on the research of the college of agriculture in the field of vine pests and diseases.
"California Commerce." 3 vols.
"California Miscellany." 20 vols. in 2.
"California Pamphlets." 30 vols.
"California Viticulture and Wine Making." Special reports of the State Board of Viticultural Commissioners for the various counties are to be found in this collection.
Hayes, Benjamin. "Scrapbooks." 138 vols. See especially the following: "Agriculture," "California Notes" (5 vols.), and "History of Los Angeles County" (10 vols.).
Hilgard, Eugene W. "University Papers." Contains the important report of Arpad Haraszthy to Governor Waterman, April, 1888.
"Pamphlets of the Civil War Period." 13 vols. in 1. 2nd. ser. 63 vols. in 2. The second series contains the "Report of the Committee on the Improvement of the Grape Vine in California, 1861"; the reports of J. J. Warner and Agoston Haraszthy; and the "Official Report of the Annual Fair and Cattle Show of the State Agricultural Society, 1856."
"Pamphlets on California Viticulture." 8 vols. in 1. Indispensable collection.

Bibliography

"Pamphlets on California Wines." 20 vols. in 1. Several pamphlets are the reports of various county viticultural societies.

"Pamphlets on the Phylloxera." Paris, 1853–1889. 68 vols. in 17. Originally these volumes were a part of the library of the Board of State Viticultural Commissioners. They contain pamphlets on the phylloxera in Europe and America.

"Pamphlets on Tulare County." 26 vols. in 1. Primarily for the recent period.

"Pamphlets on Wines." 12 vols. A collection of French and English pamphlets on various aspects of viticulture in California, France, and elsewhere.

"Wines and Viniculture in California." 26 vols. in 1. Valuable miscellaneous collection.

ALMANACS AND YEARBOOKS

Almanach de la Californie Illustrée. San Francisco, 1860.

Almanach Payot, 1864. San Francisco, 1864.

Alta California Almanac and Book of Facts, 1868–1883. 5 vols., San Francisco, 1868–1883.

American Almanac and Repository of Useful Knowledge, 1830–1861. 32 vols. Boston, 1830–1861.

American Yearbook and National Register for 1869. San Francisco, 1869.

Bristol's Illustrated Almanac . . . prepared expressly for California. 11 vols. New York, 1879–1890.

Calendarios español . . . arreglado al meridiano de San Francisco . . . 1864. San Francisco, 1864.

California Almanacs. 5 vols. 1860–1890. A miscellaneous collection of almanacs bound together under a Bancroft Library title.

California State Almanac and Annual Register, 1855. San Francisco, 1855.

California State Register and Yearbook of Facts for the Year 1859. San Francisco, 1859. Particularly valuable for its statistical tables.

Carrie and Damon's California Almanac. San Francisco, 1856.

Greenleaf, Benjamin. *California Almanac for 1849*. Boston, 1849. Reprinted in 1942 by the Friends of the Huntington Library.

Langley, Henry G. *Trade of the Pacific*. San Francisco, 1870.

Pacific Coast Almanac and Yearbook of Facts, 1865. 4 vols. San Francisco, 1865–1872. Bancroft Library possesses the volumes for 1865, and 1868 to 1872.

San Francisco Almanac for 1859. San Francisco, 1859.

San Francisco Directory . . . 1864. San Francisco, 1864.

FOREIGN DOCUMENTS

Italy. Direzione Generale dell'Agricoltura. *Notizie e Studi sulla Agricoltura, produzione e commercio del vino in Italia e all'estero*. Rome, 1892. Contains a survey of California wine making.

Annali di Agricoltura. 147 nos. in 39 vols. Rome, 1879–1911. Essentially technical.

Bibliography

Rossati, Guido. *Relazione di un viaggio d'istruzione negli Stati Uniti d'America.* Rome, 1900.

NATIONAL DOCUMENTS

Browne, Daniel J. "General Principles of Wine-Making," *United States Patent Office Reports, Agriculture,* 1856, pp. 439–445.

Dunn, H. D. "California—Her Agricultural Resources." *U. S. D. A. Report,* 1866, pp. 581–610.

Emory, William H. *Notes of a Military Reconnoissance, from Fort Leavenworth in Missouri to San Diego, in California.* . . . 30 Congress, 1 session, Senate Exec. Doc. no. 7. Washington, 1848. Contains interesting notes on viticulture in California.

Hilgard, Eugene W. "The Agriculture and Soils of California." *U. S. D. A. Report,* 1878, pp. 476–507.

———, T. C. Jones, and R. W. Furnes. *Report on the Climatic and Agricultural Features and the Agricultural Practice and Needs of the Pacific Slope.* . . . Washington, 1882. *U. S. D. A. Special Reports.* No. 2.

Husmann, George. "American Wine and Wine-Making." *U. S. D. A. Report,* 1867, pp. 154–163.

———. "Grape, Raisin, and Wine Production in the United States." *U. S. D. A. Yearbook,* 1902, pp. 407–420.

———. "The Present Condition of Grape Culture in California." *U. S. D. A. Yearbook,* 1898, pp. 551–562.

Keller, Matthew. "The Grape and Wine of Los Angeles." *U. S. Patent Office Report, Agriculture,* 1858, pp. 344–348.

M'Kee, Andrew. "The Grape and Wine Culture of California." *U. S. Patent Office Report, Agriculture,* 1858, pp. 338–344.

McMutrie, William. *Report upon the Statistics of Grape Culture and Wine Production in the United States for 1880.* Washington, 1881. *U. S. D. A. Special Reports.* No. 36.

Pierce, Newton B. *Grape Diseases on the Pacific Coast.* Washington, 1895. This important report is no. 30 in the *Farmer's Bulletin.*

Saunders, William. *Papers on Horticulture and Kindred Subjects.* Washington, 1891. *U. S. D. A. Special Reports.* No. 48.

Williams, A. "Agriculture in California." *U. S. Patent Office Report, Agriculture,* 1851, part 2, pp. 3–7.

United States. Census Office. Seventh Census, 1850. *Statistical View of the United States . . . being a compendium of the Seventh Census.* . . . Washington, 1854.

———. Eighth Census, 1860. *Agriculture of the United States in 1860; compiled from the original returns of the Eighth Census.* Washington, 1864.

———. Ninth Census, 1870. *Statistics of Agriculture.* Washington, 1870.

———. Department of the Interior. *Report of the Productions of Agriculture as returned at the Tenth Census . . . 1880.* Washington, 1883.

———. Congress. *Congressional Record.* 45th Cong., 2d sess. February 13–

Bibliography

March 25, 1878. Resolutions and petitions regarding the proposed Chotteau treaty.

———. 3d sess. December 2, 1878–February 3, 1879. Petitions on the tariff controversy.

———. House. *Resolution of the State of California in Relation to Tax on Native Wines.* 38th Cong., 1st sess., H. Misc. Doc. 7. 1863.

———. Senate. *Resolution of Senator Sargent.* 45th Cong., 3d sess. S. Misc. Doc. 61, 1879. A resolution on the proposed wine tariff and taxes.

———. *Joint Resolution of the Legislature of California in Favor of ... Modification of the Internal Revenue Law. . . .* 41st Cong., 2d sess. S. Misc. Doc. 103. 1869–1870.

———. Department of Agriculture. *Report of the Secretary of Agriculture ... 1847-1893.* 46 vols. Washington, 1848–1894. Continued in 1894 as the *Annual Report.*

———. *Farmer's Bulletin,* 1889–1943. 1,950 nos. in 77 vols. Washington, 1889–1944. See particularly nos. 30, 471, and 1689.

———. *Monthly Report of the Department of Agriculture.* Washington, 1867–1876.

———. *Yearbook of Agriculture.* Washington, 1894–.

———. Patent Office. *United States Patent Office Reports.* Washington, 1858–.

———. "Grapes and Wine." *U. S. Patent Office Report, Agriculture.* 1858, pp. 296–306.

———. Tariff Commission. *Annual Report.* 2nd. ser. 152 nos. in 16 vols. Washington, 1931–1944. See especially no. 134, *Grapes, Raisins, and Wines, a Survey of World Production.*

STATE DOCUMENTS

California. Agricultural Experiment Station. Berkeley. *Report of the Viticultural Work during the Seasons 1883–1884 and 1884–1885, 1885 and 1886, 1887–1889, 1887–1893.* 4 vols. in 1. Sacramento, 1886–1896. An indispensable collection of reports, studies, and statistical data.

———. *Appendix to the Senate and Assembly Journal.* San Jose, San Francisco, Sacramento, 1850–. Title varies. Important for reports, resolutions, and action of the state legislature.

———. Bureau of Labor Statistics. *Biennial Report.* Sacramento, 1884–1929.

———. Department of Agriculture. *Descriptive Catalogue of California Agriculture—Grapes.* Sacramento, 1922.

———. Department of Natural Resources. Division of Mines. *Reports.* 41 vols. Sacramento, 1881–. The volume for the year 1884 has a good collection of statistics of wine and grape production. Title varies.

———. *Journals of the Assembly of California.* San Jose, San Francisco, Sacramento, 1850–.

———. *Journals of the Senate of California.* San Jose, San Francisco, Sacramento, 1850–.

———. *Report of the State Engineer to the Legislature of the State of California,*

Bibliography

Session 1880–1881. 2 vols. Sacramento, 1880–1881. Contains valuable discussion on irrigation and grape culture.

———. State Agricultural Society. *Transactions.* 31 vols. Sacramento, 1885–1911.

———. State Board of Agriculture. *Report.* 8 vols. Sacramento, 1912–1923. The volume for 1911 has one of the best collections of statistics and historical data on the California wine industry.

———. State Commissioner of Horticulture. *Reports.* 13 vols. Sacramento, 1883–1902.

———. Board of State Viticultural Commissioners. *Annual Reports of the Chief Executive Viticultural Officer.* . . . 2 vols. Sacramento, 1882–1884. Important for material on phylloxera and role of this officer in viticultural affairs in general.

———. *Annual Reports.* 6 vols. Sacramento, 1881–1894. Contains activities of the S. B. V. C. for each year.

———. *Directory of the Grape-Growers and Wine-Makers.* . . . Sacramento, 1891. List of important viticulturists of California.

———. *Reprints of Reports on Viticulture.* 4 nos. in 1 vol. Sacramento, 1887–1890. Valuable reports of various district commissioners with excellent statistical tables.

———. *Reports of the Annual State Conventions.* Sacramento, 1884–1888. Valuable collection of speeches and issues at annual meetings of California grape growers and wine makers.

———. *The Vine in Southern California, Being Reports by Commissioners Bichowsky and Shorb.* . . . Sacramento, 1892.

———. *The Vineyards in Alameda County, Being the Report of Commissioner Charles Bundschu.* . . . Sacramento, 1893.

———. *The Vineyards in Napa County.* Sacramento, 1893.

———. *The Vineyards in Sonoma County.* Sacramento, 1893.

———. *Viticulture and Viniculture in California, Statements and Extracts.* . . . Sacramento, 1885. This pamphlet was prepared expressly for distribution at the New Orleans World Fair, 1885.

———. *Statutes of California.* San Jose, San Francisco, Sacramento, 1850–.

———. Surveyor General's Office. *Reports.* 46 vols. Sacramento, 1852–1928. Important source of statistics in spite of inaccuracies.

Grape Growers' and Wine Makers' Association of California. *Report of the Fifth Annual State Viticultural Convention.* San Francisco, 1887. Also called *Report of the Year 1887.*

Hayne, Arthur P. *Resistant Vines, Their Selection, Adaptation, and Grafting.* Sacramento, 1897. An important technical study published in series of University of California, College of Agriculture, Agricultural Experiment Station publications.

Southern District Agricultural Society. *Annual Fair of the Southern District.* . . .

Bibliography

2 vols., Los Angeles, 1872–1873. Lists the wine exhibits and premiums awarded.

University of California. College of Agriculture. *Agricultural Experiment Station Bulletins.* Berkeley, 1884–. Largely technical.

Wetmore, Charles A. *Treatise on Wine Production and Special Reports on Wine Examination, the Tariff, Internal Revenue Taxes, and Chemical Analyses.* Sacramento, 1894. Published as Appendix B to the *Annual Report of the Board of State Viticultural Commissioners, 1893–1894.* Very useful for the tariff and revenue problems of the 'eighties and 'nineties.

LOCAL DOCUMENTS

Buena Vista Vinicultural Society. *Reports of the Board of Trustees and Officers.* San Francisco, 1864.

By-Laws of the Eisen Vineyard Company and Prospectus Addressed to the Board of Directors and Stockholders by E. T. Eisen, President. San Francisco, 1885.

Estee, Morris M. *Address delivered by Morris M. Estee at the Opening of the Twenty-second Industrial Exhibition of the Mechanics Institute, September 1, 1887.* San Francisco, 1887.

Mechanics Institute of San Francisco. *Annual Reports.* 50 vols. in 7. San Francisco, 1868–1941.

Official Report of the California State Agricultural Society's Third Annual Fair. San Francisco, 1856.

Official Report of the Session of the International Congress of Viticulture. San Francisco, 1915.

Report of the Annual Meeting of the State Viticultural Society. San Francisco, 1879. Contains important addresses by Arpad Haraszthy, Charles Wetmore, and others.

San Francisco Chamber of Commerce. *Franco-American Commerce: Statements and Agreements in behalf of American Industries against the proposed Franco-American Commercial Treaty.* San Francisco, 1879. An indispensable collection of materials, speeches, resolutions, and statistics against the proposed Chotteau treaty.

Vineyard Homestead Association. *Indenture, Rules of Order, and certificate of incorporation.* San Francisco, 1865.

MEMOIRS, DIARIES, AND CONTEMPORARY ACCOUNTS

Bowles, Samuel. *Across the Continent.* . . . New York, 1865.

———. *Our New West.* . . . New York, 1869.

Bryant, Edwin. *What I Saw in California.* . . . New York, 1848.

Carmany, John H. *A Review of the Year 1866. Compiled from the Mercantile Gazette and Prices Current.* San Francisco, 1867.

Carr, John F. *Anaheim, Its People and Its Products.* New York, 1869.

Codman, John. *The Round Trip.* New York, 1879.

Bibliography

Colton, Walter. *Three Years in California.* New York, 1850.
Cox, Isaac. *Annals of Trinity County.* San Francisco, 1858.
Cronise, Titus F. *Agricultural and Other Resources of California.* San Francisco, 1870.
———. *The Natural Wealth of California.* San Francisco, 1868.
Davis, William H. *Seventy-five Years in California.* . . . San Francisco, 1929. Contains probably the best account of Jean Louis Vignes.
Fabian, Bentham. *The Agricultural Lands of California.* San Francisco, 1869. A guide to promote immigration.
Ferry, Hippolyte. *Description de la Nouvelle Californie.* Paris, 1850. A guide for immigrants.
Forbes, Alexander. *California: A History of Upper and Lower California from Their First Discovery to the Present Time.* London, 1839.
Gibbons, Henry. *The Wine Culture of California.* San Francisco, 1867. One of the earliest anti-prohibitionist tracts.
Greeley, Horace. *An Overland Journey from New York to San Francisco in the Summer of 1859.* New York, 1860.
Haraszthy, Agoston. *Grape Culture, Wines and Wine Making: with Notes upon Agriculture and Horticulture.* New York, 1862. The official report of Haraszthy's tour of Europe in 1861.
Haraszthy, Arpad. *California Grapes and Wines.* San Francisco, 1883.
Hittell, John S. *Resources of California.* 6th. ed. San Francisco, 1874. First edition published in 1863.
Hyatt, Thomas. *Handbook of Grape Culture.* 2d ed. San Francisco, 1876.
Levy, Daniel. *Les Français en Californie.* San Francisco, 1884.
Melrose, Richard, ed. *Anaheim, The Garden Spot of California.* Anaheim, 1879.
Menefee, C. A. *History and Descriptive Sketch Book of Napa, Sonoma, Lake and Mendocino.* Napa City, 1873. Contains several important biographical sketches of the important wine men in these counties.
Millard, Hannah. *Grapes and Grape Vines of California.* San Francisco, 1877. A publication sponsored by the California State Vinicultural Association to instruct the growers of California of the value of the different grape varieties.
Morris, William Gouverneur, and H. C. Bennett. *An Essay on the Manufacturing Interests of California.* . . . San Francisco, 1872.
My Vineyard at Lake View. New York, 1866.
Newmark, Harris. *Sixty Years in Southern California, 1853-1913.* 2d rev. ed. New York, 1926.
Northern California Historical Records. *Calendar of the Major Jacob Rink Snyder Collection of the Society of California Pioneers.* San Francisco, 1940. Valuable manuscript collection printed by the W. P. A.
Player-Frowd, J. G. *Six Months in California.* London, 1872.
Powers, Stephen. *Afoot and Alone: A Walk from Sea to Sea by the Southern Route.* Hartford, 1872.

Bibliography

Price, Major Sir Robert Lambart. *The Two Americas; an Account of Sport and Travel*. Philadelphia, 1877.

Quigley, Hugh. *The Irish Race in California and on the Pacific Coast*. San Francisco, 1878. Important source of agricultural information.

Robinson, Alfred. *Life in California*. . . . San Francisco, 1891. 1st ed. 1846.

Sayward, W. *All about Southern California*. San Francisco, 1875.

Stevenson, Robert Louis. *Silverado Squatters*. Boston, 1884. Several editions. Chapter iii discusses Napa County viticulture.

Stillman, Jacob Davis. *Seeking the Golden Fleece, a Record of Pioneer Life in California*. San Francisco, 1877.

Truman, Major Ben C. *Semi-Tropical California*. San Francisco, 1874. Important agricultural information.

Wetmore, Charles A. *Ampelography of California*. . . . San Francisco, 1884. "A discussion of vines not known in this State, together with comments on their adaptability to certain locations and uses."

SECONDARY WORKS

Allen, John F. *A Practical Treatise on the Culture and Treatment of the Grape Vine in the . . . United States*. 2d enl. ed. Boston, 1884.

Anaheim, Southern California, Its History, Climate, Soil and Advantages. Anaheim, 1885.

Arthaud, J. *De la vigne et ses produits*. Paris, 1858.

Atchison, Topeka and Santa Fe. *Wine of California: The Stirring Story of a Great American Industry*. 1937. Popular and brief historical account.

Bancroft, Hubert H. *History of California*. 7 vols. San Francisco, 1884–1890. Volume vii contains valuable material. Excellent references to sources.

Brown, John, and James Boyd. *History of San Bernardino and Riverside Counties*. 3 vols. Madison, Wis., 1922.

Bush & Co. *Illustrated descriptive catalogue of American Grape Vines*. 4th ed. St. Louis, Mo., 1895.

Callahan, James M. *American Foreign Policy in Mexican Relations*. New York, 1932.

Carrier, Lyman. *Beginnings of Agriculture in America*. New York, 1923.

Chorlton, William. *The American Grape Growers' Guide*. New York, 1856.

Cleland, R. G., and O. Hardy. *March of Industry*. San Francisco, 1929.

Colburn, Frona Eunice Waite. *Wines and Vines of California*. San Francisco, 1889. Good account of the viticulture of the 'eighties. Important list of California's outstanding vintners of the period.

Curtis, Edward. *Two California Sketches*. San Francisco, 1880.

Davin, C. *État actuel de la viticulture américaine*. Draguignan, France, 1879.

Delay, Peter J. *History of Yuba and Sutter Counties*. Los Angeles, 1924.

de Lôme, Enrique Dupuy. *La Producción y el Comercio de Viños en los Estados Unidos*. Madrid, 1895. Very important because de Lôme was in charge

Bibliography

of the viticultural exhibits at the Chicago World Fair of 1893. Largely based on the reports of the State Board of Viticultural Commissioners.

Eldredge, Zoeth S., ed. *History of California*. 5 vols. New York, 1915.

Emerson, Edward. *The Story of the Vine*. New York, 1902.

Faust, Albert B. *The German Element in the United States*. 2 vols. Boston, 1909. Volume II contains valuable information on the prominent Germans engaged in California viticulture.

Fitz-James, Marguerite. *Grande Culture de la vigne américaine, 1881–1883*. 3 vols. in 1. Paris, 1884. Especially valuable on diseases of the vine in California and Europe.

Gregory, Tom. *History of Sonoma County*. Los Angeles, 1911.

Grossman, H. J. *Grossman's Guide to Wines, Spirits, and Beers*. New York, 1940.

Hall, Charles V. *California the Ideal Italy of the World*. Philadelphia, 1875.

Hedrick, Ulysses P. *Manual of American Grape Growing*. New and rev. ed. New York, 1924.

Historical Souvenirs of El Dorado County. Oakland, 1883.

History of Placer County. Oakland, 1882.

History of Napa and Lake Counties. San Francisco, 1881.

Hittell, John S. *The Commerce and Industries of the Pacific Coast*. San Francisco, 1882.

Hittell, Theodore H. *History of California*. 4 vols. San Francisco, 1885–1897.

Hodges, R. E., and E. J. Wickson. *Farming in California*. San Francisco, 1923.

Hunt, Rockwell D., ed. *California and Californians*. 5 vols. New York, 1926.

Husmann, George. *Grape Culture and Wine Making in California*. San Francisco, 1888. Primarily a manual for grape growers.

Hutchins, Claude B., ed. *California Agriculture*. Berkeley, 1946.

Joly, Charles. *Mélanges*. 22 vols. in 2. Paris, 1881–1890.

Jones, Idwal. *Vines in the Sun: A Journey through the California Vineyards*. New York, 1949.

Landfield, Jerome. *California—America's Vineyard*. San Francisco, 1945.

Lord, Eliot. *The Italian in America*. New York, 1905. Contains a good account of the early history of the Italian Swiss Colony.

Mabon, Mary F. *ABC of America's Wines*. New York, 1942.

Memorial and Biographical History of the Counties of Fresno, Tulare, and Kern, California. Chicago, 1891.

Memorial and Biographical History of Northern California. Chicago, 1891.

Millardet, Alexis. *Histoires des principales variétés et espèces de vignes d'origines américaine*. Paris, 1885. Treatise on the use of native American vines to combat the phylloxera in France.

Murphy, Celeste G. *The People of the Pueblo*. Sonoma, 1935.

Murray, W. H. *The Builders of a Great City: San Francisco's Representative Men*. 2 vols. San Francisco, 1891.

McGroarty, John S., ed. *History of Los Angeles County*. 3 vols. Chicago and New York, 1923.

Bibliography

Nesfield, David. *The Vineland of the West*. San Francisco, 1883.

Nordhoff, Charles. *California for Health, Pleasure and Residence*. New ed., New York, 1882. Excellent material on the Anaheim experiment and a valuable chapter on the history of California wines.

———. *The Communistic Societies of the United States*. New York, 1875. Valuable material on Anaheim.

Raup, Halleck F. *The German Colonization of Anaheim, California*. University of California Publications in Geography. Berkeley, 1932.

Rifford, E. H. *The Wine Press and the Cellar*. San Francisco, 1883.

Schoonmaker, Frank, and Tom Marvel. *The Complete Wine Book*. New York, 1934.

———. *American Wines*. New York, 1941.

Shand, P. Morton. *A Book of Other Wines than French*. New York, 1929.

Shear, Sherwood, and Gerald Pearce. *Supply and Price Trends in the California Wine-Grape Industry*. Berkeley, 1934. A valuable collection of statistical tables and charts.

Southworth, John R. *Santa Barbara and Montecito Past and Present*. Santa Barbara, 1920. Interesting, if not entirely accurate, history of the Montecito vine.

Spooner, Alden J. *The Cultivation of American Grape Vines, and Making of Wine*. 2nd ed. Brooklyn, 1858.

Tinkham, George H. *History of San Joaquin County*. Los Angeles, 1923.

Vandor, Paul E. *History of Fresno County*. 2 vols. Los Angeles, 1919.

Vischer, Eduard. *Briefe eines Deutschen aus Californien. 1842*. San Francisco, 1873. Interesting references to the types and quality of California wines.

Wagner, Philip M. *A Wine-Grower's Guide*. . . . New York, 1945.

Weeks, George F. *California Copy*. Washington, 1928. A defense of the quality of California wines.

Wine Handbook Series. San Francisco, 1943–.

Wood, A. *The Truth about the Wine Interest*. 3rd ed., San Francisco, 1883. A prohibitionist attack against the wine industry.

TRADE PERIODICALS

American Wine Press and Mineral Water News. 42 vols. New York, 1897–1918. This journal devoted to the American wine interests. Each issue carried a California section. Particularly valuable for its coverage of legislation affecting the liquor industry.

Bonfort's Wine and Spirit Circular. 89 vols. New York, 1871–1919. Largely a journal for foreign wines, but contains valuable statistics on American and California production, prices, and exports.

Bulletin international du vin. 9 vols. Paris, 1935–1939. Valuable for the articles and statistical tables for the early post-prohibition period.

California Grape Grower. Berkeley, 1924. Several important articles are to be found in this one volume.

Bibliography

California Farmer and Journal of Useful Sciences. 52 vols. San Francisco, 1854–1884. Especially valuable for the period between 1854 and 1875.

California Fruit News. 114 vols. San Francisco, 1888—. Many important historical and business articles as well as good statistical tables.

California Rural Home Journal. 24 nos. in 1 vol. San Francisco, 1865–1866. See particularly the valuable historical sketch on California grape and wine culture by Colonel Agoston Haraszthy.

California Wine, Wool, and Stock Journal. 2 vols., San Francisco, 1863–1864. An indispensable periodical. Contains the only complete account of the meetings of the California Wine Growers' Association of 1862 and 1863. This journal also has several important articles by Arpad Haraszthy.

Cozzens' Wine Press. 7 vols. New York, 1854–1861. Several important articles on California viticulturists. See particularly the biographical sketch of William Wolfskill.

Grape Culturist. 3 vols. St. Louis, 1869–1871. George Husmann was editor of the periodical. Not valuable for California wine, but is useful for the attitude of a Middle Westerner toward California.

The Horticultural Review and Botanical Magazine. 4 vols. Cincinnati, 1853–1854. Largely a Middle Western and Eastern periodical, but contains some interesting material on California wines.

Hunt's Merchants' Magazine. 63 vols. New York, 1839–1870. For variations in title see the *Union List of Serials.* Not a wine or grape periodical, but contains important statistics of production, export, and valuable summaries of California grape and wine culture.

Pacific Wine, Brewing and Spirit Review. 61 vols. San Francisco, 1880–1935. Volumes I to XXII entitled *San Francisco Merchant.* For the several changes in the name of this periodical see the *Union List of Serials.* An indispensable collection. Contains important articles by the prominent growers of the 'eighties and 'nineties as well as many full and complete statistical tables. This journal is particularly important since it printed many of the texts of the meetings and conventions of the Board of State Viticultural Commissioners.

Revue Viticole: annales de la viticulture et de l'oenologie françaises et étrangères. 6 vols., Dijon, 1859–1864. Several important articles on early California wine and early California vintners are to be found only in this collection.

The Rural Californian: an Illustrated Monthly. 38 vols. Los Angeles, 1877–1918. Particularly valuable for its material on southern California.

Western Broker. 13 vols. Chicago, 1880–1891? Not a wine or grape trade periodical, but contains several valuable articles.

Wines and Vines. 26 vols. San Francisco, 1919—. Many changes in title. See the *Union List of Serials* for changes of title and frequency of publication. Many interesting historical articles on early California wine history. Articles usually written for popular consumption.

Wines and Vines, Yearbook of the Wine Industry. 7 vols. San Francisco, 1940—.

Bibliography

A compilation of the outstanding achievements of the industry during the year. Also some information on the historical development of the industry. Usually good statistical tables.

GENERAL PERIODICAL ARTICLES

"Agricultural Capacity of California," *Hours at Home*, V (Sept., 1867), 457.
"Agricultural Capacity of California," *Overland Monthly*, X (April, 1873), 297.
"Agricultural Production of the United States," *De Bow's Commercial Review*, XIII (Sept., 1852), 295.
Andreeva, Tamara. "The Vineyards of California," *Travel*, LXXXVII (July, 1946), 16–18, 30.
Barrows, H. D. "William Wolfskill, the Pioneer," *Annual Publications of the Historical Society of California*, V (1902), pp. 287–294.
Bartlett, Lanier. "Immigrant in the Land of Opportunity," *World's Work*, XVII (March, 1909), 1375–1380.
Bean, Walton E. "James Warren and the Beginnings of Agricultural Institutions in California," *Pacific Historical Review*, XIII (Dec., 1944), 361–375.
Bioletti, Frederic T. "A Short Sketch of the History of Wine Making in California," *California Journal of Development*, XXIII (Dec., 1933), 14–15, 45.
Blythe, Stuart O. "California Wineland of America," *California Magazine of Pacific Business*, XXVII (Oct., 1937), 43–44.
Brown, William E. "Devil Fish Ink: the Viticultural Commission and Its Origin," *Out West*, n. s., VIII (Nov., 1914), 275.
Butterfield, H. M. "The Builders of California's Grape and Raisin Industry," *Blue Anchor*, XV (Feb., 1938), 2–4, 23–25.
"California as a Vineland," *Atlantic Monthly*, XIII (May, 1864), 600–604.
"California Wine Growers and the Tariff," *Overland Monthly*, n. s., LIV (Sept., 1909), 285–286.
"California—Wine Land of America," *California Journal of Development*, XXV (Sept., 1935), 7–27.
Camp, Charles L., ed., "Chronicles of George C. Yount, The," *California Historical Society Quarterly*, II (April, 1923), 3–67.
Carosso, Vincent P. "Anaheim, California: a Nineteenth Century Experiment in Commercial Viticulture," *Bulletin of the Business Historical Society*, XXIII (June, 1949), 78–86.
Colburn, Frona Eunice. "Vintage Day," *Sunset*, XXIV (Feb., 1910), 206–210.
Dickson, Lucile E. "The Founding and Early History of Anaheim, California," *Annual Publications of the Historical Society of Southern California*, XI (1919), 26–37.
Edwards, Horace. "The Grape in California," *Land of Sunshine*, I (Nov., 1894), 120–121.
Fredericksen, Paul. "One Hundred Years of American Champagne," *Wine Review*, XV (July, 1947), 14–15.

Bibliography

———. "Haraszthy Comes to California," *Wines and Vines*, XXVIII (June, 1947), 25–26, 42.
———. "Haraszthy in San Francisco and San Mateo," *Wines and Vines*, XXVIII (July, 1947), 15–16, 30.
———. "Haraszthy's Early Years in Sonoma," *Wines and Vines*, XXVIII (Aug., 1947), 17–18, 37–38.
———. "Haraszthy's Mission to Europe," *Wines and Vines*, XXVIII (Sept., 1947), 17–18, 34.
———. "Busy Last Years," *Wines and Vines*, XXVIII (Oct., 1947), 21–22, 41–42.
"Grape Growing Industry in the United States, The," *National Geographic Magazine*, XIV (Nov., 1903), 445–451.
Grayson, John R. "The Farmer in California," *California Illustrated Magazine*, IV (July, 1893), 200–213.
"Great California Winery, A," *Land of Sunshine*, VIII (Dec., 1897), 53–56.
Halstead, B. D. "Fruits of California," *Chautauquan*, VII (May, 1887), 480.
Haraszthy, Arpad. "Wine Making in California," *Overland Monthly*, o. s., VII (Dec., 1871), 489–497.
———. "Early Difficulties," *Overland Monthly*, o. s., VII (Dec., 1871), 489–497.
———. "Later Triumphs," *Overland Monthly*, o. s., VIII (Jan., 1872), 34–41.
———. "Processes and Varieties," *Overland Monthly*, o. s., VIII (Feb., 1872), 105–109.
———. "Conclusion," *Overland Monthly*, o. s., VIII (April, 1872), 393–398.
"Haraszthy's Wisconsin Experiment," *Wisconsin Magazine of History*, XXIII (Dec., 1939), 182.
Heath, Sallie. "A Valley of Vineyards," *Californian*, II (Sept., 1880), 216–220.
"High Spots in Napa's History," *Wine Review*, II (Aug., 1934), 14.
Hilgard, Eugene W. "The Future of Grape Growing in California," *Overland Monthly*, n. s., III (Jan., 1884), 1–6.
Hittell, John S. "The Wines of California," *Pacific Monthly*, X (Sept., 1863), 196.
Inkersley, Arthur. "The Vintage in California and Italy," *Overland Monthly*, n. s., LIV (Oct., 1909), 406.
Jones, Idwal. "Champagne on the Coast," *Westways*, XXXVII (Dec., 1945), 8–9.
———. "He Planted the Zinfandel," *Westways*, XXXIV (Sept., 1942), 12–13.
———. "Lords among the Vintners," *Westways*, XXVII (Sept., 1935), 26–27.
Ladrey, C. "Faits pour servir à l'histoire de la vigne en Californie," *Revue Viticole*, III (1861), 15–22, 212–216.
Maitland, William. "A Mountain Vineyard in California," *Nineteenth Century*, XXIV (Aug., 1888), 251–261.
McWilliams, Carey. "Grape Vines Introduced in Livermore Valley, Alameda County, by James Concannon," *Westways*, XXXI (May, 1939), 4.

Bibliography

"Montecito Grape Vine, The," *Overland Monthly*, o. s., IX (Dec., 1872), 519–522.
Oldham, Charles F. "California Wines," *Journal of the Society of Arts*, XLII (Feb. 2, 1894) 195–201.
———. "Wines at the Chicago Exposition of 1893," *Journal of the Society of Arts*, XLII (Jan. 5, 1894), 112.
Pardee, M. R. "Romantic Wineries of the North Coast," *California Journal of Development*, XXIV (March, 1934), 8–9, 30.
Pettit, George A. "The University and California Wines," *California Monthly*, XXXII (Jan., 1934), 18–21, 45.
"Picture of the Big Santa Barbara Vine," *Mining and Scientific Press*, XXVII (July 12, 1873), 22.
Roberts, Edwards. "California Wine-Making," *Harper's Weekly*, XXXIII (March 9, 1889), 197–200.
Roberts, W. "Wine Growing in California," *Fortnightly Review*, LIX (March, 1893), 394–403.
Sbarboro, Andrea. "Vines and Wines of California," *Overland Monthly*, n. s., XXXV (June, 1900), 65–76.
Sheldon, Lionel C. "Profits of California Fruits," *Forum*, XI (Aug., 1891), 662–669.
Shinn, Charles H. "Horticulture in Early California," *Overland Monthly*, o. s., VI (Aug., 1885), 117–128.
Shipsey, Edward. "Eighty Years of Vineyards," *California Magazine of the Pacific*, XXX (Sept., 1940), 22–32.
Silver, J. S. "The Vineyards of California," *Overland Monthly*, o. s., I (Oct., 1868), 307–310.
Sneath, R. G. "Wine, Brandy, and Olive Oil," *Overland Monthly*, n. s., XIV (Aug., 1889), 175–179.
Stoll, Horatio F. "Agoston Haraszthy's Eventful Career," *Wines and Vines*, XVIII (Jan., 1937), 16–17.
———. "The Birth of California's Wine Industry," *Wines and Vines*, XX (March, 1939), 4.
———. "The Development of the California Wine Industry," *Argonaut*, CXII (March 16, 1934), 39–42.
———. "Father Serra and the Mission Grapes," *Wines and Vines*, XVIII (Feb., 1937), 16.
———. "The Mission Grape Popular with the Pioneer Wine Makers," *Wines and Vines*, XIV (March, 1932), 8–9.
———. "Napa Valley Pioneer Winemakers," *Wines and Vines*, XVIII (April, 1937), 6–7, 10.
———. "Pioneer Winemakers of the Historic Sonoma District," *Wines and Vines*, XVIII (May, 1937), 5, 11.
Thickens, Virginia E. "Pioneer Agricultural Colonies of Fresno County,"

Bibliography

California Historical Society Quarterly, XXV (March and June, 1946), 17–38, 169–177.

"Viniculture and Wine Making in California," *California Mail Bag*, I (June, 1871), xiii–xv.

"Wine-Making in California," *Harper's*, XXIX (June, 1864), 22–30.

"Wines and Vineyards," *California Mail Bag*, I (July, 1871), vii–xii.

NEWSPAPERS

The purpose of this section of the bibliography is to point out what newspapers have been most important in their coverage of viticultural interests. For the early period, 1850–1870, the two collections of newspaper clippings— "Bancroft Scraps" and "Hayes' Scraps" have proved invaluable. An attempt has been made to collect the material topically, but much pertinent information can be had only by a careful coverage of several topical headings. Sloat's *San Francisco, Prices Current and Shipping List* (October 31, 1850, to May 31, 1852) makes a highly desirable adjunct to the two clipping collections mentioned above. The other newspapers which are valuable for the early period are:

Alta California, (Jan. 4, 1849, to June 18, 1891). California State Library, Sacramento. Title varies.

California Star and *The Californian*, (Jan. 9, 1847, to Dec. 23, 1948). California State Library, Sacramento.

Sacramento *Union*, (Jan. 10, 1852, to May 1, 1880). California State Library, Sacramento. Title varies. For exact references to the title see Gregory, Winifred, ed., *American Newspapers* (1821–1936): *A Union List of Files Available in the United States and Canada*. New York, 1937.

San Francisco *Daily Herald* (1850–1862). Title varies. Between June 1, 1850, and July 14, 1863, as *Daily Herald and Mirror*. For further changes in title see Winifred Gregory, ed., *American Newspapers*.

Southern Vineyard, March 24, 1858, to June 8, 1860. Henry E. Huntington Library and Art Gallery, San Marino, California.

For the period between 1870 and 1890 the following newspapers prove exceptionally valuable:

San Francisco *Examiner*, (January 16, 1865–). Bancroft Library, Berkeley, California. Title varies.

San Francisco *Chronicle*, (1865–). Bancroft Library, Berkeley, California.

San Francisco *Call*. Bancroft Library, Berkeley, California. Title varies: 1856 to March 4, 1895, as San Francisco *Morning Call;* March 5, 1895, to December 6, 1913, as San Francisco *Call*. For further changes see Winifred Gregory, ed., *American Newspapers*.

The "Information File" of the State Library at Sacramento is a topical arrangement of various newspaper citations. It makes no pretense at being complete. Yet, it is the closest approximation to a newspaper guide for California.

INDEX

INDEX

Adulteration, wine, 25–26, 100, 107, 167; reputation injured by, 24–26, 34–35, 96, 133, 134; fight against counterfeiters, 34–35, 54; east-coast trade damaged by, 78; laws against, 83, 84; drugs used in, 84; pure wine law, 152–159
Aguardiente: early manufacture of, 8; Wolfskill production of, 12
Aliso, Don Luis del. *See* Vignes, Jean Louis
Alta California, vine introduced in, 2
Alta California: on champagne, 26; on successful grape culture, 44; on vine mildew, 46; on European commission, 49; on European viticulture, 51; on Sonoma Corporation, 69; on corporate viniculture, 72; on Wetmore study, 100
Alta California Almanac: on champagne, 88; on phylloxera, 113
Alvarado, Governor Juan Bautista, 12
American Wine Growers Association, 34
Anaheim Coöperative, 60–67, 73, 89, 183, 184, 185; spurs grape interest, 33; as grape and wine area, 76
Anaheim *Gazette*, on new vine disease, 127–128
Anaheim Landing, wharf for the colony, 66
Anaheim Lighter Company, wharf built by, 66
Anaheim vine disease. *See* Pierce's disease
Anaheim Water Company, 65, 183
Angelica, 33, 35, 77, 89
Arthaud, J., on wine and civilization, 1–2
Australia: exports to, 32; Sydney Industrial Exhibition, 101
Austria: vines of, 99; American tariff effects on, 104

Baja California, vine introduced in, 2
Bancroft, Hubert H: on importance of vine, 18; on introduction of vine, 171
Bear River, 17
Berkeley, California: experimental vineyard opened, 125; research on phylloxera, 127; Hilgard's work, 127
Black Morocco grape, 43
Black Prince grape, 43
Bleasdale, Dr. J. I., 101
Blowers, Russel B., raisin grower, 24
Board of Horticulture. *See* State Horticultural Commission
Bonfort's Wine and Spirit Circular, on pure wine law, 157
Boston: wine shipped to, 78; champagne demand in, 88; grapes shipped to, 134
Bottles: early shortage, 3, 23, 34; new business for, 35; first blown by Pacific Glass Works, 35; production expanded, 86
Bowles, Samuel, on B.V.V.S., 71–72
British Columbia, wine exported to, 133
Bryant, Edwin, on California wine and grapes, 12, 13, 14

Index

Buck, L. W., 88
Buena Vista, Haraszthy property in Sonoma, 41, 45-46, 52, 55
Buena Vista Vinicultural Society, 67-73, 77, 80, 88, 89, 97, 111
Bundschu, Charles, wine merchant, 157
Burbank, Luther, 195-196
Burgundy, 35
Butler, A. J., 43
Butte County, early northern grape area, 17

California Agricultural Society, 18, 19, 45, 79; supports Mission grape, 44; promotes viticulture, 46; forms new association, 92; promotes immigration, 94; on phylloxera, 117, 118
California Board of Health, 168
California Farmer: on Sacramento vines, 17; on major vineyards, 19; on wine costs, 20; on ideal *vigneron*, 23; on Kohler and Frohling, 31; urges foreign grape planting, 44; advocates increased wine production, 46; on distribution of Haraszthy vines, 55; on state agricultural college, 55; on legislature's inaction, 56; on wine tariff, 80; on reciprocal tariff, 103
California Legislature: Haraszthy elected to, 40; promotes grape culture, 46-47, 161; on European commission, 50; Haraszthy reports to, 52; on distribution of Haraszthy vines, 53; Haraszthy urges paternalistic attitude, 53; Haraszthy urges appointment of general agent, 54; urged to distribute vines, 55; and Haraszthy appropriation, 55, 56; predominately Republican, 57; shortcomings of, 57; Warner reports to, 57, 58, 59; Assembly committee asks federal tax relief, 82; and repeal of Fence Law, 92; urged to aid wine men, 96; Senate and phylloxera control, 118; on viticultural commission, 121; on horticultural commission, 122; urges congressional aid, 146
California Star, on adaptability of vine to California, 14
California Supreme Court: on phylloxera, 125, on pure wine law, 157-158
California Vine Growers' and Wine and Brandy Manufacturers' Association: founding of, 92; scope and functions, 92-93; appeals for immigration, 93-94; recommends emergency legislation, 95-96; shortens name, 98; on phylloxera prevention, 113
California Wine Association, merchants organize, 139-140
California Wine Growers' Association: forming of, 79; on the tariff, 80; on federal wine tax relief, 82; creates new organization, 92; inadequacy of, 120
California Wine Makers' Corporation, 139-140
Canada, exports to, 87
Cass, General Lewis, 39
Catawba wine, 46, 72
Cellar, wine. *See* Wineries
Central America, exports to, 87, 133
Central Pacific Railroad, 97
Chambers of Commerce, on Chotteau treaty, 104, 106, 193
Champagne: early experiments, 26; Sonoma production, 69-70; native district for, 77; popularity, 87-88; production figures on, 185
Chapman, Joseph, first American wine grower, 4

Index

Chicago: Kohler and Frohling distribute from, 34; wine shipped to, 97; grapes shipped to, 134; Columbian Exposition, 162-165
Chile, labor from, 62
China: exports to, 32, 78; laborers from, 42, 45, 68, 71, 135
Chotteau, Leon, 104, 105, 106, 108
Chotteau Treaty, proposed reciprocal trade treaty with France, 106, 107, 108, 146
Civil War, 57, 81, 94
Claret, 77
Cleveland, President Grover, 147, 148-149
Cognac, 164
Colfax, Schuyler, 71
College, agricultural: urged by Haraszthy, 54, by Warren, 55, by *California Farmer*, 55
College of Viticulture, proposed, 142-143
Commissioner of Internal Revenue: on wine legislation, 151; Wetmore proposes tax changes to, 152
Committee on the Improvement of the Grape Vine in California, 49-59; promotes new interest in grape growing, 78
Cooke, Jay, and Company, failure of, 94
Cooperage: casks, 3, 9, 17, 32, 80, 86, 92; business development of, 86; affected by prohibition, 167
Counterfeiting. *See* Adulteration
Cozzens' Wine Press, predicts California's wine supremacy, 48
Crystal Springs, 40
Cucamonga Ranch, 90
Cuttings: importation of, 8; of Montecito, 21; importation of European varieties, 40-41, 42-43; planted at Buena Vista, 42; importation of Catawba, 46; plans for importation, 49-50; planted at Anaheim, 63-64; cost of, 87; scarcity of, 131

Davis, William Heath, on Vignes, 8
Debanne, P., French champagne maker, 70
Delmas, A., San Jose vintner, 46, 75
Denmark, exports to, 35
Depression: of 1876-1878, 16, 85, 91, 94-98, 100, 101, 108, 114, 130, 132, 149, 152, 154; of 1886-1892, 134-141, 143, 148, 149, 152, 156; of 1920-1921, 166
De Turk, Isaac: on College of Viticulture, 143; on fortifying wines, 151
Distillers: and McKinley tariff, 148; and brandy tax, 152
Distilleries, brandy: Sonoma Corporation, 69; proposed coöperative, 137
Downey, Governor John G., 50, 53, 55
Dresel, Emil, trustee of Sonoma Corporation, 43, 68
Dubois, E., 163-164
Dudley, Assemblyman, 56
Duty. *See* Tariff

Education, viticultural, 100; plans for state-sponsored, 58; phylloxera remedies, 117; legislative aid to, 121-123; grower conventions for, 123-124;

Index

phylloxera information, 124–125, 126–128; at district level, 126; value of Commission, 129; policies of Commission, 131–132, 141–142; University of California, 142–143
Eisen, Francis T., early Fresno County viticulturist, 89–90
El Aliso, Vignes' ranch, 8, 10
El Dorado County, 89; as early northern grape area, 17; phylloxera in, 111, 126
Emigration, 39, 83
Emigration Association of Wisconsin, 39
Emory, Brevet Major W. H., on quality of Vignes' wine, 9–10
Emperor grape, 43
England, 104; Kohler wine exports to, 32; colonists from, 39; Haraszthy visits, 51; phylloxera in, 110; wine experts of, 163
Export statistics: brandy, 1870–1875, 87; wine, 1858, 28, 1859, 28, 1864 and 1869 by sea, 77–78, foreign shipments, 1860–1861, 78, foreign shipments, 1864–1869, 78, 1870–1875, 87

Federal Alcohol Control Administration, 167–168
Financial statistics: bottles, price of, 35, business incorporated for, 35; brandy, price in 1840, 9, tax on, 35, federal tax, 1862, 79, federal tax raised, 82, federal tax opposed, 82, federal tax reduced, 82, value of, 1871, 86, internal revenue tax on, 95, all-time low price, 97, duty on, 106, tariff on, 148, tax on, 150; champagne, tariff on, 148; cuttings, cost of during boom, 87; grapes, value of, 1, price of, 12, 27, 28, 45, 97, 98, 138; improvements, Sonoma Corporation, 70–71; investment, value of in Los Angeles County, 20, total California viticultural, 86, California wineries, 86, loss by phylloxera, 118; labor, cost of, 64, 71; land, price of in Sonoma County, 42, price of in Anaheim, 62, 183–184, 185, price of public and railroad, 89; produce, value of farm, 70; state aid, proposed for phylloxera research, 118, Board of Viticulture, 121, 124, University of California, 125; stock, 61, 65, Sonoma Corporation, 68; vines, planting and upkeep, 20, profit on, 20, Vallejo income from, 24, value of, 124, 128; vineyard land, price of, 10, 20, 31, 64–65, 68, 87; wine, price of, 9, 20, 45, 97, 134, 139–140, cost of, 20, value of, 28, 32, 48, 65, 77, 78, 86, tax on, 79, 81, annual business of distributing, 37, shipping rates on, 96–97, duty on, 103, 106, 147
Fitch, Asa, entomologist, 110
Flame Tokay grape, 43
Forbes, Alexander, 4, 7
France: grape culture in, 1; early vines from, 8; wines imported from, 18, 23; pioneer vintners from, 17, 23, 25, 42; Agoston Haraszthy visits, 51; cuttings from, 52; Arpad Haraszthy visits, 69; immigration from, 88, 94, 134; champagnes, 88; wines, 94, 96, 100; 1872 and 1879 imports, 99; vineyardists fail in, 99; phylloxera, 99, 110, 114, 116–117, 119; *vignerons* of, 99–100; wine making, 101; proposed reciprocal trade agreement with, 103–108; viticultural publications, 123; adopts protective tariff, 138; wine imitations of, 153; wine experts, 163; wine study by government, 163–164
Franciscans, 2
Franco-Prussian War, 88, 94
Fresno County, 36, 37, 89

Index

Frohling, John, 30–35, 135; in business with Kohler, 22; on German wine colony, 61; purchases Anaheim wine output, 66

Georgia, 80
German Concert Society, 30
German Glee Club, 30
German Savings Bank Society of San Francisco, 36
Germany: immigrants from, 17, 39, 42, 60–61, 65, 67, 68, 88, 94; wines, 18, 104; California vintners from, 25, 88; Charles Kohler's background in, 29–30; exports to, 32, 35; Haraszthy visits, 51, 52; cuttings from, 52; Sacramento vineyardist visits, 91; vines of, 99; France pays indemnities to, 103; viticultural publications, 123; wine imitations of, 153
Glen Ellen, Kohler vineyard, 37
Gold discovery, effect on viticulture, 14, 16–17, 160
Gos, François, French Commissioner of Viticulture, 163–164
Grape Culture, Wines and Wine-Making, Agoston Haraszthy, 51
Greece, earliest grape culture, 1
Greeley, Horace, on California vines, 17–18
Grower-manufacturer, 139; never totally replaced, 75; poor wine of, 90; number increases, 133
Growers, 161, 163, 164; number of grape, 1; number of wine, 1, 8, 27; background of, 7–8, 10, 17, 29–30, 38–39, 61–62, 65, 130, 183; wine makers among, 22–23; inexperienced, 90–92; education of, 117, 126; fight against phylloxera research, 127; on wine panic, 136–137, 139; difficulties with merchants, 140; attack State Board, 141; National Viticultural Association, 146; on the tariff, 146–149; on excise taxes, 149–150, 152; on sweet wine law, 150–152; on pure wine law, 152–159
Gundlach, Jacob, 43, 135
Gutadel, 35

Haight, Governor Henry H., 96
Hancock, Henry, 47
Hansen, George: on German wine colony, 61; supervisor of Anaheim, 62; lays out Anaheim, 62–63; plants vines at Anaheim, 63–64; loses confidence of shareholders, 64
Haraszthy, Agoston, 13, 33, 161; on vineyard upkeep, 20; settles at Sonoma, 22; on soil adaptability, 26; father of modern California wine industry, 38–48; on European commission, 49–51; reports on return from Europe, 52; plants European cuttings, 52; urges legislature to aid agriculture, 53; urges horticultural societies, government agents, schools, 53–54; urges general agent, 54; asks legislature for reimbursement, 55; reimbursement refused, 56; sells European vines, 57; viticultural education, 58; accomplishment as member of Vine Committee, 59; founds Buena Vista Vinicultural Society, 67–68; production figures for 1862, 69; appoints cellar master, 69; and champagne, 69–70; supervises entire Sonoma estate, 70; hires Chinese labor, 71; resigns under pressure, 72; as retailer, 75; early Sonoma viticulturist, 77; efforts toward state aid, 79; on excise tax and tariff, 80–81; phylloxera on estate of, 111; heirs refuse reimbursement, 182
Haraszthy, Arpad: on reimbursement of father, 57; appointed cellar master,

Index

69; resigns from Sonoma Corporation, 70; on scientific wine production, 90; procures commission for Wetmore, 100; on reciprocal trade treaty, 104, 106–107; on viticultural board, 121, 124; on experiment stations, 131; on grape varieties, 132; on American drinkers, 132; on depression, 134; on new wine markets, 135; on College of Viticulture, 143; on the tariff, 146; on adulterations, 154

Haraszthy, Atilla, 42
Harper and Brothers, publishers of Haraszthy's treatise, 51
Hawaii, 8; exports to, 32, 87, 133
Hearst, William Randolph, on wine panic, 136–138
Hilgard, Professor Eugene W., 24; on phylloxera, 109, 113–114, 117, 118, 125, 127; on viticultural board, 121; experimental vineyards, 125–126, 127; on Anaheim disease, 128; on wine panic, 137–138; contributions of, 141; attacked by viticulturists, 142
Hittell, John S., on number of California vines, 13
Hock, 35, 77
Horticultural Review and Botanical Magazine, on Sonoma vineyards, 41
Horticultural Society of Sonoma County, 44
Hungary; Haraszthy's background in, 38–39; Haraszthy fosters emigration from, 39; cuttings from, 40
Husmann, Professor George: on inexperienced vintners, 25; on wine trade, 99; on phylloxera, 117–118; on University viticultural work, 142

Immigrants, 7; gold-rush, 16–17; Sonoma County, 42; Chinese, 45; Anaheim, 65; to California, 73; state encourages, 86; to large cities, 88, 134; viticultural societies encourage, 93–94; aid viticultural industry, 165
Indians: as laborers, 3, 19, 62, 64; war with, 40
Insecticides, phylloxera combated by, 115
International Wine Jury, 163
Interstate Commerce Act of 1887, 135
Ireland, immigrants from, 94
Irrigation: 19; erroneous conception of, 42–43; Sonoma requirements of, 45–46; taxes for, 47; Anaheim, 62–64; Fresno County, 89
Italian Swiss Colony, 37
Italy: earliest grape culture, 1; Haraszthy visits, 51; cuttings from, 52; immigrants from, 88, 134; vines, 99; viticultural publications, 123; exports, 133; agriculturist of, 163

Japan: Kohler distributor in, 32; exports to, 133
Jesuits, introduce vine into Baja California, 2
Johnson, G. A., California attorney general, 156
Jones, Commodore Thomas ap Catesby, 9

Keller, Matthew: on cost of vine planting, 20; on Montecito cutting, 21; vineyardist of Los Angeles, 23, 32; on problem of vintners, 23; on railroads, 27; on brandy tax, 83; on poor wines, 90
Kentucky, 148
Kohler, Charles: pioneer wine merchant, 22, 28, 29–37, 48, 75, 135; on German wine colony, 61; on stockholders in Anaheim, 61; purchases Anaheim wine output, 66; fights reciprocal trade treaty, 107

Index

Kohler, Henry, 157; State v., 157
Kohler and Van Bergen, wine firm, 157
Kossuth, Louis, Hungarian nationalist, 39
Krug, Charles, Napa County vineyardist, 24, 43

Labels, 165, 167; falsification of, 25, 153; proposed specifications, 155, 156
Labor, viticultural, 93, 135; Indian, 3, 19, 62, 64; Mexican, 19, 62, 64; Chinese, 42, 45, 68, 71, 135; Chilean, 62; Sonoran 62; American 64; German, 64
Lachman and Jacobi, wine merchants, 135
Ladrey, C., 37
Lake County, first grape culture in, 17
Landsberger, trustee of Sonoma Corporation, 68
Legislation, national, 161, 162, 168; Tariff Act of 1864, 76; duties on foreign wines increased, 81; brandy tax reduced, 1867, 82–83; Pure Food and Drug Act, 84, 158; Interstate Commerce Act of 1887, 135; Tariff Act of 1883, 147; proposed reciprocity, 147–148; Mills Bill, 148; Tariff of 1890, 148; Wilson Tariff, 148–149; "Sweet-Wine Bill," 150–151, 159; Act of 1894, 151; proposed revision of brandy tax, 152; proposed pure wine law, 152, 153–155, 158; prohibition, 166; repeal of 18th amendment, 167
Legislation, state: on taxing vineyards, 47–48; to study improvement of vine, 49–50; Warner urges protective and educational measures, 57–59; Act of 1859, 58; on corporations, 68; against counterfeiting, 1861, 84; pure wine bills discussed, 84; wine organizations' interest in, 93; wine organizations recommend, 95, 96; proposed aid against phylloxera, 114, 118; on Viticultural Commissioners, 121; Act of 1880, 121, 123; Act of 1881, 122; on protecting fruit trees and vines, 124–125; on viticultural education, 130–131; pure wine law, 130, 155–156, 157–158; proposed aid for research, 131; on state viticultural board, 141–142; College of Viticulture, 143; proposed aid for grape culture, 145–146
Library, viticultural, 123, 124, 142, 197
Livermore, California, 100
Livermore Valley, 127
Lobby, wine, 80, 81, 82, 84, 148–149, 150
Lôme, Enrique Dupuy de, Spanish viticulturist, 162–163
London, exports to, 135
Los Angeles: early importance of, 3; early economy, 7–8; settlement, 9; sale of Vignes holdings in, 10; early Wolfskill undertakings, 11; general economy, 13, 14; pre-Haraszthian vintners in, 22; white and red wines, 26; trade with San Francisco, 27; early shipments to East, 27–28; Frohling buys vineyard in, 31; Kohler and Frohling business, 31, 32, 33, 36; vines planted in 1850's, 44; Sonoma rival of, 46, 77; diseases of grapes, 46; and Anaheim, 60–61; Anaheim stockholders from, 61–62; Anaheim cuttings from, 63; major grape and wine area of 1860's, 76; phylloxera, 111; protective league founded, 150; early vintners, 160
Los Angeles County, 82, 89, 160, 189
Los Angeles Vineyard Society. See Anaheim Coöperative.
Louisville Exposition of 1885, 133

233

Index

McKinley, President William, 162
McKinley Tariff, 148–149, 150
Malaga, 89
Malvoisie, 35, 161
Marsh, Dr., early vineyardist, 14
Mayacamas Mountains, 42
Mediterranean: first European vines, 1; monasteries, 3
Memorials, 92; on reducing tax and bonding requirements, 96; against Wilson Tariff Bill, 148–149
Merced, first vineyard in, 17
Mexico: vines from, 2; secularizes mission lands, 4; labor from, 19, 62, 64; exports to, 87, 133, 136
Micheltorena, Governor Manuel, 9
Mildew, 46, 99, 192
Mission Dolores, 40
Mission grape, 3, 24, 38, 42, 43, 44, 63, 70, 76, 90, 98, 99, 119, 132, 138, 161
Mission vines, 31
Missions, Spanish, 2, 3, 4, 7, 8, 160
Montecito, giant vine of, 21, 98
Monterey, 9
Morrison, Murray, 50
Muscatel, 33, 35, 89
Must, condensed juice, 135–136

Napa County, 68, 77, 82, 89, 141; early vineyards of, 4, 12; beginning of grape culture, 17; Krug vineyard, 24; residence of Husmann, 25; phylloxera in, 111, 117, 126; experimental vineyards in, 125–126
Napa Valley, 73
Napa Valley Wine Company, 93
National Recovery Administration, 168
National Viticultural Association: founded, 146; aims of, 146; considers wine trade problems, 152; on pure wine law, 158
Natoma Mining and Water Company of Sacramento County, 37
Newmark, Harris, 61–62
New Orleans, grape market in, 134
New York, 27, 151, 153; wine trade in, 27; wine men of, 102; phylloxera in, 110
New York City: wine adulteration in, 25; Kohler arrives, 30; exports to, 32, 34, 88; Kohler branch, 32, 34; Haraszthy in, 39, 51; as wine market, 78, 134

Ohio: and the eastern market, 34; wine industry expands in, 46; wine interests and the tariff, 80, 102; brandy fortification in, 151, 154
Oldham, Charles F., wine expert, 163, 164
Oldham, Grierson and Co., London wine merchants, 163
Onteverras, Juan Pacific, 62
Oranges, early planting of, 8, 11
Organizations, wine, 161; at industry level, 79–84, 92–93, 146, 154; at local

Index

level, 93, 147; need for, 120–121; coöperative, 137–138; founded, 139–140; proposed, 142–143
Osborn, Doctor William, 27

Pacific Glass Works, 35, 36
Pacific Mail Steamship Co. of San Francisco, 135
Pacific Wine Brewing and Spirit Review, on wine market, 138
Paris Exposition of 1878, 100
Paris Exposition of 1889, 133
Paris Universal Exposition of 1867, 70
Perkins, George C., governor of California, 121
Perkins, Stearn and Co., 32, 34
Peru, Kohler distributes in, 32
Petaluma County Fair, 45
Petitions, 138; on wine tax, 82; on brandy tax, 95–96; on tariff, 107, 149; on pure wine law, 153
Pettit, George A., on early grape culture, 3
Philadelphia: champagne market, 88; grape market, 134
Philadelphia Centennial Fair, 88, 97–98
Phoenicians, vine planters, 1
Phylloxera, 16, 48, 100, 108, 130, 132, 140; in France, 99, 100; damage caused by, 109–110; insect causing, 109–110; menaces European vineyards, 110; New York vines not hurt by, 110; invades California, 110–111; spreads northward and southward, 111; indifference to, 111–113; increases substantially, 115; methods of combating, 115–117; vines resistant to, 117; becomes increasingly serious, 117–118; state aid proposed to combat, 118; controlled, 119; fight against, 121, 122, 124, 125, 126, 127, 129, 141, 161
Pierce, President Franklin, 41
Pierce, Newton P., on plant disease, 128–129
Pierce's Disease, 128–129, 161
Placer County, phylloxera in, 111, 126
Port, 33, 35, 77, 89
Portugal, cuttings from, 52
Portugese-British Wine Treaty of 1840, 105–106
Price, Major Sir Rose Lambart, 91, 96
Prizes: at eastern exhibits, 35; at state fair, 43; at Paris Exposition, 133; at Columbian Exposition, 163
Produce, farm, 12–13, 42; lack of, 49; Sonoma Corporation, 70; Anaheim, 67
Production statistics: Angelica of Kohler and Frohling, 32; *aguardiente* of Wolfskill, 12; brandy, San Gabriel, 4, Kohler and Frohling, 32, Sonoma Corporation, 69–70, California in 1865–1867, 83, in 1868 188; interior shipments to San Francisco, 99, Anaheim in 1870, 185; champagne, Sonoma Corporation in 1863–1867, 185, in 1869, 70; grapes, California raisin, table, and wine, 1, Tuolumne County, 23, Anaheim, 64; tobacco, Sonoma Corporation, 70; wine, 1, San Gabriel, 4, Vignes, 10, Wolfskill, 12, Los Angeles and California, 13, Napa County, 17, Los Angeles County, 21, 189, Wilson, 22, Keller, 23, Kohler and Frohling, 32, Zinfandel, 40, Haraszthy, 42, 45, Anaheim, 65, 185, Sonoma Corporation, 68, 69, 70, California in 1850, 74, 1860, 74, 1869, 74, 1890 and 1892, 152, 1912 and

235

Index

1919, 166, 1884 and 1894, 202, Sonoma County, 189, Cucamonga Ranch, 90, interior shipments to San Francisco, 99
Prohibition, 166–167
Prosperity, 85; post-Civil War, 86–93; post 1873 depression, 96–99; in 1880's, 130–134; in mid-20th century, 143; in 1920's, 166–167
Protective Viticultural League, 150
Prussia, Haraszthy visits, 51
Pure Food and Drug Act, 84
Putah Creek, 12

Racking, of wines, 58
Railroads, transcontinental, 34, 76, 78, 87, 88–89
Railroad, freight rates, 87, 96–97, 133, 135
Raisin Industry, 111, 122
Ralston, William, patron of Sonoma Corporation, 68
Reisling grape, 43
Reisling wine, 35, 77
Republican, Springfield, Massachusetts, 71
Revue Viticole, 51; compares European and American wine, 26; on Anaheim, 64
Rhine Valley, 30, 61
Rhine wine types, 72
Riley, C. V., entomologist, 110–111
Rome, early grape culture, 1
Roosevelt, President Theodore, 84
Rossati, Guido, Italian agriculturist, 13, 15, 134, 163
Rowland, John T., early vineyardist, 23
Rural California, on useless commissions, 142
Russia, Kohler distributor in, 32

Sacramento, 14, 83, 87, 91, 92, 121, 145, 149
Sacramento County, 89; early vines in, 17
Sacramento *Union:* on legislative tangle, 56; on Anaheim, 64
St. Helena Viticultural Club, 97
San Diego, 2, 21, 40
Sandwich Islands. *See* Hawaii
San Fernando Mission, wine and brandy produced, 4
San Francisco: as early market, 9, 12, 13, 14; beginnings of viticulture in, 14; 1849 wine production, 17; vines in Bay area, 17; first Napa County shipments, 17; Los Angeles grapes, 22; Keller grapes, 23; jobbers in, 24; Sansevain champagne, 26; trade with Los Angeles, 27; Kohler arrives, 30; Kohler cellar, 31, Kohler and Frohling business, 32, 33; Kohler's public service, 36; Haraszthy holding near, 40; Haraszthy trade, 41, 42; Sonoma trade with, 42; foreign vines in Bay area, 43; grapes shipped to, 45; wine shipped to, 47; Haraszthy sails from, 50; Haraszthy returns, 51–52; vines arrive at, 52; proposed residence of a general wine agent, 54; Anaheim stockholders from, 61–62; as market for Anaheim, 66; as market for Sonoma, 67; Sonoma stockholders from, 68; Arpad Haraszthy goes into business in, 70; as grape market in 1850's, 75; as wine market, 76–77; European

Index

vines imported into, 77; chief export center, 78; center of industry, 78; vineyardists meet in, 79; merchant committee recommends tariff changes to Congress, 80; wine convention of 1862, 81–82; as market, 85, 87, 138; industrialization of, 86; foreign export trade from, 87; interior ships to, 99; Chotteau visits, 105–106; Vinicultural Society meets in, 105; Chamber of Commerce, 106; phylloxera in area of, 111; fresh grape outlet, 133–134; wine merchants of, 135; viticultural convention, 138, 162; price of wine, 140; as wine center, 143; merchants, 157; proposed exposition in, 165

San Francisco Chamber of Commerce, 104–105, 106–107
San Francisco *Chronicle*, on false labeling, 153
San Francisco *Examiner*, on viticultural depression, 136–137
San Francisco Insurance Co., 36
San Francisco Wine Dealers' Association, 95, 157
San Gabriel, 26
San Gabriel Mission wine and brandy, 4
San Joaquin County, experimental vineyard, 125–126
San Joaquin Valley, 87
San Mateo County, 40, 41
Sansevain, Jean Louis, 90
Sansevain, Pierre, 9
Sansevain Brothers, 10, 22, 26, 48, 75
Santa Ana, Anaheim cuttings from, 63
Santa Ana River, 62
Santa Ana Valley, 129
Santa Barbara, 9
Santa Barbara County, 13; Montecito vine in, 21
Santa Clara County, 89; experimental vineyard, 125–126
Santa Cruz County, 89
Sauk City, Wisconsin, 39
Sauterne, 77
Scientific viticulture: Haraszthy's contribution to, 40–45, 51–53, 59, 161; retarded, 57; Warner's report on, 57–58; proposed aid for, 121; legislation for, 121–123; library about, 123; phylloxera experiments, 124–125; experimental vineyards, 124, 125–126, 127; proposed research, 131; College of Agriculture, 141, 142–143
Sea voyages, for aging wine, 9
Seedless Sultana grape, 43
Sergent, Senator Aaron A., investigates importation of wines, 105
Seward, William H., 51
Shaw, on commission to improve vine, 50
Sherry, 33, 35
Shorb, J. de Barth, 148, 150
Sierra Nevada Mountains, early northern viticultural area, 17
Snyder, Major Jacob R., 43, 100
Solano County, 56, 89; Wolfskill holdings, 12; phylloxera in, 126
Sonoma, 2, 3, 22, 33, 38, 40, 41, 42, 44, 46, 52, 55, 67, 73; major grape and wine area of 1860's, 76; outranks Los Angeles, 85; phylloxera in, 110
Sonoma Corporation. *See* Buena Vista Vinicultural Society

Index

Sonoma County, 3, 36, 44, 71, 77, 82, 89, 189; phylloxera in, 111, 113, 125; experimental vineyards, 125–126
Sonora, labor from, 62
South America, 50; imports from, 49; exports to, 78
Southern Californian, on sale of El Aliso, 10
Southern Vineyard: on northern vintner competition, 21; on a native wine, 26; on Sonoma, 45–46
Spain: early grape culture in, 1; Haraszthy visits, 51; cuttings from, 52; immigrants from, 88, 134; vines of, 99; viticultural publications, 123; imitations of wine from, 153; viticulturist of, 162
Spanish Mataro, 189
"Sparkling Sonoma," first successful champagne of Sonoma, 70
Speculators, 63, 90, 98, 119, 160
Stamps, wine, 156, 157–158
Stanford, Leland, 131
Star, Los Angeles, on founding of German wine colony, 61
State Agricultural Society. *See* California State Agricultural Society
State Board of Viticultural Commissioners, 130, 160, 162, 165; formation of, 79, 120; precursor of, 92–93; Wetmore prompts establishment of, 100; phylloxera control, 118–119; duties of, 120–122; accomplishments of, 123; on phylloxera, 125–127; on experimental vineyards, 125–126; on Anaheim disease, 128; value of, 129; viticultural education, 131; educating American public, 132; on labor, 135; on the depression, 136; meets in seventh convention, 138; establishes cellar and café, 138–139; attacks against, 139, 141–142; contributions of, 141, 142; suspended, 142; proposed successor, 142–143; proposes legislation, 145; against all reciprocity treaties, 147; attack on Wilson Bill, 149; on "Sweet Wine Bill," 151; discusses wine trade problems, 152; on wine adulteration, 153; on proposed national pure wine law, 153–155, 158; on state pure wine law, 155–156, 158
State Fair: of 1856, 18–19; of 1863, 69
State Horticultural Commission, founded, 122
State Vinicultural Society: 118; at Philadelphia Exposition, 98; and wine industry recovery, 99–100; tariff fight by, 103; reciprocal trade treaty fight by, 104–108; on phylloxera, 113, 118
State Viticultural Convention, 162
State v. Henry Kohler, 157
Stevens, Thaddeus, 82
Stockton, beginning of grape culture in, 17
Submersion, phylloxera combated by, 115-116
Subsidy, legislature against, 56
Sugar, to fortify sweet wine, 85, 151, 154, 155
Sulphur, as mildew cure, 46
Switzerland, immigrants from, 39
Sydney Industrial Exhibition, 101

Tarbell, Ida M., 147
Tariff, 131, 138, 144, 152, 161, 168; on foreign wines, 76; need to replace ad valorem rates, 80, 82; foreign merchants defraud, 80; specific duty called for, 80–81; duties increased by legislation, 81; as protection, 83, 85; high

Index

American, 94, 99; ad valorem rates fought, 102–103; proposed rates of reciprocal treaty, 103; small Parisian group presses for, 103–104; San Francisco Chamber of Commerce on, 104–107; fight against Chotteau treaty, 104–107; proposed protection, 146; "Mongrel Tariff," 147; reciprocity attempted, 147–148; Mills Bill, 148; Tariff Act of 1890, 148; Wilson Bill, 148–149; Democratic view of, 150; Republican view, 150

Tax: federal excise on wine, 35, 71, 79, 80, 81, 82, 83, 85, 146; on vineyards, 47, 58; causes sale of unripe wine, 58, 59; federal excise on brandy, 71, 79, 80, 81, 82, 83, 95–96; on distilled spirits, 81, 82; proposed relief from excise on brandy, 146, 149–150, 152; proposed on adulterated wine, 155

Taylor and Co., 35

Tehama County, 131

Tokay wine, 35, 89

Trade: brandy, declines with tax, 81, problems solved, 82–83; grape, 26–27, 41, 45, 166–167, 168, coastwise, 12–13, early out-of-state, 27–28, out-of-state from San Joaquin Valley, 87, to eastern cities, 88–89, Fresno County, 90, reduced by high freight rates, 96–97, prospers, 133–134; raisin, 87, 89; wine, coastwise, 9, 12–13, 27, 34; early out-of-state, 27–28, 32, 33, 34, 35; early Anaheim insufficiency of, 66; large demand and short supply, 76; hopes of eastern market, 76; of the 1860's, 77; exports to United States and foreign markets, 77–78; exports suffer from European competition, 80; regression, 81; tax hurts, 81; more profits from, 83; grows into real business, 85; export by rail and ship, 87; foreign export, 87–88; decline in, 94–95; reduced by high shipping rates, 96–97; damaged by Philadelphia showing, 98; resumes after depression, 98–99; threatened by proposed reciprocal treaty, 103–104, 106; expands, 108; in Los Angeles area, 111; increase in, 114; limited export, 120; increased demand, 131, 133, 134; low prices and slow sales, 134–139, 148; export, 145; hurt by counterfeiters, 154; and pure wine law, 157; 1895–1918, 165–168

Traminier grape, 43

Trinity County, early northern grape area, 17

Tulare County, 89

Tuolumne County, French growers in, 23

Tyler, President John, wine sent to, 9

Ugarte, Father Juan, 2

United States Bureau of Internal Revenue, 155

United States Congress: wine bloc, 80; and specific duty on wine, 80, 81, 85; House reduces brandy tax, 82; and brandy tax, 96; on Chotteau treaty, 105, 107–108; urged to protect grape culture, 145–146; and the tariff, 146–149; sweet wine law, 150; pure wine law, 153, 155

United States Department of Agriculture, 111, 128

United States Mint, Haraszthy employed by, 41

United States Patent Office, 53

University of California, 118; founded 1868, 55; Board of Regents, 130, 142

University of California College of Agriculture, 3, 24, 92, 109, 121, 123, 125; on phylloxera resistant vines, 125; oenological research center, 126; on Anaheim disease, 127; viticultural education, 130, 131; Haraszthy urges research, 132; experimental work at, 141–142; takes over viticultural com-

Index

missioners' functions, 142; attacked by viticulturists, 142-143; great viticultural center, 143

Vacaville, California, 88
Vallejo, General Mariano G., first commercial vintner of Sonoma County, 24, 41, 77
Viala, Professor P., French vineyardist, 128
Vigilantes, in Los Angeles, 8
Vigilantes Committee, 36
Vignes, Jean Louis, first to make wine a business, 7-15, 18, 90
Vignes, Jean M., 8
Vignes, Louis, 160, 161
Vina Vineyard, Stanford's ranch, 131
Vines: varieties, 1, 2, 52, 53, 76, 86, 87, 99, 110-111, 116-117, 119, 126, 127, 132, 134; classification of, 19; imports, 31, 33, 42, 43, 44, 49-50, 72, 73, 110, 122, 126, 127, 134; experimentation, 33, 38, 40-41, 44-45, by State Board of Viticultural Commissioners, 124, by University of California, 125, 127; diseases, 46, 67; distribution, by Haraszthy, 50, 52-53, 56-57, and legislation for, 122, 126; deposited at consulates, 51; importing rooted, 52; Haraszthy plants rooted, 52-53; Haraszthy asks reimbursement for, 55, but legislature refuses, 56; Haraszthy sells vines, 57; Haraszthy plan for teaching planting, pruning, and training, 58; pruning, 92; grafting, 110, 116-117; phylloxera infected, 113, 115, 125, 126; resistant, 115-119, 125-127, 196; quarantine, 126-127
Vines, acres or numbers of: 1; J. Chapman, 4; Los Angeles, 8, 13, 21, 176; Vignes, 9, 10; Wolfskill, 11, 12; Sacramento County, 17; California 1856-1858, 22, 47, early 1860's, 75, 76, 1873 and 1876, 95, early 1880's, 124; Wilson holdings, 22-23; Tuolumne County, 23-24; Blowers, 24; Vallejo, 24; Kohler and Frohling, 32, 33; Kohler, 37; Buena Vista, 42, 45; Anaheim, 63-66; Sonoma Corporation, 68; Sonoma over Los Angeles, 85; Eisen planted, 89; killed at Anaheim, 128; Vina Vineyard, 131
Vinegar, 97, 99
Viticultural Club of Sonoma, 110-111
Vitis californica, 117, 125
Vitis vinifera, 2, 125, 160, 161; phylloxera attacks, 110-111; phylloxera combated, 116-117

Warehouse, government, 83
Warehouses, bonded, 152
Warner, J. J.: on commission to improve vine, 50; report to legislature, 57, 58, 59; accomplishment as member of Vine Committee, 59
Warren, James, 55
Washington, D. C., 80, 82, 83, 103, 105, 107, 146, 148, 149, 150, 154, 158
Wells Fargo, 52, 57
Wetmore, Charles A.: founder of Cresta Blanca Wine Co., 100, 101, 118, 134, 138, 163; on reciprocal trade treaty, 105, 106, 107; viticultural library data collected by, 123; Chief Executive Viticultural Officer, 126; on College of Viticulture, 143; on wine taxes, 146; president of national wine group, 146; on McKinley Tariff, 149; on Wilson Bill, 149; "Sweet Wine

Index

Bill," 150; Act of 1894, 151; proposes brandy tax revision, 152; on false labeling, 153; on pure wine law, 154
Weyse, Otto, 61
White, Doctor T. J., early scientific vintner, 23
Williams, General Charles H. S., 43
Wilson, Benjamin D., early Irish vineyardist, 22–23, 26
Wilson Bill, 148–149
Wine Bank, proposal for, 136
Wine Bloc, 80
Wine Experts, at Chicago Exposition, 163–164
Wine Growers' Association, 82–84, 92
Wine Growers' Union of Napa County, 141
Wine Institute, 167
Wine war, 140
Wineries, 18, 23, 27, 75; Vignes, 9; Wolfskill's cellar, 11; depots in San Francisco, 27, 29, 69; Kohler, 31, 32–33, 37; Haraszthy's cellar, 42; organization of cellar, 58; Buena Vista viticultural holdings, 67–68, 69, 73; proposed coöperative depot, 137; eastern interests purchase, 168
Wisconsin, Haraszthy's projects in, 39–40
Wolfskill, John, 11
Wolfskill, William, 10–13, 22, 32, 75, 160
Wood, Fernando, 103
World War II, 168
World's Columbian Exposition, 162
Wratten, George L., 43

Yolo County, 24; Wolfskill holdings, 12; phylloxera in, 111, 126
Yount, George C., first white settler in Napa County, 10, 14, 171–172
Yuba County, early northern grape area, 17, 89

Zinfandel, 40, 43, 76, 132, 138, 161